# THE
# HINDU
# GODS

# THE
# HINDU
# GODS

**ETHEL BESWICK**

**CREST PUBLISHING HOUSE**
(A JAICO ENTERPRISE)
G-2, 16 ANSARI ROAD DARYA GANJ
NEW DELHI- 110002

THE HINDU GODS
ISBN 81-242-0004-1

First Edition : 1993

Published by :
Crest Publishing House
(A JAICO ENTERPRISE)
G-2, 16 Ansari Road, Darya Ganj
New Delhi-110002

Printed by :
Efficient Offset Printers
215, Shahzada Bagh
Industrial Complex
Phase II, Delhi-110035.

# CONTENTS

# List of Plates

1. Smiling Bramha *(Sikar, Rajasthan)*
2. Lord Vishnu *(Sikar, Rajasthan)*
3. Siva-Parvati marriage performed by Bramha *(Ajmer, Rajasthan)*
4. Ganesh-Parvati and Kartikay *(Amber, Rajasthan)*
5. Standing Surya *(Amber, Rajasthan)*
6. Seated Lord Vishnu *(Sikar, Rajasthan)*
7. Bearded Lord Bramha *(Ranthambhore, Rajasthan)*
8. Dancing Ganesha and his Consort on the eastern terrace of Harshad Mata-ka-Mandir *(Abaneri, Jaipur)*
9. Chaturambha lings *(Ajmer, Rajasthan)*
10. Standing Vishnu in Harshad Mata-ka-Mandir *(Jaipur, Rajasthan)*
11. Lord Vishnu *(Jaipur, Rajasthan)*
12. Seated Bramha *(Sikar, Rajasthan)*
13. Seated Garuna *(Nahargarh Fort)*
14. Surya in Sun Temple *(Nahargarh Fort)*
15. Radha-Krishna *(Jaipur, Rajasthan)*
16. Standing Lord Vishnu *(Sikar, Rajasthan)*
17. Siva-Parvati *(Jaipur, Rajasthan)*
18. Laxmi Naryan *(Jaipur, Rajasthan)*
19. Standing Lord Vishnu *(Jaipur, Rajasthan)*
20. Bansi Gopal *(Jaipur, Rajasthan)*
21. Sculpture of Siva of Adai-Din-Ka Jhopra *(Ajmer, Rajasthan)*
22. Lying Lord Vishnu *(Sikar, Rajasthan)*
23. Dancing Siva in Madwa Temple
24. Narasimha—fifth incarnation of Vishnu
25. Parasurama—sixth incarnation of Vishnu
26. Rama—seventh incarnation of Vishnu
27. Krishna—eighth incarnation of Vishnu.

India is a land whose past is ever receding in time and it is therefore not surprising that her myths and legends take us back to the misty dawn of mankind and lead us through the centuries to the Great War 5,000 years ago. Cosmic events, heroic events, tales of the invisible, of human nature at its best and at its worst, of the nearness of gods and nature spirits to man, of the great powers of nature and those that can be gained by man—all these make up the drama which is unfolded to our gaze. But cosmos and man can never be separated and therefore all myths have a cosmic and a human, an astronomical and a psychological meaning.

We can understand but little of them unless we remember that the powers and attributes of nature are given names as though they were persons, and their actions are described in terms of life as we know it. The gods ride in chariots; they are given human forms and are subject to human feelings. The eclipse is personified; the thunderbolt is thrown by the great god of the elements, and tussles between the sun and the clouds are turned into wars between personal beings.

The celestial weapons won from the gods by heroes are powers in nature which they have learnt by their own efforts to control and master. The hundreds of sons possessed by some of the kings and princes refer to their passions and evil tendencies. For instance, the story of the sixty thousand sons of Sagara destroyed in a moment by a glance from the eye of Kapila the sage, refers to the instantaneous destruction of evil when brought into contact with good or truly spiritual force.

There is the dramatic and awesome account of the God Siva* who carried his dead wife on his shoulders and stamped over the earth in such an agony of grief that it trembled with fear, the rains

* This is Siva in his destructive aspect.

stopped and famine came. This surely refers to some time of desolation, to an upheaval of cosmic forces that struck the earth.

Lankā, Ceylon, said to be a lump of rock thrown from a mountain range, reminds us of the earthquakes and disturbances that took place before our earth became as it is today.

When we read that the Vindhya mountain range was jealous of Mount Meru and the Himālayas, and issued a command to the sun telling it to revolve round it as well as round Mount Meru, are we learning something of the movement of the earth's axis before she settled into the present position? The sun refused, it is said, and Vindhya in anger raised up its head so that it was higher than Mount Meru. Then the gods complained and asked Agastya, "the spiritual guide of Vindhya", to do something about it. He asked the mountain to bow down and make a passage so that he could travel to the south and return to the north. The mountain obeyed—but Agastya never returned and so the Vindhya range remains today lower than the Himālayan.

Earthquakes occur when Sesha, the serpent of time, turns round.

With reference to the evolution of man we learn that woman was made from the best parts of the animals (the eyes of the deer, for example), while the birth of Mārishā from the sweat of her mother who "flew" through the air, suggests another method of generation in the forgotten early stages of man's evolution, sometimes called "sweat-born".

Running throughout the myths and legends are two important ideas: (1) the nearness and relationship of the invisible to the visible, and (2) actions in time bring effects which, to be understood, must be traced back to the cause. This on the moral as well as on the physical plane.

The legends and stories bring out the human qualities of love and tenderness as well as of courage and steadfastness and, as in all great dramas, they show the triumph of the human spirit through sorrow, suffering and tragedy and the final destruction of evil. They must be read as psychological studies of human nature.

Rāma and Krishna show what man ought to be and can be; Sitā and Rādhā show a perfection towards which woman should aim. Sāvitri and Damayanti are two very poignant studies of the faithfulness and love of a wife for her husband, while Prithā and Draupadi show the anguish of a widow and mother and the regal pride of the princess-wife.

The myths and legends are told in the *Vedas*, and the *Purānas*, and in the two great epics, the *Rāmāyana* and the *Mahā-bhārata* with which is the *Bhagavad-Gitā*.

The *Vedas* are the oldest of the sacred writings and are said to have been "heard", that is, passed on by word of mouth for thousands of years. They are not the work of any one person but of many. Some are signed and some are anonymous. As they exist today they are written in a form of Sanskrit which is not known except by the most learned Brāhman pundits.

There are four *Vedas* in existence: the *Rig*, the *Yajur*, the *Sāma* and the *Atharva*. The *Rig-Veda* consists of over a thousand hymns dealing with visible and invisible nature, the dawn of manifestation and the great plan of the cosmos. The *Sāma-Veda* contains hymns of peace and praise to the living intelligences and powers in nature. The *Yajur-Veda* gives details of the religious rites and sacrifices, and the *Atharva-Veda* is composed of sacred incantations.

The other main Sacred Writings of the Hindus are the *Upanishads*. These are interpretations of the *Vedas*. They give their essence, as it were, which has been passed on from teacher to pupil for ages. One meaning of the word is "sitting down near", as pupil and teacher. Another meaning is the "secret doctrine".

There are over a hundred *Upanishads,* ten of which are looked upon as the chief ones, and on these the great Indian teacher, Sri Sankarāchārya (A.D. 900), wrote many commentaries. Anquetil Duperron, a Frenchman, and the first European who is known to have read them wrote:

> Here, reader, is the key to India's sanctuary somewhat rough with rust. Enter, if thou darest, if thou canst, with pure and clean heart, drawing near to the highest being and merging in it. Let the outer sense rest; awaken the inner. Let the body be as dead, and sunk in the ocean of wisdom and unwisdom. Know it—after Indian custom—as a divine law, that thou seest nothing Eternal; that nothing is, but the Eternal.

Schopenhauer thought very highly of them for he wrote:

> From every page of the *Upanishads,* deep, original, lofty thoughts step forth to meet us; while a high and holy earnestness breathes over all.

> This is the richest and loftiest study possible in the world; it has been the comfort of my life, and will be the comfort of my death.

> Throughout these works one supreme Spirit is recognised, Self-existent and Unknowable, yet the light and life of all. Manifestations and forms may come and go, but the Unknowable remains.

There is a conversation in the *Brihad-āranyaka Upanishad* between the teacher and the learner which deals with this subject. The teacher is asked how many gods there are, and when the answer is given that there is only one god, the further question comes: should one meditate on Fire, Air, Breath, Brahmā, Siva, Vishnu or any other aspect of the world? The teacher answers that all things can be meditated on, or not, for they are only manifestations of the One. The *Taittiriya Upanishad* gives this description: "For fear of him the fire burns, for fear of him the sun shines, for fear of him the winds, the clouds and death perform their office." In the *Mundaka Upanishad* we find: "The moon and the sun are its eyes, the four quarters of the sky its ears, the wind its breath?" Everything is It.

A study of these books leads to the recognition of Sat-Chit-Ānanda, Bliss. But these conditions are not without, they are within, and the inner search for the Reality, the difference between the known and the unknown, the real and the unreal, runs like a thread throughout. It is perhaps best epitomised in the wellknown phrase; "Lead me from the unreal to the real, from darkness to light, from death to immortality." But few will seek for the inner until they are dissatisfied with the outer, and it is through sorrow and suffering that man wakes up and begins to ask what is it in life that perishes and what ever remains? To the sufferer's cry, "What is life for, why do I live, where am I going?" the answer is *given,* but it cannot be *known,* until effort is made to learn and understand. It is not enough to say that the world is unreal and the Reality is God, or even *vice versa:* the Truth must be learnt by experience, study and meditation. Man must learn to know what *in him* is perishable and what real; what a mere passing shadow, and what a reflection of the Real. When the Buddha taught that the heart of Being was celestial Rest, he also taught that which would lead men from the Ocean of Samsara (illusion) to the knowledge of that "Power divine which moves to Good," and beyond. So the *Upanishads* lead to the recognition of Sat-Chit-Ānanda.

A graphic story illustrates the kind of teaching that enables man to realise, even if it is forgotten time and time again, that the body is not the real man. It is said that if we look at ourselves in a mirror or pool we see the details of the body and the clothes worn. If we change the clothes, or become blind or lame, the reflection will show that which is placed before it. The pupil is therefore made to see that the body cannot be the self. He is then told that the self is the happy dreamer. But he says, just as the "self is not rendered faulty by faults of the body, nor lamed if the body is lamed," so in dreams he can feel pain as well as pleasure, and therefore the dreamer cannot be the self. He is then told that "when a man being asleep, reposing and at perfect rest, sees no dreams, that is the self". But the pupil can see no real value in this either, for if the self does not know anything it must have gone into annihilation ! He is then told that the self is that which is the continuity throughout all experiences; it is the self which sees, the eye is the instrument; the self smells, the nose is the instrument; the self is, the body is the instrument. The self is the basis of all.

The *Māndukya Upanishad* deals with the three conditions of consciousness, waking, dreaming, sleeping, and also with the higher state of *turiya*. What is the consciousness during sleep ? What is the difference between the deep dreamless condition and the higher spiritual condition, *turiya* ? These questions are answered, and the pupil is led to dwell on self. To make the points clear, well-known examples are used, such as archery:

Having taken the bow, the great weapon, let him place on it the arrow, sharpened by devotion. Then, having drawn it with a thought directed to that which is, hit the mark, O friend—the Indestructible. OM is the bow, the Self is the arrow, Brahman is called its aim. It is to be hit by a man who is not thoughtless; and then as the arrow becomes one with the target, he will become one with Brahman. Know him alone as the Self, and leave off other words. He is the bridge of the Immortal. Meditate on the self as the OM. Hail to you that you may cross beyond the sea of darkness.

Turning to the Epics the *Rāmāyana* tells the story of Rāma, the divine king, and his conquest of Rāvana, the demon king, and at the same time gives minute instructions as to details of government in a righteous kingdom. The *Mahā-bhārata* tells the story of the great war on the plain of *Kuru-kshetra* between the cousins, the Pandus and the Kurus. With it is the *Bhagavad-Gitā*, The Lord's Song, said to have been delivered by the spiritual teacher Krishna to his pupil Arjuna on that battlefield.

Romesh Dutt who translated much of these Epics wrote: "To know the Indian Epics is to know the Indian people better," and certain it is that to read them enriches life beyond all expectation.

Many inconsistencies can be found, but when they are analysed they are seen to be apparent rather than real and due to emphasis being placed on one or another aspect of the story. For instance Kārttikeya, the war-god, is sometimes said to be born from Siva, and at other times from Agni, or even from Gangā: a full description would make him appear to be born from them all; for the seed was from Siva, the vital spark from Agni and, for a time, Gangā held it in her waters. Further, Kasyapa is said to be the son of Marichi, son of Brahmā, and again the son of Vishnu; Vishnu was born as a dwarf, fathered by Kasyapa ! Yet all are true for Vishnu is the Preserver aspect of the Trimurti, Brahmā-Vishnu-Siva, and the Trimurti is indivisible. The dwarf incarnation of Vishnu came naturally from Kasyapa as he was the progenitor of the human race.

The whole mythology is so vast in its concept, so infinitesimal in its detail, that it would take tomes fully to explain, even if anyone *could* fully explain it today. The attempt here to put down a tiny portion of it is fraught with difficulties, and the only excuse is that perhaps such a simple statement of that tiny portion may help the ordinary man of the West to understand to some extent the vast heritage of India.

Very little has been said of Kāli or Durgā or of the many degrading forms of religious rites which have in so many cases sprung up in the passage of years. Such degradations take place in all religions in the course of time, but the inner core of spiritual truth is eternal.

## PART I

THE COSMIC GOD

THE NATURE GODS

# CHAPTER I

# THE COSMIC GOD

*Nor aught nor nought existed; yon bright sky*
*Was not, nor heaven's broad woof outstretched above.*
*What covered all? what sheltered? what concealed?*
*Was it the water's fathomless abyss?*
*There was not death—yet was there nought immortal,*
*There was no confine betwixt day and night;*
*The only One breathed breathless by itself,*
*Other than It there nothing since has been.*
*Darkness there was, and all at first was veiled*
*In gloom profound—an ocean without light—*
*The germ that still lay covered in the husk*
*Burst forth, one nature, from the fervent heat.*
*Then first came love upon it, the new spring*
*Of mind—yea, poets in their hearts discerned,*
*Pondering, this bond between created things*
*And uncreated. Comes this spark from earth*
*Piercing and all-pervading, or from heaven?*
*Then seeds were sown, and mighty powers arose—*
*Nature below, and power and will above—*
*Who knows the secret? who proclaimed it here,*
*Whence, whence this manifold creation sprang?*
*The Gods themselves came later into being—*
*Who knows from whence this great creation sprang?*
*He from whom all this great creation came,*
*Whether His will created or was mute,*
*The Most High Seer that is in highest heaven,*
*He knows it—or perchance even He knows not.*

*Atharva-Veda*, trans. by MAX MULLER

Hindu mythology, like all other mythologies, has as its starting

point the one great God, the Father of all other gods, the
background and container of all, eternal and self-existent. All
mythologies have realised the necessity of postulating that
which contains all there is, while itself remaining unfathomable,
beyond the reach of the mind, (which, by its very nature gives
form or colour or sound to anything it conceives), unchanging
and unchangeable, yet essential. During periods of non-
manifestation it is said the "One breathed, windless, self-
dependent. Other than That there was nought beyond." The
*Upanishads* say It can only be described as "Not this, not that".
All that we can know of It are the powers and faculties shown
through the forms which appear in It and of which It is the Source.
Such forms and powers and faculties are personified in the gods
and goddesses, the inner and outer side of all manifested
Nature.

The nearest approach that can be made to It is to liken It to the
sky, shining and glorious, enclosing everything, unaffected by
anything, unfathomable in its spatial depths, but the home in
which all floats. The ancient Hindus called It Dyaus, a word
meaning sky, and in course of time the word became the proper
name of the personalised god. The same thing happened in the
case of the other gods and goddesses; a power or quality of
nature became in time known as a god of that name. Hence
Dyaus is the shining one, recognised as essential but beyond
thought, the background to all that there is.

With him is Aditi, the broad expanse of space-matter, the
Mother of all, boundless also and infinite. From this duality of
spirit-matter arise the gods and goddesses, the "sons in time
and space." As in the Christian Trinity—Father-Mother-Son—so
here we have Father-Dyaus, Mother-Aditi, and the Ādityas, sons
of Aditi, seven, eight, ten or twelve in number according to the
degree of manifestation from spirit to matter-form. All manifestation
is an expression of this Trinity: it is the ONE breaking into
multitudinous facets of Itself. As all comes from It so all will be
merged in It again for a time, only to reappear, for Life is eternal:
only forms come and go. It is this Trinity throughout all Nature—the

background of Spirit, the visible forms of Matter and the invisible Life—that is the key to the understanding of the universe and of man himself.

It is only when we leave Dyaus and Aditi to remain as the background that we come to manifestation, just as in the Christian scriptures we leave the God "around whose pavilion is darkness" and "in whom we live and move and have our being,"and turn to God manifested.

Such a god is Varuna. He also stands for Space, the universal encompasser, the maker of heaven and earth. He marks the uttermost boundaries of the earth as does the horizon. He "covers the worlds as with a robe, with all the creatures thereof and their dwellings." He is the chief of the Ādityas (sons of Aditi); he keeps the great cosmic laws, moral as well as physical; he regulates the seasons and the movement of the heavenly bodies; he marks out the river beds, causes the waters to flow into the ocean though it never becomes full; he holds the waters of the heavens in the sky and, at times, lets them fall on to the parched earth; he gives rise to all the intelligence in the universe. Everything is his servant and ally. He rides on the sun, using it as his eye during the day, and, when darkness falls, he sees by means of the moon.

As it is clear that duality pervades the manifested universe—positive and negative, light and darkness, life and death, etc.—so Varuna is linked with his brother sky-god, Mitra or light. Sometimes both brothers ride through space with light as a chariot, and, just as the sky changes from gold to grey from dawn to dusk, so the chariot is sometimes golden and bright, and sometimes grey. Mitra awakens men and nature to day and its work; he watches the actions of men, avenging the evil and forgiving the penitent.

Many hymns were composed to both brothers, the finest of which is probably the following:

Sing a hymn, pleasing to Varuna the King—to him who spread

out the earth as a butcher* lays out a steer's hide in the sun.—
He sent cool breezes through the woods, put mettle in the
steed [the sun], milk in the kine [clouds], wisdom in the heart,
fire in the waters [lightning in the clouds], placed the sun in the
heavens, the Soma on the mountains. He upset the cloud-
barrel and let its waters flow on Heaven, Air and Earth, wetting
the ground and the crops . . . .

Varuna laid out the sun's path . . . . He leads forth the great,
the holy sun-steed, that brings a thousand gifts.—When I
gaze upon his face, I seem to see him as a blazing fire, as the
King causes me to behold the splendour of light and darkness
in the heavens. . . . Varuna's ordinances are immutable . . . he
is seated in his mansion protecting the law, Varuna, Almighty
King, and looks down attentively from there on all that is
hidden, on all that has been and is still to be done. Arrayed in
golden mail, he wraps himself in splendour as in a garment
and around him sit his spies [the stars at night, the sunbeams
by day].

*Vedic India*—Zenaide A. Ragozin

With the passage of time this magnificent concept was lost
sight of and Varuna became the god of the ocean, king of the
waters. As such he lives in the ocean with Varuni his wife, sister
of Lakshmi, wife of Vishnu. In the great depths he has his palace
with its vast Assembly Hall. There he sits on his throne with
Varuni enthroned beside him. The pure whiteness of the Hall is
a background for his magnificence, for he is covered with
sparkling jewels, golden ornaments and flowers. His attendants
are the other Ādityas, the Nāgas (part-human, part-serpent) and
the spirits of the rivers and oceans, lakes and ponds, and
mountains. The guardians of the heavens are also there. The
outside walls of his palace are pure white and the whole is
surrounded by many coloured trees, always in full bloom and
sparkling with jewels.

* Tanner.

All gods have their *vāhana* or vehicles in the form of some animal, bird or fish, and Varuna's vehicle is an antelope with a fish tail, a kind of sea animal or Leviathan. Sometimes it is pictured as a dolphin or, reminiscent of Egypt, as a crocodile.

A noose is also associated with him, for with it he binds the transgressor against his laws even while he is gracious to him.

# CHAPTER II

## THE NATURE GODS

When we pass from this most sublime concept we come to the Nature gods, the three greatest gods of the Vedic Trimurti, Agni, god of fire; Vāyu, god of wind or air; Sùrya, god of the sun. All are Ādityas, sons of Aditi. They long ante-date the more well-known Trimurti of Brahmā-Vishnu-Siva.

*Agni,* fire, is not merely the physical fire we know but the ramifications of the fire element throughout all nature. He is the vital spark in the earth; lightning in the sky; and Surya the sun. He is the sap in the plants which is carried down to them by the rain. He is present even in the dry sticks for, by friction, he can be brought to birth from them, and, when freed, soars to heaven. He brings fire down to earth as the lightning which escapes from the ocean of clouds which hide it; he is electricity itself and the vital element in man, power over which gives complete freedom and mastery over life. Just as there are seven notes to the scale and seven colours in the spectrum, so fire is sevenfold in its nature, and as each seven can be subdivided seven times, we have the forty-nine fires spoken of.

Fire has always to be *brought forth* from where he is hiding, but, when he has been released by friction, he has the power to light innumerable things. Fire by friction is one of the earliest gifts given to man by divine beings who helped infant humanity, it is said, and sacrifice by fire has been part of religious rituals down the ages.

There are many descriptive passages in the old scriptures of this great nature-god. He is described as raging in the forest like a lion whose golden mane flies in the wind. He eats up everything that is in his path, and breathes out smoke as he burns up the living trees, leaving behind him blackened stumps. Even the wheels of his swift chariot leave dark tracks in the forest, and the sparks, flying out on all sides, turn the grass into a withered mass. All nature is terrified of his approach. He is also likened to a bull among a herd of cows, or to the onward rush of huge masses of water.

These are his destructive aspects. On the other hand he is the friend of man, for he gives him warmth and light, and is a great purifier.

*Vāyu,* god of wind or air, is a fierce god. He drives his horses furiously, sometimes a thousand of them. He is thought of as the god of rapid motion and therefore the father of the fleet-footed. As such he is the father of Hanumān, who could move with the speed of air, and of Bhima, brother of Arjuna, who was called the swift. The storm-gods, the Maruts, are his children, born from a daughter of Twashtri the divine carpenter. Many hymns have been written to him.

As with the other gods Vāyu can be prayed to for help. One legend says that Nārada the sage asked him to blow strongly enough to break off the top of Mount Meru, the holy mountain. Vāyu blew and blew, but in vain, for Garuda, the vehicle of Vishnu, spread his wings over the summit to shelter it and even the most terrific storm failed to move it. Then Nārada told him to watch Garuda, and if for a moment the great bird lifted his wings, he could try again to break the summit away. Such a moment came, and Vāyu blew the top of the mountain off, and it landed in the ocean where it now rests, as Lankā, or Ceylon.

*Surya,* the sun-god, the third of this early trinity, is not only the shining sun we see but also a god, powerful and free, master of his actions but obedient to the great Cosmic laws which bind all Ādityas. He brings light by rolling darkness up and dropping it into the waters. He rides in a chariot drawn by seven swift and fiery horses. At night time he dies as he disappears over the horizon, or, alternatively, he travels to other places until the time comes for his reappearance. One early poem asks how he is able to keep in the sky when there are no visible means of support, and also how does he travel along the same path every day when there are no roads to guide him.

Beautiful descriptions are given of this journey across the sky. Sometimes he is said to fight a hard battle with the cloud-demons; sometimes the god Indra comes to his aid and destroys the clouds which are hiding him from the earth. At other times Indra is called in to help the earth against him when he is too strong, and there is a great battle in the sky. On one such occasion, aided by Soma the moon, Indra struck off a wheel of Surya's chariot and sent it spinning down to earth.

Sometimes after a hard day fighting with the clouds Surya sinks wearily to rest in the arms of night. At other times he plays all day with the fleecy clouds in the blue sky, and then slowly sinks down in all his glory at the end of the day. But, as the dawn-myth tells us, he is for ever rising, crossing the sky and sinking out of sight.

The dual aspect appears here again, for with him is Sāvitar to whom the Gāyatri, the most holy text of the *Rig-Veda,* is addressed: "Let us keep in mind the adorable light of the divine Sun of Life, who may illumine our souls." All the aspects of Sāvitar are golden—his eyes, arms and hands—also his car which passes through the well-known paths in the sky. He is the higher aspect of the sun we see, and is said to be existing even when the physical sun has dropped below the horizon, for it is he who controls the bright stars that people the midnight sky. Some of the hymns addressed to him raise him to the height of Varuna, for he is the enlightener of the spirit of man, as Surya gives light to the physical sun.

Surya, as Vivaswat, married Saranyu, daughter of Twashtri and had twins, — Yama and Yami. Afterwards, as she was unable to stand the intense heat of Vivaswat, the gods took pity on her and carried her away, leaving in her place another so like her that her husband did not know the difference. The substitute became the mother of Manu the progenitor of the human race.

Saranyu escaped in the form of a mare, but some say that Vivaswat discovered this, and assuming the form of a horse, went after her. While she was away she bore the twin Aswins, the divine physicians. In time she returned to her husband for, in order to reduce his heat, he cut off some of his bright rays. It was from these rays that Vishnu's discus, Siva's trident and the weapons of Kārttikeya and Kuvera were made. (Kārttikeya is the war-god. Kuvera, the god of wealth, is not a nice person, he is deformed in body, pale in colour, with three legs and eight teeth. He is keeper of all gold, silver and jewels.)

Some say that Saranyu (also called Sanjnā) stands for night, daughter of Twashtri the bright hard sky; Yama for the moon. In time night vanishes, as did Saranyu, and gives birth to the twilight twins, the Aswins.

The *Aswins* are the divine physicians, young, beautiful, gracious and bright. They are immortal, for they partook of the Soma juice, much to the annoyance of Indra, it is said. They are the friends of man and rescue him from storms. They drive away darkness and enable him to see, and therefore to kill evil demons. One twin brings the moisture over the earth while the other brings the bright light. Symbolising twilight and dawn they are the physicians of man, for all know that night brings rest and healing, and dawn an uprising of energy. They are also the physicians who look after the sun and the dawn during the night, refreshing them for the next day's activity. Their chariot is golden and is drawn by horses or by birds. They are the reputed fathers of the twins Nakula and Sahadeva of *Mahā-bhārata* fame.

Connected with the sun is the dawn-myth, one of the loveliest in the mythology.

*Ushas* is the dawn. The word means "to burn or to glow". She is the auspicious, the beautiful; she is a gentle maiden who rides in a chariot of faint pink and gold, drawn by red horses.

There is pathos as well as love and worship in this myth for, after piercing the evil darkness and making a way for the sun to come, she spends the rest of the day fleeing from his love as he chases her across the sky. At the end of the day both of them fall into the arms of twilight and then vanish from sight until the next day. In the dark unknown of night the beneficent Aswins take her into their care and make her ready for the next day and her battle against darkness. Then, once more, she drives the night away by her rosy rays and floods the sky with soft light, and again the chase across the sky begins. Eternally the chase goes on for she keeps the cosmic laws and wakes all nature to activity. Just as the birds greet her with song so man should, it is said, greet her with his sacrificial fires and his praise. And he who would prosper in his day's work must be the first to greet her.

Rise! Our life, our breath has come back! The darkness is gone, the light approaches! Ushas has opened a path for Surya to travel; we have reached the point where our days are lengthened. The priest, the poet, celebrating the brightening Ushas, arises with the web of his hymn; shine, therefore, magnificent Ushas, on him who praises thee. . . . Mother of the gods! manifestation of Aditi! banner of the sacrifice, mighty Ushas, shine forth !

*Rig-Veda*

Ushas follows the track of the Dawns that are past and is the first of the unnumbered Dawns that are to come. . . . How great is the interval that lies between the Dawns that have arisen and those which are yet to arise ? Ushas yearns longingly after the former Dawns and gladly goes on shining with the others [that are to come]. Those mortals are gone who saw the earliest Ushas dawn; we shall gaze upon her now; and the men are coming who are to behold her on future morns. . . . Perpetually in former days did the divine Ushas dawn; and now today the radiant goddess beams upon this world: undecaying immortal.

*Rig-Veda*

But there is another side to this story for at certain times her arrival is dreaded. In tropical countries in times of drought, dawn begins another day of horror, of thirst and heat and struggle, and only the comparative cool and darkness of night brings any relief. Then the storm-gods help man, for they fight and vanquish Vritra, the drought demon, and a great battle takes place between Indra and Ushas. The Maruts and Indra, drunk with Soma juice, war against the sky and set free the cows (or rain) that are being held back by the sun. Once, Indra struck her car and broke it, and she fled in terror. Some say this taught her a lesson, but whether or no, her loveliness is so great that she still remains for most of the time the bringer of joy and happiness.

Sometimes she and night are said to be sisters, both daughters of the sky. At other times she is the daughter of night and she and her twin sister are dawn and twilight, each perpetually weaving gorgeous garments and as perpetually undoing the work of the other.

The *Maruts* are the storm gods. They travel, always with great speed, in chariots drawn by yellow horses or dappled deer. They can be so destructive that they are called Rudras or destroyers, or howlers—and their chariot can be so filled with rain that it spills over and falls to the earth. The speed of their passing can be such that the mountains shake and the great trees bend before them. At other times they are not so fierce and then their chariot is light and shining.

The birth of the Maruts was not simple. Diti, their mother, had a feud with Indra and wanted to destroy him. Kasyapa told her that if she carried the baby in her womb for a hundred years, and did not allow her thoughts to be for one moment impure, but always pious and good, she would bear a son who would destroy him. Unfortunately the god heard this and throwing his thunderbolt at her, divided the embryo into seven portions and each portion into seven. These became the Maruts.

According to another version Siva and Pārvati saw the lumps

of flesh and Pārvati asked Siva to turn them into boys. This he did and gave them to her for her own. This version brings out a deeper symbolical aspect for the Maruts also stand for the human intelligent ego of man which makes of the lumps of flesh, "boys", namely human beings.

*Twashtri.* All the gods have chariots and weapons. Who made them? Twashtri, or Viswa-karman, the divine architect. He it was who made Indra's thunderbolt of gold, with a thousand points and edges. He sharpened the axe of Brihaspati. He made the cups from which the gods drank the Soma juice. In fact he makes everything that has to be made.

He is connected with the seasons also as the following legend tells.

Twashtri had three very promising pupils, brothers, who became nearly as good workmen as he himself. They made Indra's chariot and horses, and the three-wheeled chariot which the Aswins drive. They also restored youth to their old parents and rejuvenated Surabhi the sacred cow who could, at will, produce anything which was desired. Yet in spite of their cleverness they were not gods but only good, pious men.

One day Agni came to them with a message from the gods asking them to make four cups from the one precious cup their master had made. If they would do this they were promised a great reward. So they set to work. Dividing the cup into four cups, they took their chariot and drove up to heaven with them. The gods were so pleased that they granted them the boon of immortality and allowed them to drink the Soma juice and attend the great Soma sacrifice.

When Twashtri saw what had been done he was very angry and rushed up to heaven to kill them, but as they had already drunk the waters of immortality he was thwarted and went away to hide himself among the wives of the gods.

This myth refers to the birth of the four seasons. At first there was but one season all the year; then three seasons—the three brothers. The moon stands for the one season, or cup, which the brothers had to divide into the four stages of the moon. As there are nearly thirteen times four phases of the moon in the year, the extra time was taken by the twelve days rest that the three brothers took in the heavens.

The seasons bring the different weapons of the gods into use, for at certain times the thunderbolt appears, and Indra's chariot and horses are necessary if he is to carry on his wars—at other times other weapons are in use. It is also the seasons that bring back youth and vitality to the heavens and the earth, and to the ever-productive cow.

High among the nature gods is *Indra,* son of Twashtri. As soon as he was born he drank the Soma juice and immediately grew so strong that he threw his father down in order to kill him. Sometimes he is said to be the child of *Kāma* (love), born from the heart of Brahmā. He is also indentified with Agni, for fire or spirit gives life. Combining these ideas, we see that he was made by the divine architect from the love, or heart, of Brahmā and given life by fire.

He is regarded as a great god, and heaven and earth bow down to him in fear. He is the thunderer who rides in a shining chariot, holding a whip of gold in his hand, and the thunderbolt under his arm. At times he drives so fiercely that his golden beard flies in the wind. He joins forces with other gods, Vāyu and Agni, and also with the Maruts, and together they storm the heavens to make the clouds give up their moisture. The rain is likened to cows, and the rain-clouds to pent-houses in which these cows are kept by demons. The heavy thunder-clouds on the horizon are likened to caves in which they are hidden. The gods are the herdsmen. The little fleecy clouds are also called cows.

In one story when Vala, the cave-demon, stole some cows and hid them in a cave so that they could not be found Indra sent his ambassador, Saramā the dog, to search for them. She found them in the dark caves low on the horizon, for she heard their lowing, but when she asked Vala to set them free he refused to part with them. She returned to Indra with the news and he decided to go and rescue them.

He set out with the help of Brihaspati and the Agnirasas, and with Saramā as guide, and broke down the walls of the cave with his mace, setting the cows free. Then Brihaspati drove them along the horizon. But Vala wept, it is said, for his beautiful cows, "like the tree mourns for its foliage when it is stripped bare by the frost."

In this story it is not the Maruts who help, but Brihaspati, the Lord of the sacrificial fire and the Angirasas, the heavenly singers and sacrificers, so that we obviously have a reference to religious ritual and sacrifice.

In times of drought when the drought demon Vritra is in power, Agni asks Indra and the Maruts to a great sacrificial banquet where they drink the immortal *Amrita,* and, full of energy and strength, set out to fight him. In the fierce battle that follows they cut him into pieces and fling them down the mountain sides where they fall as refreshing rain.

Indra's heaven, Swarga, is on Mount Meru, the holy mountain, but it is built like a chariot and can be moved from place to place. As in the other heavens there is a great Assembly Hall in which Indra sits robed in white, his upper arms covered with bracelets, and a crown on his head. With him is Indrāni his wife. He is surrounded by the Maruts and the "spirits" of the elements, of wind and rain, thunder, fire and clouds. Everything is there, and life is not dull, for religious rites are performed and tournaments are given by those battle warriors who have entered the kingdom after their death. Messengers, shining like the bright moon and riding in chariots, are constantly visiting him. All is happiness; there is no fear, no suffering, no sorrow, and, as usual, the palace is full of flowers. Here are the Apsaras, the dancing nymphs, and the Gandharvas and Kumāras the musicians; the Gandharvas number 6,333 and represent the sounds in Nature. The Apsaras were often sent down to earth to disturb human beings who were growing too godlike, as shown by the following story.

Kandu, a sage, had developed such marvellous will-power through his austerities and sacrifices that the gods were worried. Indra* therefore sent down Pramlochā, one of the most beautiful Apsaras, with orders to try and disturb him and beguile him from his austerities. This she did to such effect that for nearly a thousand years—years which seemed to him as only one day—he forgot everything else but her. Then he awoke from this state of intoxication and cursed her so vigorously that she fled in terror. Flying through the forest she wiped the beads of perspiration from her body on to the tree tops, and dried herself with the leaves. The wind gathered the drops together, the moon shone on them and they were transformed into a young and beautiful girl, Mārishā.** She was known as the "offspring of the trees." Then the moon gave her in marriage to Prachetas who personifies those solar beings who are said to have spent ten thousand years in the ocean of matter, deep in meditation, only coming forth when the world was very wicked, and then destroying almost the whole of the vegetation on the earth. It was to pacify them that the moon, lord of the vegetable world, offered them Mārishā, and thus the powers of the sun and moon became allied. Mārishā became the mother of Daksha who figures in the Siva stories.

*Soma* the moon is another Āditya. This is a difficult symbol to understand, for three main ideas are incorporated—King Soma, regent or spirit of the moon; Indu, the visible moon; and the juice of the Soma plant, an intoxicating drink usually kept for the use

* Or Kama—the god of Love. This story seems to resemble that of Adam and Lillith at a very early period of evolution.

** Have we here an early mode of birth of the human form through drops of sweat, the sweat-born 2nd race of mankind, Kandu standing for the 1st race?

of the priests in their religious ceremonies.

The Soma juice is said to open up the spiritual vision as ordinary intoxicants open up the lower vision. In its highest aspect it is the water of immortality which came from the Churning of the Ocean and which is drunk by Indra and the other gods before they go into battle. The plant is said to have been brought to earth by supernatural beings and planted by King Varuna.

Indu, the physical moon, is likened to a golden bowl which holds the juice, or like a well of sweetness from which the gods drink when the moon is new. The more they drink the brighter the moon becomes, and as it decreases in size the Pitris, spirits of the dark, drink from it. According to another explanation it is the gods who drink when the moon is at the full and the Pitris when it is new.

King Soma is wise. He brings about the seasons and marks the times for special rites and prayers. He is also a warrior, waging war against the powers of darkness and bringing light to the earth. He preserves the sacred waters. He married the twenty-seven daughters of Daksha (personifying the twenty-seven lunar asterisms). One of them, Rohini, became his favourite and this so angered the other sisters that they complained to their father. He tried to help them but failed, and so cursed Soma to be childless and to waste away. This was more than the jealous sisters had bargained for, and they begged him to modify his curse. This he could not do but he relented so far as to make the wasting away periodical, and so the moon waxes and wanes.

Soma once stole Tārā, wife of Brihaspati (Jupiter) and thus caused a great war among the gods, shaking the very earth itself. Usanas (Venus) came to his aid, while Indra and Rudra helped Brihaspati. Once Rudra threw his trident and cut Soma in half and Brahmā had to intervene and stop the war, making Soma return Tārā to her husband. While away Tārā had borne a son, Budha, and when Brihaspati saw him he liked him so much that he took him as his own son.

One explanation to this myth is that Tārā, personifying the soul of man, was married to Brihaspati, who stands for ritual and faith, but longed for wisdom and drinking of the Soma juice, gained Budha, or wisdom as her son. Brihaspati, ritual and faith, saw that wisdom was much greater than he and adopted Budha as his son.

One other war in heaven can be referred to before passing on to Yama. Such wars were frequent, both between the gods and between the gods and demons. In one such war the gods were led by Brihaspati, and the asuras, or demons, by Usanas. This war continued for a long time without a decided victory, for Usanas, who shines by night as well as day, had the power to bring back to life those who had been slain during the day. At last the gods asked Kacha, son of Brihaspati, if he would go to Usanas and learn from him the power of awakening the dead. He was told, also, to make himself devoted to Usanas's daughter Devayāni. Kacha agreed and was accepted as a pupil by Usanas.

For five hundred years, half the time of his pupilage, happiness reigned. Then the followers of Usanas, discovering Kacha's motive, decided to remove him, and killed him in a lonely part of the forest where he was minding the sheep. They cut his body into many pieces and the jackals and wolves devoured them. When at evening the cattle returned home without him, Devayāni felt that he must be dead for otherwise he would have come back, and she asked her father to revive him. He did so by the mere process of calling to him, and all the pieces of his body tore themselves out of the animals which had eaten them, joined themselves together, and Kacha was once more whole.

Another time when he was gathering flowers in the forest for Devayāni he was killed, his body ground into minute pieces and mixed with the ocean. But he was again brought to life by Usanas.

Still another attempt was made. He was again killed, his flesh burnt to ashes, bones powdered and put into the wine which Usanas drank. Even Usanas now said that he was powerless to revive him for to do so would be to kill himself. Devayāni said she could not live without both of them and eventually Usanas thought of a plan. He gave Kacha the power to revive the dead and then called him to come out of his body. Kacha did this, and his first act was to restore Usanas to life.

Five hundred more years passed in peace for Usanas made the demons refrain from further persecution.

When the time came for Kacha to return home Devayāni asked him to take her with him, but in spite of all her entreaties and even curses, he would not do so for as his master's daughter she was like a sister, and he said he would not sin. Later she married king Yayāti and became the mother of a long line of princes and tribes of Asuras.

*Yama* king of the dead is somewhat different from the other gods. His symbol is the earth. He is also the progenitor of the human race for he was the first man to attain a physical body and, as physical bodies must be laid aside after a time in what is called death, he was the first to reach the kingdom of the dead. That is why he is able to welcome and guide all who come to that kingdom.

There is something very beneficient and "human" about Yama. He is pictured as having dark garments over his green body and he rides about on his black he-buffalo—that gentle sad-looking creature which seems to have no will of its own and to whom time is as nought. He is aided in his work by recorders and counsellors, and by his messengers, the two dogs called *Sārameyas,* a word meaning children of Saramā, the dog-messenger of Indra. These dogs roam the world to find those who are about to die, and take them to Yama each morning and evening. They are not very prepossessing in appearance for they have four eyes, wide snouts and spotted skins.

In the early conception Yama's kingdom was not dark and fearsome, nor was he a judge and accuser, but in his hands there was perfect trust. The kingdom was bright and happy, and people went to live there gladly for, just as all know that the setting sun will rise again, so they knew that they could come out again after a period of rest. Nārāyana says in the *Mahā-bhārata* that in this kingdom there is neither hot not cold, neither hunger nor thirst; age does not bring difficulties; no one is wretched or tired, but everyone is kind and harmonious. Fruit and flowers grow in abundance, and life is happy and gay with music and dancing. The vast Assembly Hall, built by the divine architect, shines like gold; the *Rishis,* or wise men, are clad in white, their arms are covered with bracelets, and they wear golden earrings.

But as time went on people began to fear death—something which Yama found very difficult to understand as the following story shows.

Once a husband and wife who were  very pure and good obtained from Siva a boon. They asked for a son, and the god granted their request, but he told them they had to decide whether they would like an ordinary son who would live and marry and give them grandchildren, or a perfect son, good, beautiful, clever, who would die when he was thirteen years old. The father shirked the decision and left it to his wife. She decided in favour of the perfect son, and in due time he was born. They called him Kamil. He was so good and perfect that he was loved by everyone, and in their happiness the mother and father forgot all about the early death which had been prophesied.

But Yama did not forget, and when the boy was thirteen years old he sent his messengers to bring him to his kingdom. Kamil refused, saying he was quite happy and had no desire to die. Yama sent again, with the same result, and at last decided he would have to go himself, and mounting his dark buffalo he set off. Kamil still refused to go, and when Yama tried to take him by force he put out his hand and touched a *lingam,* symbol of Siva whom he worshipped, and in the strugle the *lingam* was knocked down. This angered Siva so much that he came in wrath and sent Yama back to his kingdom, telling him to stay there until he told him he could come out again!

Siva's word is law, and so death did not come; no one died, nor did the flowers, animals and birds, and as people and things kept on being born, the earth soon became so full that the people begged Siva to let death come again in order that they might be taken to the kingdom of forgetfulness and quiet peace.

Siva, however, would not go back on his word. The people then approached Pārvati, Siva's wife, and told her how weary they were and how they longed to sleep the sleep of death, and she spoke to Siva about it. But the answer was the same—Yama had insulted him and he would not go back on his word. Pārvati then began to use her ingenuity. She told him that it was true Yama had been insulting  but he had only been obeying orders when he went to take the boy at the end of his allotted period of life. She pointed out that it was Siva himself who had said the boy was to die at the age of thirteen! Siva remained silent. Pārvati then said that perhaps it was all due to a mistake. Perhaps Siva had meant that the boy should always be thirteen years old to look at, and therefore could be allowed to live to any age. Siva still remained silent. Then Pārvati said that Yama was a very old man and surely he ought to be forgiven if he could not understand the subtlety of this explanation. This seemed a good  way out of the difficulty. Siva agreed, and ordered death to come again. The messengers went away with the good news and all the earth was glad and Yama did not send for Kamil for many years.

## PART II

THE CREATIVE GODS

Brahmā

Vishnu

The Ten Avatāras of Vishnu

Siva

# CHAPTER III

# BRAHMĀ

The well-known Tri-murti, Brahmā, Vishnu, Siva, (Creator, Preserver and Destroyer-Regenerator), belongs to a much later period than the Vedic Tri-murti, Agni, Vāyu, Surya.

Brahmā, the Creator, was born from the golden egg, Hiranya-garbha, which appeared in the "beginning" in the infinitude of space, created by the Supreme Cause—though the idea of creation cannot really be applied to the Supreme Cause. After lying in it for a year he divided it into two parts, one half of the shell became the heavens and the other half the earth. Between them was the sky.

He is also said to have sprung from a lotus growing out of Vishnu's navel, symbolising re-birth or re-manifestation from the seed of past manifestations which had been preserved in Vishnu, the preserving aspect of the Tri-murti. Or, again, he floats on a lotus on the Waters of Space—the "Moyst" principle of the ancients.

After living for aeons, a period of time counted in fifteen figures, he expires, and everything expires with him and returns to the Supreme Cause. This does not imply finality, however, for that which has been must be again. This period is known as the "Age" of Brahmā.

During his life he sleeps and wakes periodically. When he is awake the world flourishes; when he sleeps all beings cease to exist except in their hidden aspects. Sometimes the world is destroyed by fire, sometimes by water, but it is always "reborn" when he awakes. The periods of waking are called manvantaras, the periods of sleep, pralayas. As well as the periods of waking and sleeping, the "days" and "nights" of Brahmā, there is his "year" and his "age" which equals 100 years. The "day" lasts for

2,160,000,000 years—earthly years, and the "night" is of equal length.

When personified he has four heads (once he had five, but Siva's fire destroyed one), and four arms. He carries a sceptre, or bow, and is generally red in colour, red standing for the creative or active principle in nature. Like all gods he has his *vāhana* or vehicle, Kalahansa, the swan.

From his body came the four castes of the Hindus: the Brāhman from his mouth, the Kshatriya from his arms, the Vaisya from his thigh and the Sudra from his feet. These represent the four types of work needed in the world: the Brāhman is the teacher, the Kshatriya the soldier or statesman, who preserves order in the kingdom and guards it from the enemy; the Vaisya is the merchant who buys and sells and therefore looks after the needs of the people, and the Sudra or servant gives his service to others whether in the house or in the State.

The four *Vedas* also came from his mouth.

As he has four heads he has four faces, and legend tells us how this came about. When he took on human shape he created a woman from a half of himself. She was so beautiful that he fell in love with her and looked at her so continuously that to avoid his gaze she turned to one side. He then created another face so that without moving he could still see her. She turned away twice more and each time he created another face.

He is intimately connected with the Arts for architecture, painting, dancing, music and the drama are associated with Spirit: all are efforts to glorify the divine and to bring some glimpse of the divine to earth.

Legend tells how the gods, bored with heavenly inactivity, sent one of their number, Indra, to Brahmā and asked him if he would write a play which they could see and hear and which would give them an understanding of what was the real nature of joy. Brahmā therefore began to write a *Veda,* known as the Fifth *Veda,* or the *Nātya-Veda,* for which he took parts from the other four *Vedas.* He took recitation from the *Rig-Veda,* song, mime, *rasa* from respectively the *Sāma,* the *Yajur* and the *Atharva Vedas.* This was, and is today, the Veda of the theatre. He then called on Viswa-karman, the Divine Architect, and ordered him to build a theatre in Indra's heaven and when this was completed the Sage Bharat took over the production of the play. Siva was the dancer, and he danced the famous *Tāndava* dance which symbolised the great motion of Cosmos. Pārvati, his wife, danced the *Lāsya* dance, and Vishnu also took part. The play was such a success that Bharat was asked to bring the knowledge of the *Nātya-Veda* down to earth, and he wrote the *Bhāratanātayasāstra* the book on which all Indian drama has been based.

The legends regarding the beginnings of music deal also with the great cosmic dance of Siva. It is said that as he danced, the five *rāgas* came from his five faces. *Rāgas* are melody types in the structure of which are the seven fundamental notes C. D. E. F. G. A. B. The sixth *rāga* emanated from the voice of Pārvati. The union of Siva and Pārvati typifies the union of energy and matter transforming itself into musical forms. The notes are linked with the whole Cosmos for each note is said to have an individual value and to be connected with a planet, for the whole planetary system is the source of sound in the universe.

There are only a few myths and legends connected primarily with Brahmā, though he figures in many of them for he is often called upon for help. This help is rarely given by himself, but he suggests that the aid of Vishnu or Siva should be sought. In other words it is his preservative-permeating aspect, or his destructive-regenerating aspect that is needed when a world is in existence. At times his name is used interchangeably with that of Vishnu as is the case in the ten *avatāras* which are said to be of Vishnu or of Brahmā indiscriminately.

His wife, or female aspect, is Vāch, the Word, goddess of wisdom. All creation comes from the union of these two aspects.

His heaven is on Mount Meru and is called Brahmapura or Brahmaloka. It is surrounded by the waters of the sacred river Ganges.

One legend tells us that he had a daughter Sandhyā who was the wife of Siva, and he fell in love with her. She was so frightened that she changed herself into a deer, and in order to follow her, he changed himself into a stag and chased her across the sky. Siva saw this and was so angry he shot an arrow which cut off the stag's head, and Brahmā resumed his own form. But the arrow and the stag's head remain in the sky, the former in the sixth moon mansion, Ārdrā, and the latter in the fifth mansion, Mrigasiras.

Another legend says that he fell in love with his daughter Ushas. (Sandhyā means twilight and Ushas means the dawn). He turned her into a deer and committed the first sin. The gods were so terrified of the consequences of this sin that they united with the spirit of evil to destroy the child. When Brahmā saw this he was ashamed, and repented of his folly so deeply that while he was chanting the prayer of purification he dropped a tear, the hottest ever shed, and it fell to earth and became the sapphire.

His son, Marichi, became the father of Kasyapa who is said to be the greatest of the Prajā-patis or creators for he married Aditi and twelve other daughters of Daksha. By Aditi he became the father of the Ādityas and of Vivaswat. The other wives were the mothers of reptiles, birds, demons, serpents and all other living things.

Garuda, the great bird, vehicle of Vishnu, was born from the daughter Vinatā. He was so brilliant that the gods worshipped him, for they thought he shone as if he were Agni himself. His eagle-like head, wings, talons and beak, are joined to a human body, so that he is half man, half bird. His wings are red, his body like gold, and his face is white.

His mother had a quarrel with one of the co-wives, her sister, whose children were serpents, and Garuda is therefore the enemy of serpents. For some reason his mother had been imprisoned by her sister Kadru, mother of the serpents, chief of which was Vāsuki, and in order to free her he had to fetch the *amrita,* the waters of immortality, from the mountain of heaven. To do this he had to pass through flames, fanned by the wind to enormous proportions. He put them out by drinking up all the rivers and pouring the water on the flames. Then he found that the *amrita* was further protected by a wheel, with edges sharp as knives, which revolved with great speed. He therefore made himself small enough to get between the spokes, but was then hindered by two snakes. These he blinded with dust and killed. Then, breaking the wheel, he took the cup which held the *amrita* and flew away with it. Unfortunately Indra saw him and threw his thunderbolt at him. But Garuda flew on and was just able to give the cup to the demons, who then released his mother, before Indra snatched it away so that the demons could not drink. In the tussle some of the water was spilt and the snakes drank up what they could by licking the grass on which it had fallen. From that day the grass, called Kusa, has possessed special properties and is used by the yogis to sit on during their meditations.

# CHAPTER IV

# VISHNU

Vishnu, the second of the Tri-murti, is the Preserver and Pervader. He is a dark god, with four hands, one holding a club, another a shell or conch, the third a discus and the fourth a lotus. He is usually pictured with a yellow robe and a necklace, Vaijayanti, comprising five precious gems, the pearl, ruby, emerald, sapphire and diamond, symbolising the five elements. He has other jewels, notably Kaustubha which came from the Churning of the Ocean.

He is said to take three strides which cover the universe; on earth as Agni, fire; in the atmosphere as lightning; and in the sky as Surya the sun. Sometimes they are said to refer to the rising, culmination and setting of the sun. During the periods of rest or Pralaya he reclines on the coiled serpent Ananta, and during manifestation he rests on Sesha, the other aspect of the serpent, symbol of Time. His vehicle is the great bird Garuda.

He is represented as having four arms which symbolise his power throughout the four directions of space. The right lower hand holds a conch or shell formed of a spiral with ever-increasing spheres. The sound given forth when it is blown symbolises the "Sound" which brought the universe into existence, the Great Word, the Voice of God. Its name is a word meaning born-of-five, the five elements.

The higher right hand holds the discus with six spokes, symbolising the ascending tendency and the mind. It is called Su-darsana, a word meaning Beauteous Sight, and refers to the Universal Mind. Where the spokes join one another at the centre is the Holy Word, representing the changeless, motionless centre, while the outer circle represents the *māyā* of all existing things.

In the upper left hand, representing the descending tendency towards dispersion, is the bow, symbol of *māyā,* and the lotus, symbol of the universe. The bow symbolises the active form of individual existence and is the origin of the senses, for from it we send out our arrows, our senses, through which we perceive and act. The lotus represents the Universe for it rises from the depth of the water, immaculate and pure.

The lower left hand, representing individual existence, holds the mace, symbol of Primeval Knowledge. It is the power of the intellect, and the essence of life. By knowledge alone can Time be conquered and used, and therefore the mace is identified with the goddess, Kāli, the Power of Time, which destroys all who oppose it.

On his chest is the great shining jewel Kaustubha, born from the waters surrounding the earth. It represents the consciousness which is in all living beings, and is the enjoyer of all.

On his left breast is a lock of golden hair, symbolising all the forms of the world, all that which the enjoyer enjoys.

Round his neck is a garland of five rows of flowers or of jewels, representing the five senses. The garland is called the "Garland of the Forest", and is also *māyā,* the Power of Illusion.

His earrings are formed like sea monsters (Makara the fish) and represent knowledge and intuitive perception.

On his arms are armlets representing the three aims of worldly life, righteousness, prosperity and pleasure.

His crown stands for the divinity, the Unknowable Reality. Round his hips is a thin yellow scarf reminding us that the Divine Reality shines through the eternal wisdom as Vishnu's dark body shines through the golden veil.

Across his chest is the scared thread, representing the three syllabled AUM.

His chariot stands for the mind and moves at will. From the mind come the five spheres of perception. Divinity which rides in the mind fits the arrows, the senses, to the Bow of Time and aims at objects.

His body is represented as black or dark blue. In his various incarnations the colour differs, for in the first age, the golden, he is white; in the second, red; in the third, yellow; and in the fourth, our dark age, he is black.

The following story tells of the greatness of Vishnu.

Once Siva visited Vishnu, going to him on his bull and taking Pārvati with him. He wished to ask Vishnu if he would show him the woman form by which he had bewitched the asuras at the Churning of the Ocean so that the Waters of Immortality could be taken from them and given to the gods.

When he heard the request, Vishnu laughingly complied, and vanished.

Immediately a woman appeared playing with a ball in a garden gay with flowers and trees. She was young and beautiful, and as Siva watched her she returned his gaze with coy looks. He became so enamoured of her that he forgot Pārvati and everything else and ran after her. For a time she ran away and hid behind the trees, darting from place to place, but at length he caught her up and tried to hold her. Struggling free she fled and he followed. The chase led them past rivers and lakes, mountains and forests and gardens, until his passion was exhausted. Then he realised that his mind had been deluded by appearances and he became calm once more and unashamed.

Seeing him thus returned to his normal state Vishnu reappeared in his own form. He told Siva that he knew that only for a time could he be deluded by illusion.

Satisfied, Siva asked leave to depart and after walking round Vishnu, as was the custom, he walked away, followed by Pārvati. On the way he told her that if he, the most powerful of the aspects of Vishnu, could thus fall under the power of illusion, how difficult it must be for those who are weak and dependent.

But all over the earth where the seed of Siva fell as he pursued the form mines of silver and gold appeared.

In another story Siva is saved from death by Vishnu.

Once an Asura, hearing that Siva was more easily pleased than either Brahmā or Vishnu, began to perform austerities in the hope of gaining a boon from him. He began by cutting off bits of his flesh and throwing them on his sacrificial fire. But nothing happened. In despair he took up an axe and started to cut off his head, having first moistened his hair with holy water.

At this stage Siva appeared from the middle of the sacrificial fire and stopped him, and by the touch of his hand made him whole. Then he said that if he wanted his protection all that was necessary was to ask for it, and he ought not to hurt himself as he had done. And he promised him a boon.

The Asura asked that if he touched anyone's head that person should die at once. Siva granted the boon, though it distressed him.

The reason for this request then became clear for the Asura raised his hand to touch the god's head ! Seeing this Siva ran away, and the Asura following, the chase took them through earth and heaven until the abode of Vishnu himself was reached.

Vishnu saw them approaching and changing his appearance into that of a mendicant clad in deer skin, with a stick and rosary and chain round his hips, he approached the Asura and asked him why he did not rest and tell him what had happened.

This the Asura did, but Vishnu said since Siva had been cursed by Daksha his word could not be trusted and he advised the Asura to find out for himself whether his word was true by touching his own head. If the boon did not work then the giver of it ought to be put to death.

The Asura accordingly put his hand to his own head and immediately died.

All the heavens rejoiced and flowers rained down in gratitude that Siva had been saved. But Vishnu told Siva that the man had been killed by his own fault for there could not be happiness when any one committed a fault against the great, and even less so when against the Lord of the Universe.

# CHAPTER V

# THE TEN AVATĀRAS OF VISHNU

Vishnu is said to incarnate ten times: these incarnations are known as *avatāras*. Nine have already taken place but the tenth is still to come. Each incarnation is in order to save the world from evil and destruction.

## MATSYA

The first incarnation is known as the *Matsya* or fish incarnation and it reminds us of the story of Noah and the Ark.

How long ago one does not know, but at some time there lived a king Manu, whose father was Vivaswat the Sun, and whose brother was Yama.* He was a holy man, and after a time he gave up his throne to his son and spent a million years in a certain part of what is known as Malabar, performing great austerities and ascetic practices.

One day when he was washing his hands in the river Chirini he found a small fish in them. It spoke to him saying that as it was so very small it was frightened to be in the river, and it asked if he would take care of it and place it in a smaller container. This Manu did, using a jar, "bright as a moon-beam". He looked after it so well that it grew rapidly, and finding the jar too small, asked to be placed in something larger. Manu put it in a pond, but soon this was too small and he put it in the Ganges. Even this sacred river became too small and the fish asked to be taken to the ocean.

Manu did so, but before the fish disappeared it told him that the world was shortly to be destroyed by water because the time had come for it to be purified. It advised him to build a ship, with

---

* Yama (not the god of death) stands for the first human being.

a rope attached, and take on board the seven Rishis and all the seeds of life when the flood came. Then Manu should look out for it, recognising it by its horn, and it would come to his aid.

Manu did as he was advised, and when the waters rose the ship floated on them. Then Manu saw the fish swimming towards him and tied the rope to its horn. Thus the ship was taken over the rough waters to the only land visible, the highest peak of the Himālayas. The fish told Manu and the Rishis to tie the ship firmly to the peak, which is known today as the "Binding of the Ship"— Naubandhana. But it warned them to begin to descend when the waters receded or they would not be able to leave the peak ! As it was swimming away the fish disclosed to them that it was Brahmā (or Vishnu) in the form of a fish, and it asked Manu, when the waters had gone, to begin to create all creatures.

The rope attached to the ship is said to be the serpent Ananta.

The *Vedas* were also saved. They were recovered from the demon Haya-griva, who had stolen them when they fell from Brahmā's mouth when he was asleep during one of his "nights."

## KURMA

The second incarnation was that of *Kurma* the Tortoise at the Churning of the Ocean.

Once again there was great trouble in the world for Indra had been cursed by a Rishi and had lost all his power. The world had begun to decay, all energy had been lost, nothing lived, and the battles between gods and demons, devas and asuras, raged long and fierce. And because Indra's energy had gone, the gods began to lose the battles and became very disheartened. At length they went to Brahmā and asked for his help. He took them to Vishnu's dwelling and they explained their trouble. Vishnu consented to help, provided they did what he asked.

He told them to gather one of every kind of plant and herb that grew in the world, and throw them all into the Sea of Milk. The Sea must then be well churned until the Waters of Immortality, the *amrita,* came from it. He said he would take the form of a tortoise to help them. As this was a great task he suggested they should stop fighting the asuras and ask them to help. But he promised that though the asuras helped they would not get any reward.

So the gods took the great mountain Mandāra to the Ocean of Milk to use as a churning stick. The serpent Vāsuki, king of the serpents, came to be the rope by which the churning stick could be revolved, Twashtri made the churn, and Vishnu, as a tortoise, supported the mountain on his back and became the pivot. He also gave his energy to the participants in this exercise. The devas took the lowly place and held Vāsuki's tail, but the asuras went to the serpent's head and consequently suffered, for as Vāsuki became hot, the flames of his breath blackened their faces and made them hot also, while the swish of his tail created a cooling breeze which fanned the faces of the devas !

As the churning went on great waves appeared and many wonderful things were thrown up. First Surabhi, the sacred cow, appeared. Then followed Uchchaih-Sravas, the many-headed horse; Airāvata, the white elephant, guardian of the east, which was taken by Indra to be his own; Pārijāta, a wonderful tree which was afterwards kept in Indra's heaven and much loved by Indrāni. (Once Krishna stole this tree at the request of his wife and planted it in Dwārkā, but when he died it was given back to Indra.) Many other things came up: Kaustubha, a jewel, afterwards worn by Vishnu or Krishna; Sankha, the conch; the Moon, which Siva placed on his brow; troops of water-nymphs; the apsarās from Indra's court; the goddess Lakshmi, wife of Vishnu, who arose out of the waters seated on a lotus, looking so beautiful that everything sang her praises, the sky-elephants poured refreshing waters from the Ganges on her and the Ocean of Milk gave her a garland of imperishable flowers. The four *Vedas* then appeared, and finally Dhanwantari, the divine physician, holding in his hands the cup of *amrita.*

But poison had also come. Some say Siva drank it, and hence became known as Nila-kantha, the blue-throated, for his throat was turned blue by the poison. Others say Vāsuki took it for himself and his race.

In the meantime the asuras had fallen in love with Lakshmi and wanted to fight the gods and possess her, and a battle began. Then Vishnu took the form of a very beautiful woman, and the asuras began to fight over him, so that he was able to take the cup and give it to the gods who drank deeply from it.

One demon, Rāhu, making himself appear as a god, stole a drink. The sun and moon saw him and complained to Vishnu. Vishnu flung his discus at the culprit and cut off his head, flinging him up in the sky where he remains today, for, having drunk of the waters, he is immortal. In revenge his head with its wide open mouth follows the sun and moon across the heavens, and at what we call eclipses, he swallows them.

In the battle between the gods and asuras thousands of the demons were slain by Vishnu's discus, which has the power to return to him every time it is sent out. Those who were not slain hurried to hide in the depths of the earth or the ocean, but before they went, they hurled down great rocks and overthrew mountains in their effort to defeat the gods.

At last all was well. Indra sang a hymn of praise to Lakshmi, and she was so pleased that she promised never to forsake anyone who sang Indra's hymn to her. That is why she is still evoked today as the goddess of prosperity.

### VARAHA

The third incarnation was that of *Varāha* the boar.

Once again the earth was suffering, due to the pride of Hiranyāksha, a demon, the golden-eyed Daitya who had won a boon from Brahmā through spending many ages in austerities.

(It should be noted that even Brahmā cannot prevent the attainment of powers won through effort; it is the use to which these powers are put which makes them good or bad. When used for bad purposes Brahmā helps to destroy the culprit.) The boon was that he should become king of the whole world, and that no animal which he mentioned by name should have the power to harm him. In his catalogue of animals he forgot the boar! When in his pride he had dragged the earth down into the ocean it complained bitterly to Vishnu. Vishnu therefore took the form of a boar, with great white tusks, and plunged into the ocean to free the earth. It took him one thousand years to kill Hiranyāksha and to lift the earth up with his tusks.

In one account Prajā-pati, or Brahmā, found the earth covered with water and caused the wind to blow to dry it. Then he lifted the earth up. As she dried she grew, so that her name is Prithivi, a word meaning "the extended one."

Another account says that when Brahmā saw a lotus leaf on the waters he realised that its roots must be on something firm, and taking the form of a boar plunged into the water, and breaking off a portion of matter, rose to the surface. This portion he placed on the lotus leaf and it became the earth.

## NARA-SINHA

The fourth *avatāra* was that of *Nara-sinha,* half-man, half-lion. This was in the reign of Hiranya-kasipu, twin-brother of Hiranyāksha. It is said that Hiranya-kasipu was born again at a later date as Rāvana, and to explain these incarnations of evil, its said that once he had been offered a choice, either to succeed in his evolution as an enemy of Vishnu in three lives, or to be a friend of Vishnu and take many lives. He had chosen the first course.

In this particular incarnation he was so great that even the sun and moon ruled by reason of his power, and the saints sang his praises. He had won this eminence through ten thousand years

of austerities, gaining lordship over the three worlds, and freedom
from harm at the hands of gods, men, and animals, at night time
or in the day time, within doors and out of doors, on earth and in
heaven. But this comprehensive freedom from harm had a
loophole, and he was destroyed from a *pillar,* at the *threshold* of
a room, *i.e.,* neither in a room nor out of doors, at *evening, i.e.,*
neither day nor night, after a fight lasting one hour so that his
actual death took place at the moment between night and day !

He had a son, Prahlāda, who was wise and good, and he sent
him to the priests for his education. After some time he sent for
him and asked him what he had learnt. The boy said he had
learnt that Vishnu was the great Lord of the Universe and he
worshipped him.

This made Hiranya-kasipu so angry that he sent for the priests
and complained of their teaching. But they said he must have
learnt of Vishnu from the God himself, for they had not taught
him. Prahlāda agreed, and told his father that Vishnu dwelt in
him and had taught him this truth. More angry still Hiranya-
kasipu sent the boy away to learn wisdom.

After a while he called him again and asked what he had now
learnt. In answer the youth chanted a prayer and hymn to
Vishnu. Infuriated, his father ordered his servants to beat him.
When the king thought the beating was sufficient he ordered
them to stop, and asked his son to recant, but he would not, for
he had felt no pain as he had kept his thought on Vishnu.

Again and again he was tortured, once being thrown into the
ocean, where large rocks were piled on him. But he rose up
unharmed because of his thought of Vishnu.

At last the king asked the boy where was this Vishnu he
worshipped? The youth answered that he was everywhere.
Scornfully the father said: "Then he must be in this piller,"
pointing to, and striking, a pillar by his side. Immediately the pillar
opened, and Vishnu, in the form of Nara-sinha, man-lion, sprang

out and killed him.

Thus the demons were destroyed and the reign of gods once more blessed the earth.

## VAMANA

The fifth incarnation was that of *Vāmana,* the dwarf, at a time when the earth was ruled by Bali, grand-son of Prahlāda who, by his austerities, had defeated Indra and become greater than the gods. But he was not a bad king, and so was not destroyed. As the gods had been defeated they appealed to Vishnu and he took on the form of a dwarf, son of Kasyapa and Aditi, and went to Bali. He sought an audience and then asked if he might have a piece of land, just as much as he could cover with three strides. Bali at once consented, thinking to himself that it would indeed be a small piece of land ! Vāmana then asked if he would ratify his promise in the usual way, *i.e.,* by pouring water on the supplicant's hands, and he agreed. As the water fell on Vāmana's hand he began to grow. His first stride covered the whole sky, the second the earth, and the third the heavens, so that once more the whole world belonged to Vishnu and righteousness flourished.

Sometimes it is said that Vāmana covered both heaven and earth with two strides and having therefore nowhere to go for the third, left the infernal region to Bali.

## PARASU-RAMA

The sixth incarnation was that of *Parasu-rāma,* Rāma-with-the-axe, and ushers in a different kind of period, for now the incarnations are in human beings as we know them, and deal with life more as we know it.

Parasu-rāma was the son of a Brāhman descended from Bhrigu, the Vedic sage who had officiated at Daksha's sacrifice, (see section on Siva), and whose beard was pulled off by Siva. His mother was of royal descent. At the time of his birth the world was once again in trouble through the activities of the Kshatriyas, the warriors, who had now gained control, and he came to destroy them. Siva instructed him in the use of weapons and gave him an axe, and because of the axe he was known as Rāma-with-the-axe.

One day a king visited his father's hermitage and was entertained by his mother as his father was away. As he left he stole a calf which had been prepared for sacrifice. When Parasu-rāma heard of this he followed him, cut off his thousand arms and killed him. The dead king's sons, in revenge, killed Parasu-rāma's father, and his mother burnt herself to death. Parasu-rāma was so angered that he fought the whole Kshatriya race and cleared them from the world twenty-one times, leaving the Brāhmans in power. Legend says that he rescued Malabar from the ocean by driving the water from the land. Also he made great cuts in the Ghats, those mountains which cover so much of South India. He is also said to have carved a way down the Himālayas from Kailāsa in order to be able to descend more quickly, the path being called to this day Krauncha. Other legends say this pass was made by Kārttikeya who had a race with Indra round the mountain. As they did not agree as to the result, they appealed to the mountain who decided in favour of Indra. Kārttikeya, feeling this decision unjust, flung his lance at it thus making the pass.

Parasu-rāma seems to live during other incarnations for he fought Rāma when he broke Siva's great bow, was visited by Arjuna, took part in one of the Kuru's councils and fought with Bhishma.

## RAMA

The seventh incarnation was that of *Rāma,* the whole story of whom is given in the *Rāmāyana.* Sufficient here to say that Rāma was the divine king of Ayodhyā and Rāvana the demon king of Lankā (Ceylon). In the war between them Rāvana was killed and righteousness flourished under Rāma's rule.

## KRISHNA

*Krishna,* the eighth incarnation, like Rāma is god and man. Though he knew himself as Vishnu, God incarnate, and Rāma had to be reminded that he was Vishnu in reality, yet he seems nearer to man. As child, youth and adult he lived among ordinary human beings, playing with them, protecting them, working for them and teaching them. In his infancy and early youth he was surrounded with mystery, for he destroyed demons, won a victory over Indra, and defended his friends by performing miracles—hanging on the throat of a cloud demon, holding up a mountain with his finger and resuscitating the dead. His flute is a magic one, for even the river changed its bed to hear him play.

In later life the miraculous does not appear so frequently, but his loyalty to his friends, his integrity and vision as a prince, and his great compassion and courtesy, as when he visited the aged Prithā to give her news of her banished sons before paying his respects to the king, give a depth to his character that demands tribute.

As teacher of Arjuna on the battlefield he stands supreme. Not only did he lay down a code of conduct based on philosophical understanding, which all men must follow if they would live righteously and at peace during this age of darkness, but he granted to his disciple the divine vision of himself as God, and, as this was recorded, it is within the reach of all. The pæan of praise that flowed from Arjuna's lips as he beheld this divine vision is surely one of the greatest songs of praise ever thought of by man. It thrills the soul of the striver after truth today, as the call of Krishna's flute stirs the heart with magic.

The universe, O Hrishikesha, is justly delighted with thy glory and is filled with zeal for thy service; the evil spirits are affrighted and flee on all sides, while all the hosts of saints bow down in adoration before thee. And wherefore should they not adore thee, O mighty Being, thou who art greater than Brahmā, who art the first Maker? O eternal God of gods ! O habitation of the universe! Thou art the one indivisible Being, and non-being, that which is supreme. Thou art the first of Gods, the most ancient Spirit; thou art the final supreme receptacle of this universe; thou art the Knower and that which is to be known, and the supreme mansion; and by thee, O thou of infinite form, is this universe caused to emanate. Thou art Vāyu, God of wind, Agni, God of fire, Yama, God of death, Varuna, God of waters; thou art the moon; Prajapati, the progenitor and grandfather, art thou. Hail! hail to thee! Hail to thee a thousand times repeated! Again and again hail to thee ! Hail to thee ! Hail to thee from before ! Hail to thee from behind ! Hail to thee on all sides, O thou All ! Infinite is thy power and might; thou includest all things, therefore thou art all things !

Having been ignorant of thy majesty, I took thee for a friend, and have called thee "O Krishna, O son of Yadu, O friend", and blinded by my affection and presumption, I have at times treated thee without respect in sport, in recreation, in repose, in thy chair, and at thy meals, in private and in public; all this I beseech thee, O inconceivable Being, to forgive.

Thou art the father of all things animate and inanimate; thou art to be honoured as above the guru himself, and worthy to be adored; there is none equal to thee, and how in the triple worlds could there be thy superior, O thou of unrivalled power? Therefore I bow down and with my body prostrate, I implore thee, O Lord, for mercy. Forgive, O Lord, as the friend forgives the friend, as the father pardons his son, as the lover the beloved. I am well pleased with having beheld what was never before seen, and yet my heart is overwhelmed with awe; have mercy then, O God; show me that other form, O thou who art the dwelling-place of the universe; I desire to see thee as before with thy diadem on thy head, thy hands armed with mace and chakkra; assume again, O thou of a thousand arms and universal form, thy four-armed shape !

*Bhagavad-Gitā*

The intermingling of the divine and the human runs as a thread throughout the life story of this wonder among men, who was born 5,000 years ago at the beginning of this age of darkness called Kali Yuga, which is said to last 432,000 years !

He was born at a time of discord. The seeds which would flower in the great war (see the Mahā-bhārata) between the two branches of the royal family at Hastinā-pura, the Pandus and the Kurus, were already well advanced towards their fruition, and at Mathurā, Kansa had dethroned his father, the king, and imprisoned his sister, Devaki, and her husband, Vasu-deva.

It is dangerous to know the future, for one is tempted to try and thwart it by dubious means as did Kansa. Hearing that a child of his sister would be the cause of his death, he not only imprisoned her and her husband, but ordered that every child she bore should be killed at birth. This fate overtook six of Devaki's children. When she was about to give birth to her seventh child who, it was said, was to be an incarnation of Ananta, the serpent on which Vishnu rests, Vishnu took it from her womb and gave it to Rohini, another wife of Vasu-deva, who lived with the cowherd Nanda and his wife Yasodā, at Gokula. In due time the child was born and called Bala-rāma. (A variant of this legend says that Vishnu gave two of his hairs to Devaki, one dark and one fair. Bala-rāma was born from the latter, and Krishna from the former.)

Later, Devaki gave birth to the eighth child and the heavens were full of joy, trees flowered in profusion, there was no drought, and the gods rained down flowers from heaven, while the gandharvas filled the earth with their music. As soon as he was born Krishna appeared to his father and mother with his crown and jewels, clad in yellow, holding conch, discus, mace and lotus, and they bowed to him in reverence. He told them to take him to Yasodā and bring back the daughter to whom she was then giving birth. The vision faded, and the parents saw the human baby just born to them. Though the voice and the vision were strange, they decided to obey, and Vasu-deva put the child in a basket on his head and started to leave the prison. His fetters fell off, doors opened at his approach, the guards slept, the massive gates of the courtyard opened silently, and he went safely on his journey.

On the way he had to ford the river Yamunā. When half way across, the child suddenly became so heavy that he could barely hold him, the water rose almost to his head, and progress was impossible. But the child touched the water with his foot and it receded again so that the bank was reached in safety.

When they arrived at Nanda's dwelling the voice told Vasudeva to enter, place the baby by the side of Yasodā and take the baby girl back to his prison.

This was done, but neither Nanda nor Yasodā knew of the change, and the little boy was brought up by his foster-mother as her own.

Hearing of the birth Kansa tried to kill the little girl but she changed into a goddess and told him that his slayer was already living near the village of Go-kula, on the other side of the Yamunā. Kansa therefore sent out his demons to kill every child who had just been born.

Many tales are told of Krishna's babyhood. Often Yasodā was worried by his strange behaviour, for at one moment he would appear as the usual baby, and at the next, he would be the Lord of the Universe. She was also worried by Kansa's efforts to kill the child. Once he sent the vampire nurse, Putanā, to destroy him and she, changing herself into a beautiful and gracious woman, took the child on her knee and tried to feed him. Krishna touched her breast which was full of poison and drew out her life. She fell to the ground and resumed her real shape, horrifying the people who had thought her a graceful and kind woman.

At another time a demon, in revenge for the death of Putanā, attempted to destroy him. Yasodā was playing with him one day when she was called away, and so that he should not come to harm, she left him under an old bullock-cart in the yard. The demon got into the cart meaning to break it so that it would fall on him and kill him. But Krishna knew what was in her mind and, lifting his toe, threw the cart to the other side of the yard and the demon was killed.

Once when Yasodā and the child were together a black cloud covered them from sight, and when it lifted, Yasodā saw the child hanging on to the throat of the cloud-demon and being swept along by it. It looked as if nothing could save him. As she watched, full of terror, a lull came and the cloud floated slowly down into the village with the tiny child still holding its throat.

Krishna was always up to pranks, and to keep him near her Yasodā one day tied him by a rope to the heavy axle of a cart-wheel and left him to play. But he was not content to stay there and, dragging the axle with him, went towards two tall trees which had grown close together. He forced his way between them until the axle was wedged. Then, with a pull, he passed through and the trees fell down with a loud crash. Two shining spirits appeared from them. They said they had been imprisoned in the trees until Krishna could release them, and in their gratitude they offered him their oblations and worship.

Often the little boy stole the curds that the women had made and gave them to the monkeys or to other children. One day he swallowed some clay, but when the mother told him to open his mouth, she saw there, not to clay, but the whole universe. Another time she tried to tie his hands together with her churning rope to keep him out of mischief, but though she tied together all the ropes she could find she could not make one long enough to go round his small wrists ! When she began to despair, Krishna suddenly let her tie his wrists with a piece os string !

The spirit of this period has been well epitomised in the following lines by the Irish poet A. E:—

I paused beside the cabin door and saw the
    King of Kings at play,
Tumbled upon the grass I spied the
    Little heavenly runaway.

The mother laughed upon the child
    Made gay by its ecstatic morn,
And yet the Sages speak of It as of the
    Ancient and Unborn.

When he was six or seven years old he was allowed to go to the pastures with Bala-rāma and the other boys who tended the cattle. During this period he is often referred to as Go-vinda, the cowherd. It was a happy, gay period spent in the forest of Brindāban to which Nanda had moved to escape Kansa. He played with the gopis (shepherd-girls and boys), and the forest rang with their laughter and with the sound of his flute. Even the Yamunā strayed from its course to hear him play, and the lotus blossoms which lay in its surface opened to their full glory in gladness.

Many delightful stories are told of this time for it covers the period of boyhood to manhood and it has woven itself into the fabric of India's thought and heart. But there must be contrast in life, and Kansa appeared again in this otherwise idyllic scene.

Once a huge dragon appeared and hid itself so that only its mouth could be seen. This it opened widely and the boys and girls thought it was a cave and went towards it to look inside. Then the dragon drew them and the cattle into its mouth with its strong hot breath, and they called out to Krishna. He allowed himself to be caught also, but when inside, he grew so large that the dragon burst and all the gopis and the cattle came out unhurt.

A crane appeared one day as large as a mountain and sat on the river bank. Krishna allowed it to take him up in its beak and then became so hot that it had to let him go. Krishna then forced the beak apart until the crane was killed.

Another attempt was made, this time by Metrāsur, the demon-sheep, who, disguised as a ram, seemed to be quietly grazing one day when it suddenly rushed at Krishna. For a moment it looked as if nothing could save the boy, but Krishna waited quietly until it was near him, then put out his hand, took it by the neck and swung it round and round, finally dashing it against a tree. This event is still celebrated annually, when an effigy of a ram is burnt, and water, coloured red with powder, is sprinkled on the members of the family, and on the following day on any passer-by in the streets.

One very hot day the gopis went to drink from Lake Kāliya. They did not know the waters were poisoned and so they all died. When Krishna saw this he looked at them and wept, and his tears brought them to life again. He decided however to destroy the snake which lived in the lake. This poisonous snake, Kāliya, had been forced to leave his own place through fear of Garuda who, it will be remembered, was the foe of all snakes. Garuda could not come to Brindāban for he had been cursed by a yogi to die if ever he should go there, and thus Kāliya felt safe. His poison entered into the waters of the lake, and even the ground around was poisoned by the spray, so that no living thing grew near,—except one tree. This tree was unaffected because Garuda, as the bird of god, vehicle of Vishnu, had once stayed on it, and therefore it could not be harmed. One day, when the gopis were playing, their ball fell into the lake. Krishna climbed the tree and jumped from it into the lake.

Kāliya was angry that his waters were so disturbed and raised his hundred heads to find the cause. Seeing the youth he coiled himself round him, dragged him to the bottom of the lake and tried to bite him to death. But as fast as his teeth tore the flesh it grew together again. Then Krishna grew in size so that Kāliya had to let him go.

Meantime the gopis watched in fear. Some ran to fetch Yasodā and Nanda, and great consternation filled their hearts. Yasodā wanted to jump in the water, but Bala-rāma told her to be comforted, for Krishna could not be harmed and he would soon come back. He, too, climbed the tree and blew a tune on his horn which would tell Krishna that his mother was worried. Krishna heard it, and to show that he was all right, threw his flute up through the water. This frightened the friends all the more, for they thought he would never willingly part with his flute. Balaráma then sounded another tune, asking Krishna to show he was alive, and hearing this, Krishna raised himself in the water till he stood on the snake's head, and the peacock feather in his cap showed above the water. As Káliya lashed about, the feather danced, and the people thought he was being killed ! Soon, however, Káliya was exhausted and Krishna cut off all his heads save one. Then as he was about to kill him the serpent's wives and children begged him to spare their husband and father. This he did, but on the condition that he left the lake and went to his own place. Káliya said that if he went to his own place, Garuda would kill him ! But Krishna told him to have no fear, for when Garuda saw the mark of his (Krishna's) feet on his head, he would not harm him.

It was now too late for them all to return home so it was decided that they, and the cattle, should stay in the forest for the night and they all settled down under a large banyan tree. In the middle of the night a great forest fire began. The gopis woke and called on Krishna for help. He told them not to worry and not to watch him. Then he opened his mouth and drew in the fire in three large mouthfuls and the forest was saved. No one would have known how he had destroyed the fire had not Yasodá glanced at him through her eyelashes as he inhaled the last mouthful !

Once when the monsoon season was about to begin and the usual sacrifices to Indra were to be made, Krishna said it was foolish to sacrifice to Indra in order to have good harvests. Good and bad harvests were the results of their own destiny and it was more sensible to make sacrifices to the forest, the priests, the cows and the great mountain which overshadowed them, than to Indra. This infuriated Indra and he determined to show

Krishna that *he* was the more powerful. He made the monsoon rage, and the rain poured down in greater volume than it had ever done before, the Yamunā overflowed, trees were washed away, and it began to look as if everything would be destroyed.

Then Krishna called all the people together and they went, with their cattle and possessions, to the mountain Govardhana. Krishna lifted up this huge mountain with his finger so that it made a covering for them all, and for seven days and nights they remained there, sheltered and dry.

Indra now saw that Krishna was greater than he was himself, and allowed the sun to shine again. The river lost her anger, her waters became calm once more, the people left the shelter of the mountain and it sank down again to its own place. Indra himself mounted his white elephant, Airāvata, and went down to Krishna to make his submission to him.

One day Krishna stole the clothes of the gopis as they were bathing in the river and he climbed a tree with them. When the girls came out of the water they could not find their clothes and when they saw that Krishna had them, they begged him to give them back to them. But he would not do so unless each one came herself to fetch them, and at last, overcoming their modesty, they did so. As a reward he promised to dance with them on a certain full-moon day.

This story has been given a sensual twist but, as with so many other stories, it is an allegory pointing to a truth. It has been explained in a metaphysical work, the *Nyāyamuktavali:* cows stand for the sense organs, mind is the herdsman, intellect is mind's mistress, and her garment is ignorance. To steal ignorance, therefore, is to reveal truth.

At the time of full moon the sound of Krishna's flute reached the ears of the gopis and made them restless. One and all left their husbands and homes and went to the forest, following the call of the flute deep into its depths, until at last they found him.

But after a short time he told them they ought not to have left their homes and it was time they returned for they had already seen the beautiful banks of the river by the brightness of the moon. In their disappointment they wept. They told him it was he who had called forth their love, and now that he rebuked them, they were lost. Taking compassion on them he said he would dance with them. While he made a great golden terrace on the river bank, the girls bathed in lake Mānasarovara (the holy lake) and decked themselves to look their best. Then they played and danced round him as though round a shining moon in a starlit sky. But they became proud and he vanished from their sight, taking only one of them—Rādhā—with him. The girls were desolate and went through the forest calling for him and asking the birds and the flowers and trees if they had seen him. Soon they came to a bank of leaves which bore the impress of a form, and by the side, there was a jewelled mirror, so they knew he had been there. Later they came upon Rādhā, also weeping and calling for him, for she, too, had lost him in her pride. She was so happy and proud that he had gone with her that she asked him to carry her, and he suddenly vanished from her sight.

They went through the forest while they could see any pathway by the light of the moon, and then returned to the river bank and wept. Seeing them thus Krishna came to them. He made many illusionary figures of himself and danced with the girls so that, forming a large circle, each girl thought it was Krishna by her side, holding her hand. As they danced it is said they looked like a necklace of gold and sapphires—the dark Krishna and the radiant girls.

When it was time for them to return home Krishna told them to meditate on him always, and he would be with them for ever. Satisfied and happy, they each returned, and none knew they had been absent.

Many stories are told of Krishna's love for Rādhā and hers for him. One poem, written in the seventeenth century, tells of their meeting one day at the trysting place where Krishna found her surrounded by her family. Not being able to speak to one another:—

He, with salute of deference due,
A lotus to his forehead prest;
She raised her mirror to his view,
Then turned it inwards to her breast.

Another poem of the fourteenth century refers to Rādhā slipping out of her chamber at night and escaping from her handmaids in order to meet Krishna. Indian girls, as is well known, wear anklets and bracelets, and the poet wrote:—

Softly, softly, my anklets, I pray,
Let your music my handmaids not wake!
Gently, gently, my bracelets, I say,
Dim your jingle as I my way take
To my lover who for me today
Sweetly, sweetly his reed flute doth play.
Shine not brightly, O moon, for my sake
Lest the watchman, e'er wakeful, me take
For sleepwalking nymph straying away.
Sweetly, sweetly floats song from the brake:
Gladly, gladly, I'll follow his wake;
Fondly, fondly will he lead the way.

Translated by Dr Sudhin N. Ghose

Two short poems by present-day writers show the spirit engendered by the love for Krishna. The first is by Sarojini Naidu, the nightingale of India, who died a few years ago.

My foolish love went seeking Thee at dawn
Crying O Wing, Where is Kanhya gone ?

I questioned at noonrise the forest glade
O rests my Lover in thy friendly shade ?

At dusk I pleaded with the dove-grey tides
*O tell me where my Flute-player abides.*

Dumb were the waters, dumb the wood, the wind,
They knew not where my Play-fellow to find.

I bowed my weeping face upon my palm
*Moaning Where art Thou, O Sweet Ghanashyām ?*

Then like a boat that rocks from keel to rafter
My heart was shaken by Thy hidden laughter,

Then didst Thou mock me with Thy tender malice,
Like nectar bubbling from my own heart's chalice.

Thou saidst, O faithless one self-slain with doubt,
Why seekest thou My loveliness without ?

And askest wind or wave or flowering dell
The Secret that within thyself doth dwell ?

I am of thee, as thou of Me a part,
Look for Me in the mirror of thy heart.

The following is by Laurence Binyon:

Be still my heart, and listen,
    For sweet and yet acute

I hear the wistful music
    Of Krishna and his flute.

Across the cool, blue evenings,
    Throughout the burning days,

Persuasive and beguiling,
    He plays and plays and plays.

In linked and liquid sequence,
    The plaintive notes dissolve,

Divinely tender secrets
That none but he can solve.

O! Krishna, I am coming,
I can no more delay,

My heart has flown to join thee
How shall my footsteps stay ?

At last the time came for Krishna to return to Mathurā and the opportunity arose when Kansa, tired of trying to kill him in Brindāban, sent for him and for Nanda and the shepherd boys, asking them to a great festival. Sorrowfully his foster-mother watched him depart, begging him to come back to them sometime. When they arrived at Mathurā the shepherds and Nanda stayed outside, while Krishna and Bala-rāma went through the city and came to the place prepared for the festival celebrations. There, in the royal pavilion, they saw the great bow of Siva which Kansa always had with him on such occasions as a mark of his power. It was said to be unbendable and unbreakable, but Krishna lifted it easily in his hands and broke it in two. The sound of the rending wood was so great that it struck terror into the whole city, and Kansa hearing it recognised it as his death knell.

Next day all was ready for the tournament, and Kansa took his seat. Then Krishna, at the head of the other contestants, and accompanied by Bala-rāma, began to walk towards the arena. Kansa had ordered that a large elephant should stand at the entrance to kill the youths as they entered, and as Krishna went forward it was goaded by its rider to advance on him. When they met, Krishna allowed it to take him up in its trunk. Then he touched its foot, and immediately the elephant released him. This happened again. Then Krishna took it by the tail and dragged it along as easily as if it had been a calf, and killed it. He killed the attendant, too, for he had urged the beast on. Taking the tusks, the victor entered the arena, with Bala-rāma, and wrestled with the king's wrestler and overthrew him. Kansa was so angry that he ordered his soldiers to arrest the brothers, but Krishna sprang up on to the dais and killed him, much to the pleasure of the gods.

When order had been restored, the funeral rites were prepared and Krishna himself set light to the pyre. He also comforted the bereaved queens, telling them that death, in time, comes to all and they should not grieve. He then put Kansa's father, whom Kansa had deposed, on the throne again, and set his own father and mother free. They recognised Krishna first as god, then the vision faded, and they saw him as their son.

For a few years Krishna stayed in the kingdom helping to ward off its enemies. While there, he killed the sea-demon Panchajana who dwelt in a shell in the sea, and he used the shell as his conch throughout the remainder of his life. Many enemies raided Mathurā and were driven off, but when the invading army was too great Krishna, by his magic, asked Viswakarman, the divine architect, to build a city by the sea, which he called Dwārakā. Then in the night he transported all the people from Mathurā to Dwārakā, and in the morning they wondered how the sea had come to surround them! After destroying more enemies Krishna went to Dwārakā which is always called Krishna's city.

While at Dwārakā Indra visited him and asked him to kill a demon called Naraka because he had stolen the earrings which had once come from the Churning of the Ocean of Milk. Krishna did so, and later visited Indra in his heaven. He took his wife Satya-bhāmā with him, and they were shown the famous tree, Pārijāta, which had also come from the Churning of the Ocean of Milk and now belonged to Indrāni, Indra's wife. Satya-bhāmā liked it so much she asked Krishna to take it home with them. Indra was furious but could do nothing to prevent the theft.

Once, during this period, Krishna conquered Siva himself for, at a critical moment, he used magic and made the Mahādeva yawn !

Krishna married many thousands of wives—an absurdity, as are the many wives of Solomon, unless we remember that wives are the *shaktis,* the female, passive energy, which fructified by the active male element produces an effect *i.e.,* a son. Rukmini, who ultimately became the chief wife had, from her early years, worshipped Krishna and determined to marry him. When another marriage was arranged for her by her brothers, she wrote a letter to Krishna and sent it to Dwārakā by a Brāhman. She avowed her devotion, and asked him to come for her. He immediately set out, and though the wedding festivities were just about to take place, he rescued her and took her to Dwārakā. The son born to them was Pradyumna, said to be, Kāmadeva himself, the god of love. Each of Krishna's wives had ten sons and one daughter. All, as was Krishna, were blue in colour, had lotus-eyes, and wore yellow and blue.

Once Nārada visited Krishna in order to see how he managed with his many wives. He visited their houses and was amazed, for each one thought that Krishna was with her and happiness reigned among them all.

One day Rukmini asked Krishna to tell her who was his best devotee. He answered, Rādhā. As she belonged to his early life, none of the wives at Dwārakā had ever seen her, and they begged Krishna to send for her that they might see what she was like. When Krishna's messenger found her she was deep in meditation, constantly repeating the name Krishna, and when he told her his mission, she was not eager to go. But obeying Krishna's wish she agreed to do so and, also in accordance with Krishna's wish, arrayed herself in all her glory and set forth. When she arrived at Dwārakā:

> Just as a lamp or the moon appears dim before the sun, so the wives of Sri Krishna became pale and insignificant before the indescribable brilliance of Rādhā, like a lotus in the night.

When it was time for her to leave she did not want to go, but Krishna comforted her, reminding her that as he was in the whole world and the whole world was in him, "know then, Rādhā, that none can separate thee from me."

The human side of this love story forms the basis of many paintings, and often a debased conception of "love" is implied. But in its purest meaning it expresses the perfect love of the devotee, for Rādhā is the human soul which longs to unite itself with spirit in that mystic union spoken of by the Christian Saints, the Sufis, and, in fact by all religions.

The rest of Krishna's life is taken up in the Section on the *Mahā-bhārata.*

## THE BUDDHA

The ninth incarnation was that of *Gautama,* the Buddha. (Some do not accept this birth as an *avatār* of Vishnu in the same sense as the other incarnations.)

The Buddha took birth as Prince Siddārtha in the royal family of King Suddhodana and Queen Māyā, in Kapila-vastu in north-east India about 500 B.C. Many legends have gathered round his birth and life: his mother dreamt that a star fell from heaven and entered her womb on the right; he was born without pain or suffering, in a garden where his mother was resting while on her way to visit her parents. A spring miraculously appeared for the first bath and the trees made a bower to cover them. When the child touched the earth with his foot, a beautiful lotus appeared. Queen Māyā died on the seventh day after the birth. Some say that on the day of his birth Yasodhara, the princess who was to become his wife, Ānanda, his friend and favourite disciple, his horse Kantaka, and his charioteer, Channa, were also born.

Wise men visited the young baby and foretold that he would either reign as a king, or would take up another mission which would save the world from misery and sorrow.

As the child grew he astonished his tutors for he knew everything they had to teach. Many other strange things made both the king and the courtiers remember the wise men's prophecy, and his father ordered that he should be brought up in ignorance of the outer world, of pain and suffering, of ugliness and misery.

When he was of marriageable age, the king arranged a festival during which the young prince would give a jewel to all the ladies of the realm. But after the prince had distributed the jewels one princess remained—Yasodhara. As he looked at her their eyes met, and he took off one of his own rings and gave it to her. Seeing this the king was delighted, and, according to the custom of the time, he sent out messengers to say that on a certain day there would be a trial of strength for the hand of Yasodhara. To the surprise of those who thought Siddārtha had been brought up too tenderly, he easily won on all points and the marriage was solemnized.

For some years they lived very happily in a wonderful palace given them by the king. It was surrounded by a garden round which were three walls, each with only one gate. In this way the old king hoped that all knowledge of the misery of the world should be kept from his son, so that he would not choose the path of sacrifice but would rule the kingdom in his turn.

Time passed. But the world was waiting anxiously for deliverance, and the devas began to fill the air with the refrain, "It is time." The prince began to be restless, and asked his father if he might see the city and the land which he would one day rule. His father agreed, but he sent out messengers ordering that all the streets should be cleaned and made festive, and all who were sick or old should hide themselves and not appear outside.

But who shall thwart the gods! A deva took on the appearance of an old infirm man, hardly able to walk, and crossed the prince's path. Siddārtha in surprise at this object asked Channa, his charioteer, what was the matter with the man. Channa replied that he was only an *old* man. In reply to a further question he answered that all must grow old and wrinkled in time. The astonished prince asked if Yasodhara would herself grow old. And when he heard that even her beauty must fade in time, he turned back to his palace, full, not only of sorrow, but of bewilderment.

On another occasion he met a man who was ill. Then he encountered one who was being carried to the cremation ground. And he learnt that these things come to all. He asked a wandering monk many questions, and he learnt that the yogi had left the world in order to gain peace, and to have the freedom of the Self. When he reached the palace the young prince asked his father if he could not also leave the world and seek the answer to the changeable and impermanent in life. But the worried king only set more guards to watch his son's palace, and ordered that the delights which surrounded him should be increased.

But it was all in vain. Some say that after a son was born to him, some say before he was born, the prince made up his mind to search for a way out of the sorrow and suffering of the world, not for himself alone, but for Yasodhara and for all men. In the darkness of night he left his sleeping wife and started on his search. With his eyes turned towards the East he stared at the skies and thought of all the enlightened ones who had been before him. His resolution to make the search was strengthened by the devas, and those spirits who rule the four quarters of the earth, for they filled the air with the silent refrain, "The time has come." Surely, thought the prince, the secret of the cessation of sorrow must be found, and who had a better chance than he to find it! He was not running away from the world because he was tired of life; he was not even old or ill; he had all there was of good in life. And if he were ready and eager to sacrifice them to seek for this truth, surely he must succeed.

> Oh, summoning stars ! I come ! Oh, mournful earth !
> For thee and thine I lay aside my youth,
> My throne, my joys, my golden days, my nights,
> My happy palace—and thine arms, sweet Queen !
> Harder to put aside than all the rest !
> Yet thee, too, I shall save, saving this earth; . . . .
> Wife ! child ! father ! and people ! ye must share

A little while the anguish of this hour
That light may break and all flesh learn the Law.
Now I am fixed, and now I will depart,
Never to come again, till what I seek
Be found—if fervent search and strife avail.

He called for Channa and told him to bring Kantaka, his horse, for he would leave the palace. Kantaka neighed with joy, the devas made his feet just not touch the earth so that they were unheard, the gates opened at his approach, and with Channa they silently left the palace grounds. Then dismounting, Siddārtha asked Channa to cut off his hair and to return to the palace with Kantaka. No arguments or entreaties could move him, and with a heavy heart, Channa kissed his feet and prepared to go back to the palace, taking Kantaka with him. Before turning away Kantaka licked his master's feet in homage. Back in the palace Channa told the king all that had happened and gave him the prince's message that he should not grieve, but rather he should rejoice.

When Siddārtha met a hermit he exchanged his royal robes with him and set out towards the home of a group of hermits who, by austerities, were trying to reach the secret of life. After a while he left them and went to a famous sage, but he did not gain the wisdom for which he was searching and he travelled on. At length he stopped in a wood outside a village near Gayā and sat down to meditate, eating only the smallest amount of food. Day by day his body became more emaciated but he did not find the wisdom he sought. Instead he nearly passed out of his body.

At this time there was in the village a lady, Sujāta, who had given birth to a son, and in thanksgiving had prepared a dish of rice as an offering to the gods. She had made the dish of milk which had come from fifteen cows she had reared on the milk from thirty cows, themselves reared on the milk from sixty cows, reared from one hundred and twenty cows, and so on, starting with one thousand chosen cows. This most perfect food she placed in a golden dish and offered it to the prince-ascetic when he went to the village for alms. He took the dish and passing from the village crossed a river in which he bathed. But the current was very strong and he would not have crossed in safety had not the spirit of a tree stretched out its branches to save him. When he had eaten, he threw the dish into the river, and it was taken by a serpent into its palace. Garuda, however, rescued it and took it to heaven.

Refreshed with his meal the prince walked towards the great Bo-tree at Bodhi-Gayā, determined never to leave it until he had gained the secret he sought. As he went, he was followed by five hundred peacocks and many birds and animals, while kingfishers circled round him and then joined the throng. As he passed near a serpent king who had seen other Buddhas pass that way, the serpent praised him, and his serpent queen and her followers strewed flowers in his path. The spirits of the earth-world hung flags on the Bo-tree and on the trees leading to it, so that he might not lose his way. Then the Buddha-to-be thought of Māra, the king of illusion. As he thought the dreams of Māra were disturbed, and when he awoke he called his army together and went towards the Bo-tree.

At last the prince reached the tree and sat at its eastern side. He was so radiant that he looked like a mountain of gold. Māra hastened to him saying that Devadatta, his cousin, had usurped the throne and was being very cruel. But the prince thought that Devadatta could not be cruel unless the nobles allowed him to be. It was their duty to stop the cruelty while he sought for the real meaning of suffering.

As he sat meditating, the deva or spirit of the Bo-tree rained her jewels over him, and at his feet, begging him to persevere in his search. The spirits of the other trees came to ask the Bo-tree who was the glorious being seated under her shadow, and when they heard, they too covered him with flowers and rich perfumes, and sang their hope that he would persevere.

Māra's three daughters next tried their wiles, but with no success, for he remained, "like a lily on quiet waters, and firm as Mount Meru, like the iron walls that gird the universe."

Māra himself now flung his weapons at him—but they changed to flowers and fell at his feet. In despair, he mounted his elephant, Cloud-mountain, and rode towards the prince, flinging his discus at him. This discus was powerful enough to cut Mount Meru as easily as if it was made of bamboo, but when it reached the prince it floated round his head like a wreath of leaves.

Māra refused to give up, and called his army as a witness to his great power. But the prince called on the earth to witness for him, and the Earth Goddess rose up at his feet and bore witness to his greatness. Even Cloud-mountain turned away with its tail between its legs, and Māra himself finally acknowledged his greatness and slunk away in shame.

All through the night the prince sat, gaining insight into the world. He learnt the nature of the universe, the knowledge of the causes that make for life, the secret of the laws that guide the stars in the heavens, and the meaning of the great heart of the universe which is Bliss. In the morning he arose, radiant. All nature felt the thrill of his triumph and the spirit of peace reigned over the whole world.

It is said that he, now a perfect Buddha, spent seven more days under the tree, seven more in thought, seven more in a palace, where every event of his life to come became clear to him. After eight weeks of thought he realised that the doctrine he had to teach was far too great for people to understand, but at this point Brahmā appeared to him and said that if he did not teach the world it would perish. The earth too cried out to him in anguish lest all men should perish, not knowing the Law, and his great heart responded to the call. He took up the burden of helping the world by preaching that "Law which moves to Righteousness."

First he went to the mendicants near Benares to whom he had gone at the beginning of his search, and he preached his first sermon in the deer-part at Sārnāth, just outside the city. As he preached, men and gods came to listen; it is said that Mount Meru danced with joy, the great seven mountains of the world made their obeisance, and the devas surrounded him, so that the whole invisible world was full of noise like a storm. But when the lords of the Heavens sounded their conches, there was perfect silence. In this sermon he preached the good Law, or the good Doctrine, which is "good in the beginning, good in the middle and good in the end."

Leaving the grove he visited the various places he had previously passed through, and finally arrived in his father's kingdom.

When his father heard of his preaching he sent some of his nobles to enquire whether he would not come home, but as they listened to him they were converted, and did not return to the king. Other messengers were sent, but with the same result, and at last the king sent a trusted messenger who had been with the Buddha all through his early life. He succeeded in telling him that his father awaited him, and the Buddha said he would now return home. Though at first the king was furious that his son should come as a begger, eating food gathered from the householders, he became converted by the teachings. Yasodhara had come to the palace door to see her husband, and the king invited her to come and worship him. But Buddha went to her palace instead, and though it was unlawful for any one to touch the body of a Buddha, she fell at his feet, clinging to him and weeping. The king told him that when the prince left his home, Yasodhara had taken off her royal clothes, cut her hair and eaten as she had heard he had done, for her love was so great. The Buddha told them that for many lives she had been with him as his companion and helper. Later she entered the Path, and when the order of Buddhist nuns was instituted, she was admitted to the ranks. She died two years before the Buddha.

For forty years the Buddha taught. At the age of eighty he died, saying to his disciples that they should not grieve for, "All compounds are perishable." We cannot seek the permanent in the impermanent. After his death the disciples met, and from their memories of his teachings compiled the *Dhammapāda*, or footsteps of the Law.

Many parables and stories he used in his teachings have come down to us, and in the *Jātaka Tales* we are given stories of the progress of this great spirit through the lower kingdoms of nature before he became man, and afterwards as man.

The Buddha's message was a way of life. He taught that sin bred sin, righteousness, righteousness, for law rules the universe. Man is free, free to sink lower than man, or to rise higher than the gods themselves. He showed that all nature is united in the one great Life: forms perish, but only to give place to better forms. Progress is inevitable, because of the upsurging of life and, in spite of any appearance to the contrary, the "Heart of Being is celestial Rest." "There is a Power Divine which moves to good, only its Laws endure."

There is much that is metaphysical in Buddhism, but there is much that is simple, and the kernel is love and compassion, renunciation and good deeds. The four noble Truths he taught (Sorrow exists, the cause of Sorrow, the end of Sorrow, and the Way), the noble eightfold Path, and the Pancha-sila, or five rules are becoming more known to the West today. They are the same simple rules of all time—kill not, steal not, slander not, lie not, shun drugs and drink.

The Books say well, my Brothers! each man's life
    The outcome of his former living is:
The bygone wrongs bring forth sorrows and woes,
    The bygone right breeds bliss.

Enter the path! There is no grief like Hate!
    No pains like passion, no deceit like sense!

Enter the path! far hath he gone whose foot
Treads down one fond offence.

*The Light of Asia* by Sir Edwin Arnold

His fight was not, as with most of the other *avatāras,* a fight
against evil powers but against ignorance, against those would-
be teachers who keep back the priceless knowledge from the
people. He wanted to free men from fear, from priests, from ritual
and ceremonies, from prayer and supplication, and turn them to
self-deliverance. He taught that the self of man is not the body
and its passions, but that eternal One Life. Man can become
divine by his own efforts though the struggle is hard. To do this
man must not only pass through life as free from harmfulness as
possible, but he must also stamp all evil out of himself, all
selfishness and love of pleasure so that when he dies he owes
no debt to man or Nature. Then he is able to merge himself with
the Divine.

The second great lesson of his teaching is that having
acquired, having reached the place where complete bliss is
possible, and all thought of the suffering world can be left behind,
he must voluntarily take up birth again so that he can help all
living things.

## KALKI

The tenth *Avatāra,* the *Kalki,* will come on a white horse. It is
said that the heavens will open, and Vishnu will appear like a
comet, for he will be on a milk-white horse and carry a sword
which will shine like a comet. This will happen at the end of this
period of Kali Yuga some 400,000 years hence. Then all evil will
be destroyed and righteousness will flourish; the earth will
undergo great changes, continents will disappear and other
continents will appear.

It is interesting to note that the first and second *Avatāras* deal
with the help of the gods against natural forces and demons, the

third, fourth and fifth with the fight against a particular demon, the sixth destroys the whole fighting caste of the human kingdom, the seventh wars against a particular demon but also governs in righteousness and sets an example of perfect living, the eighth fights again against the warriors, against deceitfulness and evil; but does so more through helping others to so fight than by fighting himself. With the ninth—if we accept the Buddha as such—we have the complete absence of fighting and the emphasis on teaching a Way of Life to the common people. What will the tenth do ? Some say he will conquer for all time the evil in the world for, according to some, his white horse stands for the envelope of the spirit of evil which he mounts and destroys.

From another point of view the incarnations can be taken to refer to enormous periods of the evolution of the various species of life on this earth. The life-germ, planted by the Creator Brahmā in the "matter" of the earth, goes through the Palaeozoic and Mesozoic times from the fish, living in the water, to the tortoise. Then, through the Cenozoic, where it passes from the boar to the man-lion, half-human half-animal, while with the fifth, we reach the human stage, the dwarf. Parasu-rāma, the first human hero, is by no means a perfect specimen of humanity. It is Rāma who is the first perfect man, with his ally and friend Hanumān, the monkey endowed with speech. Krishna is God man—the Buddha is man made perfect.

# CHAPTER VI

SIVA

*Siva* the third of the Tri-murti, is beneficent and maleficent. He is the power which destroys and regenerates the Cosmos after its destruction, and constantly destroys and regenerates during Cosmic activity. He lives also in the passsions and lives of men. In the early days of the *Vedas* he was called Rudra, the howler, and his activities were mainly Cosmic. Now he is more known as the Mahādeva or Mahāyogin, the patron saint of all yogis, the sound of whose drum urges man on towards perfection.

Sometimes he is said to be superior to Brahmā; at other times to be born from Brahmā's brow. Such speculations are however useless, for all three functions, creating, preserving and destroying-regenerating, are co-existent, and always in action.

One legend brings this out clearly. During the Night of Brahmā when all activity had ceased and harmony reigned, Brahmā saw Vishnu in his aspect of Nārāyana (the soul of the world) floating on a lotus leaf on the Waters of Space. He asked him who he was. Vishnu addressing him as "child" told him he was Vishnu—the creator of the Universe. Brahmā was infuriated at being addressed as "child," and said *he* was the creator and destroyer of all! Vishnu disagreed and replied that he himself was the creator, preserver and also the destroyer of worlds, and Brahmā had been born from his body. An angry argument took place between them until, suddenly, they saw a column of fire reaching so far up that it seemed to have no end, and so far down it seemed to have no beginning. In amazement they ceased quarrelling and decided to find its beginning and end. Vishnu said he would go down to its source and Brahmā said he would go to its end; then they would meet again in the middle and share their knowledge. Vishnu took the form of a boar with white tusks, Brahmā that of a white swan, whose wings were so strong it could travel as swift as thought, and they started on the journey. But though they travelled a long time they could not find a beginning or an end to the column and they returned to their starting point. Suddenly, as they talked, the air was filled with the sound of the sacred word OM; and Siva himself appeared in the column filling their hearts with joy and peace. He told them that neither of them was greater than the other, but Brahmā-Vishnu-Siva, the trinity, was one, each aspect being equally necessary to the whole.

The column was the *lingam,* Siva's symbol, represented mostly by an upright pointed stone. His vehicle is a white bull.

Statues of Siva abound. The most common one shows him standing, one foot on a small human form, symbolising man. He has four arms: in one hand he holds a drum; in another a flame; a third makes a sign or *mudrā,* and the fourth points to the human form under his foot. Symbols can be understood in many ways. One explanation of this statue is to see the drum standing for the call of the soul to man, as with Krishna's flute and Orpheus's lyre: the *mudrā* is the sign of fearlessness, or perseverance without fear; the flame stands for knowledge which destroys ignorance; the foot on the human form shows that Siva is master of all, for he has conquered the passions of man. Around his neck is a snake or serpent of wisdom, the snake standing for the passions which destroy, and the serpent for wisdom and knowledge. His hair is braided and studded with jewels; hair symbolises strength as with Samson, and jewels spiritual knowledge and virtues. A human skull can also be seen, representing death which is ever present in life.

This statue is based on a legend. Once when ten thousand sages were holding a discussion among themselves Siva appeared and joined in the discussion, confuting their arguments. This angered them for they did not recognise him and they tried to destroy him. By their magic power they created a fierce tiger which rushed towards him. But he merely took hold of it, stripped off its skin with his little finger, and threw it over his shoulder. The sages then made a serpent. Siva placed it round his neck, and then danced before them. Again they tried to kill him and made a dwarf who rushed at him. Siva lifted his foot, broke its back with his toe, and went on with his dance.

Sometimes he is called Nila-kantha or the blue-throated one, because at the Churning of the Ocean he drank the poison which would otherwise have destroyed the world and it turned his neck blue. He is also Digambara, the naked ascetic, whose home is the sky. Sometimes his body is covered with ashes to symbolise the destruction of death.

His wife or *shakti* is Sati, Pārvati, Umā, or, in the evil aspect, Durgā the dreaded goddess the destroyer of darkness, who becomes at times the incarnation of destruction and evil. Her form is terrible—as indeed are destruction and evil.

It is the Hindu festival Mahā-Siva-Rātri which celebrates the destruction and regeneration of the universe.

In one legend Siva is shown hindering the work of Brahmā. When Brahmā wanted to people the world he created four youths of great beauty who should become the fathers of the human race. But while they worshipped Brahmā by the waters of the great sacred lake, Mānasa-sarovara,* Siva, in the form of the swan, Paramahamsa the emancipated one, floated by them. He told them the world was only illusion. If they wished to be free they must refuse to become the fathers of the race. The youths saw the truth of this and sat on in meditation and worship, leaving the world unpeopled.

Brahmā then created eight great lords, the Prajā-patis. These in turn created sons and daughters. One Prajā-pati, Daksha, figures very largely in the Siva legends.

* Lake Manasa-sarovara was one of the four lakes said to have been formed when the ocean descended on Mount Meru and, flowing round it four times, became four rivers which formed four lakes. Lake Manasa-sarovara is the most famous because it is at the foot of Mount Kailasa, sacred to Siva, and legend had it that the *Vedas* were first "heard" on its shores. It is still a place of pilgrimage, and is noted for its beauty. It is covered with giant lotus blooms.

Daksha married Prasuti and became the father of sons. They in their turn refused to create offspring, and Daksha changing himself into a female gave birth to sixteen daughters, or as another legend has it, he had 24, 50 or 60 daughters by Prasuti. Among them was Vinatā who married Kusyapa and became the mother of Garuda and other birds, and Sati the youngest who married Siva. Some of the other daughters became the mothers of animals and other creatures so that Daksha could truly be called the father of all living things. He was so conceited, unfortunately, that he thought he was also superior to the gods, and when he made a feast he invited them to come and do homage to him.

Siva rarely appears as a god: he is more often covered with ashes and carries the begging bowl of the beggar, but even so when he attended one of these feasts he refused to touch Daksha's feet in homage. This made Daksha angry. He did not know that Siva had refrained from giving homage because if a superior being bowed in homage to an inferior harm would come to the inferior one.

The feud came to a head through Sati.

Sati, had from a very early age given her love and devotion to Siva. When she was of marriageable age her father arranged a feast to which he invited gods and men, and from among them she had to choose a husband by placing her garland round his neck. Her choice was final and could not be undone.

Daksha did not send an invitation to Siva, and when Sati arrived at the Assembly Hall she looked in vain for him. She recognised the gods among the guests for they shone with an inner light and cast no shadows; neither did they wink. But Siva was not among them. For some time she waited, unable to think what to do. Then, suddenly, she threw her garland into the air saying: "If I am Sati, then, Siva take my garland!" And immediately Siva appeared in the centre of the Hall, wearing the garland. As usual he was dressed as a beggar. Though Daksha was angry he could do nothing and the ceremonies were completed. Then he told Sati to go and live with her beggar husband and never come to his court again.

Siva and Sati then left the hall and went to Kailāsa beyond the Himālayas to Siva's home. Here they lived in perfect happiness either as beggars clothed in ashes, or as gods worshipped by all the gods.

But Daksha continued the feud.

One day Nārada visited Siva and told him Daksha was planning another great feast in honour of Vishnu, but he was not inviting him. Siva did not mind the insult but when Sati came to ask him why the gods were leaving heaven, and learnt the truth, she was angry that they had not been invited. She said they ought to go, whether they were invited or not, for Daksha was her father. Also Siva had by right a part in the sacrifice. But Siva told her he did not receive oblations from such sacrifices: he received them from wisdom and from the singing of the hymns of the *Sāma-Veda*. Still she was not satisfied and repeated that she wanted to go. Seeing her earnestness Siva told her that if she went she would be insulted and she would also hear things said against him which no wife should hear. As she was still not satisfied he ordered her not to go. She was so angry that he had dared to command her that she changed her form from that of the gentle Sati to the dreaded Durgā who rode on a lion and was queen of the universe. Even Siva trembled before her and acknowledged her as his equal. Then she changed back to the form of Sati and begged her husband to let her go. And, knowing what was to happen but powerless to prevent it, he let her go.

Mounting Siva's old white bull, and attended by Nandi, the servant, she started for her father's palace, not as a goddess but as the wife of a beggar. When she arrived she found her father surrounded by his courtiers all sparkling with jewels and in their wonderful robes, and she greeted him with a daughter's reverence. But he looked at her in anger. He asked why she had come when he had forbidden her to see him again, and he raved against Siva to such an extent that Sati cried she could not hear such insults about her husband and live! Rather she would give her father back the body he had given her, and, using her magical powers, she fell dead at his feet.

When Siva heard of this from his messenger he rose in great anger and, pulling from his head a lock of hair, flung it to the ground. It became transformed into a powerful demon called Vira-bhadra, terrible to look at, with three flaming eyes and a thousand arms, wearing a garland of skulls and carrying a number of dreadful weapons. Siva appointed him leader of his army and told him to destroy Daksha and make his sacrifice useless. Vira-bhadra, creating an army from the pores of his skin, went to Daksha's court, broke the sacrificial vessels, insulted the priests, broke Yama's staff, trod on Indra and cut off Daksha's head. The gods fled in terror.

Meanwhile Siva sought the body of Sati and when he found it he picked it up reverently, placed it across his shoulders and walked from the hall. Seven times round the world he went with his burden, so majestic in his wrath and in the depth of his grief, that all things were terrified. The earth trembled with fear, the soil lost its moisture, the plants died and famine came. At last the people cried to the gods for help and Vishnu came down. Striding behind Siva he hurled his discus over and over again at the dead body, breaking it into pieces which fell to the ground. The spot on which each piece fell became a holy place.

When Siva felt that his burden had gone he retired to Kailāsa and to his meditations and the earth lived normally again.

The gods who had been routed at Daksha's feast went to Brahmā for advice and he told them to make their peace with Siva. He himself went with them and they found Siva in meditation. Brahmā approached him and asked him to forgive Daksha and make good all the damage that had been done both to gods and men for, he pointed out, all sacrificial offerings belonged to him

(Siva) in reality and he should therefore allow them to be completed. Siva agreed and all became as before. One difficulty arose for Daksha's head had been lost in the tumult! However Siva found a goat's head nearby and placed it on Daksha's shoulders thus making true what Nandi had said as he left the Assembly Hall when Sati died: "If you, Daksha, live after doing these terrible things it can only be with a goat's head instead of a human head!" When the sacrifice was completed Vishnu himself, riding on Garuda, came at its close and told Daksha that he (Vishnu), Siva and Brahmā were all one.

Sati was born again as a daughter of the great mountain range Himālaya and hence she was called Umā Himavutee, or Pārvati— the daughter of the mountain. Gangā, goddess of the river Ganges, was her sister. In this new birth she continued to worship Siva, often escaping from her home during the night to place flowers and to burn lights at his shrine.

One day a sage told her father that she would marry Siva, and his heart was full of pride and joy.

But Siva showed no sign, remaining in deep meditation. Umā was accordingly sent to wait on him in the hope that her beauty would attract his attention.

About this time there was consternation among the gods for a Táraka (demon) was annoying them by altering the rhythm of the seasons and by destroying the sacrifices which were offered to them. They were powerless against him for he had obtained his power from Brahmā himself by many lives of great austerity. When they went to Brahmā for help he himself was powerless also for he could not fight against one to whom he had given power. But he made them a promise. He said when Siva and Umā married they would have a son who would destroy Táraka and make the gods victorious once more.

As Siva showed no sign of marrying, Indra went to the god of love, Kāma-deva (or desire), and asked his help, and with his wife, Passion, and his companion, Spring, Kāma-deva set out for Siva's mountain home. Spring came and the snow melted. The trees blossomed and birds and animals began to make their homes. All nature was alive and full of joy—all except Siva who remained oblivious to everything. Kāma-deva began to feel helpless. Then he saw Umā, and her beauty was such that he thought he would try again. When therefore he saw Siva was beginning to relax in his meditation and Umā was approaching he took his bow and aimed his arrow at the god. Unfortunately Siva awoke just in time to see it, and sent a lightning flash from his third eye which utterly and completely destroyed Kāma and reduced Passion to a state of collapse. Umā was so distressed that she had to be carried away by her father.

Fortunately Kāma was still alive though without a body, and Passion heard a voice telling her that Siva would in time marry Umā and would then give Kāma back to her.

As beauty had failed to reach the heart of Mahā-deva Umā tried another way. Taking off her beautiful clothes and jewels she dressed as a hermit, matted her hair and began a life of meditation and austerities on a mountain, all the time thinking of Siva.

One day a young Brāhman visited her. He asked why she, who was so young and fair, spent her time in this way, and she told him her story. He tried to turn her against Siva saying he was a horrible character who visited the burning grounds of the dead; that a poisonous snake was coiled round his neck, and that he rode on a poor bull. She was angry and said she would not listen to his insults to Siva but would continue her devotion. Then the Brāhman changed into Siva himself. He offered her his love and, immensely happy, she went back to her father with the news.

Siva then asked the seven great sages to be his ambassadors and go to Himavat with his proposal of marriage. This they did, and while Nārada, the chief messenger, was describing Siva's great virtues to Himavat, Umā who was listening, is said to have "bent her head and counted the petals of a lotus she held in her hand," overcome by her shyness and great love. Himavat consented to the marriage and arrangements were made for the ceremony to take place three days later.

On the appointed day Siva, accompanied by Brahmā and Vishnu, and followed by all the lesser gods, passed through the gaily decorated and flower-strewn streets to the palace, and the ceremony was performed. After staying with Himavat for a month Siva and Umā left for Kailāsa, visiting many mountain peaks on the way.

In the meantime Siva's attention was drawn to Kāma whom he had reduced to ashes, and he made good the damage, reuniting him with his wife Passion. Some say he gave Kāma a body again; others that he had to remain invisible though alive.

Time passed. The gods waited in vain for news of the birth of a son. At last Agni was sent to Kailāsa to ask Siva if he would fulfil his promise. Siva gave him the germ of life, and he carried it away with him. Soon, however, it became too hot to carry, and Indra advised him to drop it into the Ganges. After a while the Ganges found it too heavy a burden, and, one morning when the Pleiades came to bathe in the holy water, they took it out and laid it among the reeds on the bank, tending it with care. It grew into a baby boy and both Ganges and the Pleiades looked after it. The baby grew, "bright as the sun and beautiful as the moon," and all those who had taken care of it wanted it for his own. Agni, Ganges and the Pleiades were quarrelling over it one day when Siva and Umā appeared. Seeing the beauty of the child Umā asked Siva to whom it belonged, and was overjoyed to learn that it was their own child. This settled the quarrel to everyone's satisfaction and Siva, Umā and the child left for Kailāsa.

Kāli-dāsa the poet wrote that as the child, whose name was Kārttikeya, grew up "learnt how to get dirty, how to laugh and how to count 'One, nine, two, ten, five, seven!'"

In due time he grew to be a young man. Indra and the other gods then approached Siva asking if the youth could now fight Tārakā. Siva agreed and Kārttikeya went with the gods to Indra's heavenly city. On the way he saw the damage which Tārakā had done and became very angry and anxious to fight. Preparations for the battle began. The gods rode on their vehicles, Kārttikeya on a peacock, Indra an elephant, Agni a ram, Yama a buffalo and Varuna a dolphin. A giant who was with the army rode on a ghost. This strange array struck terror into Tārakā's army and the soldiers wanted to retire at once. But Tārakā, brandishing his sword and laughing with contempt, rushed into battle. The fight lasted a long time with no real victory on either side until Tārakā sought out the gods, meaning to destroy them with his magic arms. Then Kārttikeya went to their rescue and a duel began between the two leaders. Tārakā used all the magic weapons he had had from the god of fire and the god of wind, but Kārttikeya neutralized them and finally plunged his lance into the demon and killed him.

Some say the Tārakā was not a demon but a wise sage who had gained so much power that the gods were envious of him. Others say he stands for spiritual wisdom in contrast to religious ceremonies and hence the gods fought him—but symbols can always be understood in a variety of ways.

Kārttikeya is Mars the god of war. Also St. Michael who slew the dragon.

Siva and Pārvati—to use her other name—had another son, Ganesa or Ganapati. Many stories are told of him and many reasons given for his elephant head. In one story he is said to have lost his head because he was sleeping with his head to the north! Another says he was born while Siva was away, and when the god returned home, Kārttikeya and Ganesa guarded their mother's door and would not let him pass. In anger Siva cut off Ganesa's head. When he learnt from Pārvati that he had beheaded his own son he sent messengers to find someone or some creature who had been born on the same day and at the same time as Ganesa and to take its head. The only creature to be found was an elephant, so cutting off its head, the messengers brought it and it was placed on Ganesa's shoulders.

A legend of his birth says that one night when Pārvati was sleeping on her white, jewel-embroidered couch, in the palace at Kailāsa, among the sandalwood trees and sweet smelling flowers, Vishnu appeared, clad as a priest, old and weak from starvation, and he begged for food. Siva and Pārvati greeted him kindly and asked him what he desired. He told them that he would become their son, and immediately he took the form of a tiny baby and lay on Pārvati's bed staring at the ceiling and waving his hands and feet. His little body was perfect, his eyes more beautiful than the lotus, and it was sheer happiness to look at him. Indeed it brought a sparkle to the eyes as though something within had been lighted up!

Pārvati and Siva were delighted, and all the gods and goddesses came to see the child and to give their blessing. Vishnu gave the blessing of knowledge; Brahmā of fame and worship; Dharma of righteousness and mercy; Siva of generosity, intelligence, peace and self-control; Lakshmi promised to live always where he was, and said she would see that he had a beautiful wife; Saraswati gave him the power of speech and poetry, of memory and eloquence; Sāvitri gave him all wisdom; Himavat promised him the qualities of Krishna. Then they all gathered round Vishnu who was seated on a throne of precious stones, shaped like a lion, and the dancing girls and heavenly musicians sang and played in his praise.

Among those present was Saturn. He asked if he could see the child and approached Pārvati, who was seated on her throne of precious stones, holding the child on her lap. But he advanced with his head bent, and Pārvati, after greeting him, asked why he did not look at her, or at the child? He answered that everyone had to bear the fruits of their actions, even he himself, for one day when his beautiful wife came to see him, he had been so engrossed in his devotion to Krishna that he did not see her. She had therefore cursed him, saying that henceforth whatever he looked at would be destroyed. So he dared not look at her, or at the child. Pārvati laughed, and told him he must look at the child and at her.

Saturn could not decide whether to look or not, for either way would be bad. He decided to glance out of the corner of his eye at the child only. But even a glance was sufficient, and immediately the child's head vanished. Pārvati wept, and then fainted at the disaster, and all the other gods and goddesses, dancing girls and musicians, were stunned to silence.

Then Vishnu flew away on Garuda to a forest in the north where, on the bank of a river, he saw a king elephant asleep. He cut off its head with his discus and returned to Kailāsa with the elephant head which he placed on the headless child. Then he brought Pārvati back to consciousness and explained to her all that had happened. Hence Ganesa has an elephant head.

To continue the *motif* of "no effect without a cause," we are told why that particular elephant lost its head.

Nārada asked why, when the world is full of beautiful things, an elephant's head should be chosen to replace the human head, and he was told: Once the lord of sages, Dur-vāsa, had been given a flower from the holy Pārijāta tree which came from the Churning of the Ocean of Milk, and he gave it to Indra. This flower destroyed all obstacles, and he who wore it on his forehead would rule all men, and would never be forsaken by the goddess of fortune. His powers would be greater than those of the gods. But Indra threw the flower on to the head of his favourite elephant. It went to the forest and tossed it away. This was the elephant whose head was now on Ganesa's shoulders.

As to why this should happen to Ganesa: Once Siva, in trying to kill some demons, struck the sun with his trident and caused that great god to fall from his chariot and lose consciousness. All the gods became full of fear, and Kasyapa, father of the sun, cursed Siva, saying that the head of his son would be cut off. Siva revived the sun, but the curse remained.

When the time came for Ganesa to be married, Siva and Pārvati discussed among themselves which of their sons, Kārttikeya or Ganesa, should be married first. Both boys had grown up together and were devoted companions, though Kārttikeya had come from Siva's seed, and represented his destructive aspect, while Ganesa had come from Pārvati the female aspect from the scurf of her body. As they could not decide they called the boys together and told them that, as they loved them both equally, they could not decide this problem. They suggested, however, that the one who would encircle the earth first, should be married first.

Kārttikeya started out immediately, and began his travel round the world. Ganesa remained at home, wondering what he could do, where he could go, for because of his size, he would never have the strength to travel so far. At last the solution came to him. He took the ceremonial bath and asked his parents to sit on their thrones while he worshipped them. He went round them seven times, and sang their praises. Then he asked them to arrange his marriage.

His parents reminded him that he must first go round the earth, and advised him to go quickly so that he could come back the more quickly. But Ganesa answered he *had* encircled the earth, for the scripture said that to encircle the parents is equal to a pilgrimage roung the earth. But, on the other hand, if anyone left his parents in order to encircle the earth he was guilty of a crime.

Siva and Pārvati saw the truth of this and arranged for his marriage to the two daughters of the Prajā-pati, Lord of Creatures— Buddhi (Intellect) and Siddhi (Attainment). All the gods came to the ceremony which was performed by Viswa-karmā. In time two sons were born: Siddhi's son was called Prosperity, and Buddhi's son was Gain, a child of very great beauty.

Everyone was happy until one day Kārttikeya returned. As he came near to his home he met Nārada. He told him all that had happened, and advised him to leave again, for no wise man who wanted peace would look "upon the face of those who gravely wrong him." Kārttikeya took the advice and, after telling his parents that they had wronged him greatly, left and went to the Mountain of the Heron.

Pārvati was very sad at the loss of their son, and to satisfy her Siva sent a part of himself to dwell in that mountain and they both visited their son. But he was still angry and moved away, even though all the gods begged him to remain. And ever since then, Siva visits him on the day of the new moon and Pārvati on the day of the full moon.

Ganesa has only one tusk. The other was lost in a fight with Parasu-rāma who had come to visit his father. As Siva was asleep Ganesa would not let Parasu-rāma pass, and they fought, Ganesa swinging Parasu-rāma round and round with his trunk. When Parasu-rāma recovered his senses, he threw his axe at Ganesa. This axe was famous, for it had been given to Parasu-rāma by Siva, and recognising it, Ganesa could not fight against it, but let it fall on his tusk cutting it off.

The word Ganesa means "Lord of the Numbered," that is, the Lord of all things, for when we speak of *things*—the differentiated aspects of the One—we are dealing with that which can be numbered or counted. He is a much loved god; no worship is of real value if he is not there; he brings prosperity to everyone and is a household mascot. Joyous and friendly, grotesque and charming he is short and fat, yellowish in colour, with four hands which hold a shell, a discus, a club and a water-lily. In his statues he sits smiling, with his great stomach which contains the Universe in folds. Or he dances with his garments outspread. As with the other gods he has a vehicle—the common mouse or shrew. The word standing for mouse comes from "Mus" meaning to steal. It also stands for the Ātma or spirit, which lives in the heart, or the whole of every being.

The Ganesa festival takes place in the early autumn, and is a festival of joy, feasting and visiting. After some days—the number depending on the wealth of the family—a clay figure of the god is decked with garlands and taken in procession to a river where it is immersed. This ensures prosperity for the coming twelve months.

Siva's married life was not all bliss!

One day he sat on the sacred mountain peak of the Himālayas, clad in a tiger's skin and a lion's skin, the one round his loins and the other on his shoulders, the serpent forming his sacred thread. He was surrounded by flowers and birds, animals and spirits, all radiant because of his presence. Heavenly music filled the air, and the perfume of sandalwood rose to the nostrils. The Rishis were there, worshipping him, for to see such a vision purified them from their sins.

To this peaceful scene Pārvati came, carrying a jar of sacred water, and followed by the goddesses of all the sacred rivers. She was dressed like Siva and, as she came near to him, the flowers bloomed even more fully, and the air was filled with a wonderful perfume.

But she was in playful mood, and going to her husband she put her hands over his eyes.

The effect was tremendous: the light in the universe went out, life began to fade, and all living things became full of fear. Then a great light shone from his third eye in the middle of his forehead. It was so bright and hot that it set fire to the forests that covered the sides of the great range, and drove out the animals and birds who fled to him for protection. Almost in a moment the fire had burnt all the mountains, and the destruction of everything seemed imminent.

Then Pārvati prayed to Siva to spare her father Himavat's life, and when he saw her grief, he looked again at the mountain, this time with love, and all became as before, the trees began to grow again and the flowers bloomed and all nature rejoiced.

On another occasion Pārvati caused trouble, this time mostly to herself. One day she was sitting with Siva in Kailāsa while he explained passages from the *Vedas* to her. Her attention wandered, and when Siva looked at her, he found she was not listening, so he asked her to tell him what he was reading! Naturally she had no idea, and Siva was angry, saying she was not fit to be the wife of a god but should be the wife of a fisherman when she would not hear any sacred texts!

Immediately she vanished, and Siva returned to his meditations.

For some time these meditations were not as successful as usual, for the thought of Pārvati interfered with them, and he realised that he had been, perhaps, a little rash for, after all, she was his wife. Thinking thus he called his servant, the faithful Nandi, and told him to become a shark, and to disturb the fishermen who lived in the village where Pārvati was. This Nandi did.

Pārvati had, meantime, been found by a fisherman on the seashore who had taken her home and brought her up as his daughter. She had now grown into a beautiful young woman, so beautiful that all the young fishermen wanted to marry her. As a way out of the difficulty the foster-father promised to give her in marriage to anyone who would destroy the shark which was causing so much damage to their work. At this point Siva went to the village, disguised as a fisherman from another village, and said he would catch the shark. He threw his net into the water and the shark was caught. Then he demanded the hand of the fisherman's daughter, blessed the foster-father, and took Pārvati back to Kailāsa, after showing himself to be the great god he was.

Pārvati decided to be more careful in future, and Siva was so glad to have her back that his meditations became fruitful once more.

Siva is closely connected with the Ganges as the following legend shows.

Many many years ago Sagara was king of Ayodhyā. He had two wives, Kesini and Sumati, who was the sister of Garuda, but he had no son. At length he decided to go to the Himālayas with his wives and try by austerities to win the favour of the gods. After performing the necessary rites for a hundred years his wish was granted. He was told that his wife Kesini would bear him a son who would continue his line, and Sumati would bear sixty thousand sons, but they would not continue the line. In due time the promise came true, and Kesini bore a son Asamanjas, and Sumati gave birth to a gourd which burst open and the sixty thousand sons were born from it. They were nursed in jars of ghee (clarified butter) and grew up strong and beautiful but not good.

Asamanjas was also a disappointment for he committed many evil deeds against the citizens of his father's realm and against his brothers, and was at last banished. He left a son Ansumān who was as good as his father was bad, and was much loved.

After many more years had passed Sagara decided to make the horse sacrifice. (The horse sacrifice was very powerful. A splendid horse was set free to roam at will, and was well guarded. Any territory it entered became part of the king's realm. If the king of the territory refused tribute war was declared on him.) The horse was sent out in charge of the sixty thousand sons. Unfortunately Vāsava, an evil being, stole it, and the king sent the sons to search for it and bring it back. But though they searched the whole earth they could not find any trace of it. They dug into the earth with their hands, which were as sharp as ploughshares, and as forceful as thunderbolts, and the earth cried out in agony. As they dug deeper and deeper they killed many serpents and demons and the gods became worried for their own safety. They therefore appealed to Brahmā and he promised them that Kapila, the sage, should slay the sons of Sagara.

When the searchers did not find the horse, even in the middle of the earth, their father told them to go on digging until they did find it. As they went on with the search they met Indra's elephant of the east, Virupāksha, by whose head the world is sustained in position, and by the shaking of which earthquakes occur. They saluted him and passed on to the south, where they met Mahapadma, Yama's elephant, which holds the earth on his head. In the west they came upon Varuna's elephant, Saumanasa, and in the north they met the great elephant of Kuvera, Himapandara, white as snow, who bore the earth on his great brow. Passing on till they came to the east of the north they saw the sage Kapila, and near him the horse, quietly grazing. Thinking he was the thief they tried to kill him, but with a great roar he emitted a flame from his eye which burnt them to ashes.

When the sons did not return, Sagara sent his grandson Ansumān to search for them. He, too, met the four elephants in his search and, passing on, came to the mound of ashes which was all that remained of his sixty thousand uncles. There, also, was the horse.

His first duty was to perform the funeral rites for the dead, but there was no water to be found with which to perform them. Glancing up to the sky he saw Garuda and from him he learnt how his uncles had been killed. Garuda also told him that it was a good thing they had been killed, and under the circumstances no ordinary funeral rites would suffice. He advised him to ask Gangā, daughter of Himavat, if she would wash the ashes with her purifying waters so that the uncles could be freed from sin. Also, he said, the horse should be taken back, so that the sacrifice could be concluded.

But how could Gangā be brought down to the place where the ashes were? The mystery remained unsolved long after Sagara and Ansumān had died, even though the latter had given his kingdom to his son Dilipa and meditated for years in the Himālayas. Dilipa continued to ponder on the problem, but though he reigned for thirty thousand years he did not find any solution. His son Bhagiratha reigned after him, and soon retired to the forests and, for a thousand years performed austerities in the hope that the solution might be found.

At last Brahmā appeared to him and asked what boon he desired. He told him that he wanted the waters of Gangā to purify the ashes of his forefathers. But Brahmā answered that if Gangā fell to earth her waters would sweep it away unless Siva's aid could be evoked.

For another year Bhagiratha worshipped Siva, and then, pleased with his devotions, Siva said he would let Gangā fall to earth, and would receive her waters on his own head to break the fall. And, in a rushing torrent Gangā fell.

But pride works havoc with gods and goddesses as well as with mortals, and Gangā thought she would sweep away Siva himself! Instead, she found herself caught in his matted hair and could not even reach the earth.

Bhagiratha then performed many other austerities till Siva was satisfied and let the river fall in seven streams from his hair. One stream went in the wake of Bhagiratha's car, and the others were diverted, three to the east and three to the west, making a tremendous noise as they went tumbling down.

All nature watched the spectacle; the earth became full of river life and as the porpoises jumped, they seemed like flashes of light as their scales reflected the sun. Great devas, Rishis, gandharvas and yakshas watched from their elephants and horses, or in their chariots which moved without apparent aid. The foam that is seen on waterfalls seemed extra bright as Gangā fell over the mountain range and settled in a broad stream to flow through the valleys, or split up into many small streams to unite once more. Down and down went the waters of the stream which followed Bhagiratha's car, straight to the sacred ground of the sage Jahnu. But he was angered at the disturbance and absorbed all the water till the gods besought him to set them free. Then he let them pour through his massive ears, and again Gangā went on in the wake of the car till she met the ocean and, plunging into those dark regicns, washed the ashes of the sixty thousand sons of Sagara so that their souls could go to heaven.

Bhagiratha made his offerings to the sacred waters in the name of Sagara, Ansumān and Dilipa and, pleased with this Brahmā said Gangā should be called his daughter.

Soon Bhagiratha died and his soul went to heaven.

## PART III

THE EPICS

The Rāmāyana

The Mahā-bhárata

# CHAPTER VII

# THE EPICS

The great Epics, the *Rāmāyana* and the *Mahābhārata* with which is the *Bhagavad-Gītā,* form the background of Indian life. The former consists of twenty-four thousand verses of two lines each, and the latter of one hundred thousand verses of two lines each. Both of them have a divine source, and Brahmā is made to say in the second chapter of the *Rāmāyana:*

As long as the mountains and rivers shall continue on the surface of the earth, so long shall the story of the *Rāmāyana* be current in the world.

And in the *Bhagavad-Gītā,* Krishna, the divine teacher, is made to say:

If anyone shall study these sacred dialogues held between us two, I shall consider that I am worshipped by him with the sacrifice of knowledge: this is my resolve. And even the man who shall listen to it with faith and not reviling shall, being freed from evil, attain to the regions of happiness provided for those whose deeds are righteous.

The *Rāmāyana* is said to have been written on the banks of the river Tamasa which flows into the Ganges. According to one legend, Vālmiki the sage, was moved to pity when he saw the sorrowing of a bird whose mate had been shot down and, inspired by Nārada, he started to write the Epic of Tenderness or the *Rāmāyana.* Another legend says that when Sitā, wife of Rāma, was banished to the forest she stayed at the hermitage of Vālmiki, and there bore Rāma's twin sons. Vālmiki told the story of Rāma to the boys as they grew up and they learned it by heart. Later, when they visited their father, they sang it to him.

The *Māhā-bhārata* was written by the sage Vyāsa, who was also inspired by Nārada. He was full of sorrow for the world when he saw how men suffered, due to the injustices meted out by one to the other, and he wrote the Epic of Righteousness to show that only by righteous living could sorrow and injustices cease.

Then Vyāsa saw that righteousness was not enough, and Nārada inspired him to write the *Bhagavad-Gitā,* the Book of Devotion, the Lord's Song. Sitting on the bank of the river Jumna he recorded the teachings of Krishna to Arjuna on the battlefield of Kuru-kshetra.

Research is going on into the *Mahā-bhārata* by the Bhandarkar Oriental Research Institute of Poona, and into the *Rāmāyana* by the Research Institute of Baroda University. The latter started in 1951 will take nine years to complete.

The *Rāmāyana* used in the north of India is that of Tulsi Dās, made many centuries ago, of which a new translation has just appeared.

The *Rāmāyana* used here is that of Vālmiki and the translation by Romesh Dutt.

Of these very long Epics it is obvious that only a minor portion is given here.

# CHAPTER VIII

# THE RĀMĀYANA

The story is concerned with two great families of ancient India, the Kosalas and the Videhas, who lived many thousands of years ago in what is now known as Oudh and North Bihar. No date can be given historically, but tradition makes the era before the time of the *Mahā-bhārata* and Krishna, which, again traditionally, is put at 5,000 years ago. But times do not matter, and excavations and the findings of ancient MSS are constantly putting back the clock, so that we can leave it as having happened many, many years ago.

The events are centered round the life of Rāma, the divine king, and his fight with Rāvana, the demon king of Lankā or Ceylon. They can be taken as historical facts, or as an ordinary story, in which good triumphs over evil. But the whole is more than that: a description of how a country should be governed, what are the qualities of true kingship, what the true relation between ruler and people, what life was like in those ancient times—all these things are there. We have also a portrait of a perfect man and a perfect woman—patterns for all to follow. The nearness of the invisible nature to the visible is like an undercurrent throughout; the gods help the warriors, the birds and monkeys help in the rescue of Sitā, an aerial ship carries people where they will—it obeys the thought or the spoken word (a hint of guided aeroplanes, more perfected?). Hanumān, the monkey god, is a personality who will never die, for he is one of the most lovable characters. His devotion, his simplicity, his magic powers are wonderful—he can carry a mountain from one end of the country to the other during a night, and take it back again and he can shrink himself or enlarge himself at will.

All the characters are less coarse than in the *Mahābhārata,* less real in one sense, more idealistic. Even Rāvana the demon king, has his points. There are not the dreadful jealousies and hatreds as in the later book; but of gentle tragedy there is much. The anguish of the king as he is forced to banish his son; of the queen, as she watches him depart; and, most of all, of Sitā who, as she says, was "born to suffer", and indeed does so, not only by being abducted by Rāvana but also by having to prove her virtue by the ordeal of fire and again by the ordeal of earth. And finally, for sheer tragedy, her banishment from Rāma. Yet her devotion and stately simplicity never fail her.

The root of the tragedy lies in what are generally thought to be womanly traits!—jealousy and the love of the beautiful. It is the jealousy of the young queen that causes the banishment, but it is the wish of Sitā to possess the beautiful deer that makes it possible for Rāvana to abduct her. Yet behind both these actions is the deed of the king Dasa-ratha in his youth, caused by his pride.

At the end, one is left with the feeling of gentle sorrow, a haunting love and reverence for the gentle Sitā and the glorious Rāma, and an urge to embody the devotion and loyalty portrayed by Lakshmana and Hanumān.

In those ancient times King Dasa-ratha lived in the city of Ayodhyā, the unconquerable, in the kingdom of Kosala, the present Oudh. He had three wives but no son. As was the custom of the times he had performed many sacrifices and undergone many austerities in the hope of obtaining an heir, but to no avail. Finally he performed the greatest sacrifice of all, the horse sacrifice.

At this time the gods were troubled, for the demon King Rāvana was upsetting the peace of the world by his misdeeds, and as they were powerless to prevent him they appealed to Brahmā for help. He told them, however, that he could not help himself because Rāvana had, in the past, obtained two boons from him, i.e., that he should never be destroyed by gods or by Gandharvas. He had been too proud however to ask for immunity from death at the hands of human beings, and therefore he could be destroyed by a man.

While the gods were discussing this, Vishnu appeared, clad in his yellow robes, riding on Garuda, with his mace and discus in his hands, and the gods appealed to him. They asked if he would take birth again on earth and slay Rāvana, and he agreed.

While Dasa-ratha was performing the sacrificial rite, Vishnu suddenly appeared in the middle of the sacrificial fire like a bright fiery tiger, and advised the king to take some of the rice and milk from the sacrifice and give a portion to each of his three wives. Then, he promised, the king's wish would be granted.

Dasa-ratha gave a portion of the rice and milk to the chief queen Kausalyā, another to Kaikeyi, the "slender waisted", young and fair, and his favourite, and two portions to the other queen Sumitrā. In due time four sons were born—Rāma to Kausalyā, Bharata to Kaikeyi and twins, Lakshmana and Satrughna, to Sumitrā. At the same time the gods were active, and created a large number of monkeys which would help Vishnu to defeat the hosts of Rāvana.

For sixteen years all was well in Ayodhyā, the Righteous City, for Dasa-ratha ruled "with a father's loving grace," and the people loved their monarch. Throughout the land the people lived righteously: "Fathers, with their happy households owned their cattle, corn and gold," and famine, penury, deceit and fraud were unknown. "Poorer fed not on the richer, hireling friend upon the great... men to plighted vows were faithful, faithful was each loving wife." And "each man in truth abiding, lived a long and peaceful life." This state of happiness and prosperity was reflected in the gold and graceful garments, gems, bracelets and earrings worn by the people. There was a strong army, "troops who never turned in battle, fierce as fire and strong and brave," to guard the kingdom. In these surroundings the four princes grew to early manhood, loved and respected by all. Rāma was the most loved, for he seemed the very embodiment of all the kingly traits of honour, uprightness, gentleness and kindness, while he also excelled in all matters of bravery and war.

When Rāma was sixteen years old the yogi Viswāmitra, whose hermitage was in a nearby forest, came to Dasa-ratha and asked if the young prince could go to the forest and destroy the evil rākshasas, who were distracting him in his meditations and disturbing his sacrifices.* At first Dasa-ratha refused because of the dangers involved, but on being assured that no harm would come to the prince, and that he would be victorious, he agreed. Rāma, together with his brother Lakshmana who was very devoted to him, thus went with Viswāmitra to the hermitage, and when the demons came to disturb the sacrifice, they fought with them, killing many hundreds and driving away the two chiefs, Māricha and Su-vahu. Having accomplished this service Rāma asked what else they could do.

At this time in the nearby kingdom of Videha, the present Bihar, king Janaka was preparing for his daughter's *swayamvara,* and had made it known to all the princes and nobles that he would give her in marriage to anyone who could bend a famous bow, formerly in the possession of Rudra, and passed on to Janaka by a royal Rishi. This bow was so strong that it was said it could be strung neither by gods nor men, though efforts had often been made to do so. Viswāmitra told the princes of this, and also of Sitā's birth, for she had been found by Janaka one day when he was ploughing in the field. He had taken her home with him, calling her Sitā, a word meaning furrow, and had brought her up as his daughter. She had grown into a beautiful girl, soft-eyed and graceful, and had already earned the name of "peerless" Sitā.

---

* Hermitages were scattered over India at that time. They were situated at pleasant spots in the forests and mountains where fruit and water were within reach. Sometimes a hermit lived alone, sometimes with his family and sometimes he took pupils. They were the seats of learning of those days for some hermits were great sages and were visited by kings and learned men. The journey from hermitage to hermitage laid the foundations for future roads.

The princes were interested, and with Viswāmitra they set out for the city of Mithilā where Janaka and Sitā lived. Janaka welcomed them warmly, and Viswāmitra asked if the wondrous bow could be shown to Rāma. Janaka told his lords and warriors to: "Bring forth the bow of Rudra decked in garlands and in gold," and with great effort, for it needed an eight-wheeled car to carry it and five thousand men to pull it, it was brought from the inner hall to the king and his guests. Janaka, with pride in his voice, told the princes about it and of his vow. Rāma asked permission and then "lifted high the cover of the pond'rous iron car," and gazed at the bow. "Let me," he said, "on this bow my fingers place. Let me lift and bend the weapon, help me with your loving grace." And permission being granted, he lifted it up, strung it and drew the cord "with force resistless till the weapon snapped in twain!" The noise was so great that it sounded like a thunder clap and shook the earth. Some say that Parasu-rāma, who was still living on earth worshipping Siva, was so angry at this because the bow had once belonged to Siva, that he fought with Rāma. He was defeated, but Rāma spared his life.

However that may be, everyone else was delighted and preparations were made for the wedding ceremony. Messengers were sent to Dasa-ratha. "Three nights they halted in their journey with their steeds fatigued and spent" before they reached Ayodhyā with the invitation to attend the wedding. The next morning, as the sun began to shine on the towers and turrets of the ancient city, Dasa-ratha sent for his courtiers and ordered treasure to be gathered, his elephants and horses to be made ready, and, with his priests, he set out for the four day journey to Videha's land, followed by the "glittering ranks" of his forces. When he arrived, the two kings greeted each other and formed a close alliance of friendship, and final preparations for the ceremony were completed. Janaka gave his other daughter in marriage to Lakshmana and his brother's daughters to Bharata and Satru-ghna, and at the appointed time the "maidens, flame-resplendent.... beaming in their bridal beauty," performed their rites.

After the festivities were over, Bharata, Satru-ghna and their wives went on a visit, and Dasa-ratha with Rāma, Lakshmana and their brides, returned to Ayodhyā, to a city bedecked with banners, with flower-strewn streets, and welcoming crowds. The brides were greeted by their respective mothers-in-law to whom they paid homage, and life settled down into "days of joy and months of gladness," and, "As Vishnu with his consort dwells in skies, alone, apart, Rāma in a sweet communion lived in Sitā's loving heart!"

Rāma continued through the years to grow in grace as though favoured by the gods, doing his full duty by his father and filling his mother's heart with joy, while Sitā, "like the Queen of Beauty brighter in her graces grew."

Dasa-ratha watched the growth of Rāma as he unfolded innate virtues of steadiness of purpose, wisdom in dealing with people, a peaceful mind, patience and wisdom. As he was feeling too old to continue to carry the burdens of the State, he decided to retire and appoint him his heir-apparent. Before doing so he called his counsellors, chiefs and burghers to the Council Chamber and put the matter before them, asking for their true opinion. He told them to "speak your thoughts without compulsion," and to think if there should be any other wiser course to pursue. With one accord they decided they would wish to see "the princely Rāma" reign as Heir and Regent, "riding on the royal tusker in the white umbrella's shade," for "his heart is blessed with valour, virtue marks his deed and word."

Rāma was sent for, and acclaimed, and preparations for the ceremony of installation began. The city streets were washed and garlanded, banners floated from tall posts, lamps were prepared against the darkness of night. The people were glad and from the "confines of the empire" came to share the royal feast:

And the rolling tide of nations raised their voices loud and high,

> Like the tide of sounding ocean when the full moon lights
>   the sky,
>
> And Ayodhyā thronged by people from the hamlet, mart
>   and lea,
>
> Was tumultuous like the ocean thronged by creatures of the
>   sea!

Rāma and Sitā spent the night in fasting, prayer and preparation, while the queens watched the intense festive activities with joy and happiness. Queen Kaikeyi was happy also, for she said Rāma was as dear to her as her own son Bharata.

But evil crept in on the happy scene. An old hunchback nurse, Mantharā, who had nursed Kaikeyi as a mother does her daughter, instilled the venom of jealousy into the young queen's heart. She told her that if Rāma was regent Bharata would be under him, she herself would be subservient to Kausalyā the queen-mother, and her position would change from that of the king's favourite to that of a very secondary person. At first Kaikeyi was angry, for she said "Rāma would guard his brothers like a father guards his son," and Rāma had always offered her homage, even more than to his own mother Kausalyā. But as with "wilder, fiercer accents" Mantharā continued to poison her mind, she at length gave way and determined to follow the hunchback's advice and demand that the king should make Bharata regent and "in the deep and pathless jungle let the banished Rāma roam." Taking off her splendid clothes and jewels, she left her apartments and retired to the angry or mourning chamber, a room set apart for the queens in such cases, and there awaited the coming of the king.

When Dasa-ratha had finished his preparations he went through the gardens where the "peacocks wandered free, lute and lyre poured forth their music, parrot flew from tree to tree"; through the halls; through the "lines of scented blossoms which by limpid waters shone"; through rooms of beauty, to Kaikeyi's inner chamber, happy at heart, full of eager longing for Kaikeyi's beauty and "the glamour of her art." But Kaikeyi was not to be found! The distracted king asked a servant where she was. With terror in his voice he told him she had sought the mourner's chamber.

Dasa-ratha hurried there and found her on the unswept floor, dishevelled and weeping. In his distress he begged her to tell him what had caused this unhappiness and vowed to put it right. "Speak, command thy king's obedience, and thy wrath will melt away, like the melting snow of winter 'neath the sun's reviving ray!"

Then she spoke:

> *"By these rites ordained for Rāma,—such the news my*
> *     menials bring,—*
> *Let my Bharat, and not Rāma, be anointed Regent King,*
>
> *Wearing skins and matted tresses, in the cave or hermit's*
> *     cell,*
> *Fourteen years in Dandak's forest let the elder Rāma*
> *     dwell,"*

The horrified king refused. When he remained adamant she reminded him of his vow, given to her many years before when she had found him wounded on the battlefield and had taken him away and tended him. Then he had promised her two boons. She had not asked for them until now and as a man of honour he must grant what she asked. In vain he pleaded with her not to ask this of him.

When morning came, Rāma went to make his salutations to his father, and seeing him so upset, he begged him to tell what dreadful thing had happened. In his anguish the king could not speak, and it was Kaikeyi who told the young prince of the vow and her demand. Rāma accepted the mandate impassively, for a dutiful son must fulfil his father's vow, and turned away from the chamber to tell his mother and Sitā of the change of plans.

Queen Kausalyā said that death was preferable to life with Kaikeyi in the chief place, for already she had found it difficult to live in peace with her, but Rāma reminded her that the king would turn more to her now, and it was her duty to give him what comfort she could.

Sitā refused to be separated from her husband for:

"......let me seek the jungle where the jungle-rangers rove,
Dearer than the royal palace, where I share my husband's love,

And my heart in sweet communion shall my Rāma's wishes share,
And my wifely toil shall lighten Rāma's load of woe and care!"

Lakshmana, too, had no wish to stay behind, and though Rāma told him he ought to stay with his mother and take the place of a son to Kausalyā, he begged to go, for he could help "to fell the jungle," and his hands could build the home and seek the forest fruit. He could also help to protect Sitā. Rāma agreed, and gathering together their weapons, and distributing their treasures to the priests and sages, they prepared to depart.

The leave-taking between the three exiles and Kausalyā and Sumitrā and the other royal ladies was painful in the extreme, but the charioteer was ready and departure was imperative. As they mounted the chariot the people surrounded it, sad and stricken, begging the charioteer to drive slowly that they might see Rāma the longer. Queen Kausalyā ran beside it, while the aged and grief-laden king stood and watched it go. Rāma urged the driver to hurry so that the parting could be over, and soon Kausalyā was left behind. But the people followed throughout the day, and when night fell and the journey ended, they slept till dawn by the side of the river Tamasā, exhausted, but waiting for the morrow. After performing their devotions, with the stars shedding "their silent lustre" over them, Rāma and Sitā slept on "a bed of leaf and verdure" while Lakshmana and the charioteer kept watch.

Rising before dawn Rāma suggested that the three of them should leave while the city people slept, and by a devious course the chariot took them to the river Ganges where they stopped for the night. In the morning they took off their royal clothes and put on the bark clothes of hermits, matted their hair and sent the charioteer back to Ayodhyā. Guha, chief of the "wild Nishādas," gave them a boat in which they crossed the river and they made their way to the mountain Chitra-kuta, passing through the Yamunā forest to the Yamunā river. There was no boat waiting for them there, and Rāma and Lakshmana made a raft of forest wood, with an oar of bamboo, and they crossed the river. They travelled on until they reached the hermitage of Bharadwāja, one of the most famous of sages. He welcomed them gladly, for he had already heard of the tragic happenings, and they built huts for themselves in the middle of the forest surrounded by flowers and trees and fruits. The cries of the peacocks and cranes mingled with the gentle ripple of the streams; monkeys chattered and sprang from tree to tree in their incessant happy movement, and in these surroundings the travellers settled down happily, with their meditations and worship, living on the forest fare.

But all was not well with Dasa-ratha. The aged king grew weaker and weaker, and six days after Rāma had left his end was near. He had driven Kaikeyi away, cursing her for the tragedy, and Kausalyā was his constant companion. She tended him with loving care, but once her grief overcame her and she reproached him for what he had done. He asked her not to blame Kaikeyi too much for he had remembered that this suffering was his destiny for an action performed in his youth.

'Deeds we do in life, Kausalyā, be they bitter, be they sweet,
Bring their fruit and retribution, rich reward or suffering
  meet."

Heedless child is he, Kausalyā in his fate who doth not scan

Retribution of his *karma,* sequence of a mighty plan!"

When a young man, he had been an excellent archer, able to shoot accurately by sound as well as by sight. One day when hunting in the forest by himself, he had heard a sound such as an elephant makes when lifting water with its trunk, and he had shot at the sound. To his horror he heard a human voice cry out in pain, and hurrying to the spot he found he had shot a young hermit who was filling his pitcher with water. The youth was dying, but he begged the prince to take the arrow out of his breast and ease his pain. He told him he must go to his aged parents, who were blind and helpless, and tell them what he had done, and crave their forgiveness. Without their son they would die, but they must know that their son was dead and had not merely left them to perish. So saying he died.

Dasa-ratha, full of sorrow and remorse, went on his sad mission. When the old hermit heard him coming, thinking he was his son, he asked why he had been so long, and gently chided him for delaying his return. With great difficulty the young prince told the story of his rashness and begged for forgiveness. The hermit told him that, as a consequence of this act he would lose his own son, and die in anguish. He told him to take him and his wife to their dead son, and build the pyre for them. When this was done the hermit and his wife mounted the pyre with the dead body of the youth, and perished in the flames. The memory of this incident had faded from his mind, but now it had returned. After blessing Kausalyā and Sumitrā the king died.

Bharata had been absent from the kingdom while these events were taking place being on a visit to his uncle's country, but now he was sent for and asked to return at once, no reason for the summons being given him. When he reached Ayodhyā he was struck by the general depression and hurried to his mother's apartments, enquiring after his father and Rāma, and asking why the city was so sad. Kaikeyi, happy to see her son, and glad that he was to be king, told him all that had happened, and added, that it was she who had brought about his good fortune.

To her surprise he was angry, and blamed her for his father's death and the separation from his brother. He told her he would not rule, partly because he felt it was too great a task for him, and partly because he would not put himself in Rāma's place. He left her immediately and went to Kausalyā and the wise sage Vasishtha for comfort.

Preparations for the funeral rites were made, and in the course of the ceremony Vasishtha reminded his listeners that death must come to everyone in time, and though grief was natural, the duty of the living was to take up their tasks, even though their hearts were heavy.

Bharata was firm in his resolve not to rule, and with the sages and the royal queens and a large following, he left the city to look for Rāma and to bring him back.

After a long and trying journey he found the royal exiles, and, saluting Rāma as king, he told them of the death of their father. With the old king's death, he maintained, Rāma was free from the vow, and should return to rule. "The truth-abiding Rāma," however, would not turn from his promise, and in spite of all the endeavours of Bharata and his mother to make him change his mind, he would not return.

Queen Kausalyā's sorrow at seeing the soft-eyed Sitā dressed in bark and with her hair matted, looking worn and sad, was great. She told her that her sweet face was "like a faded lotus dry, and like lily parched by sunlight lustreless thy beauteous eye." And an anguish scathes my bosom like the withering forest fire. Thus to see thee, duteous daughter, in misfortunes deep and dire." But Sitā too answered that, "a righteous father's mandate duteous son may not recall!"

A learned Brāhman and Sophist tried to convince Rāma that he was prey to "idle maxims," and that no one owed love or friendship to his kith or kindred, but rather "seek the pleasures of the present.... take the kingdom Bharat offers." But Rāma was proof against his arguments and true to his promise: "tears nor sighs nor sad entreaty Rāma's changeless purpose shook." Bharata then asked him if he would not, for the sake of the people, return and rule. But he replied yet again that Bharata was quite capable of ruling with the aid of the wise counsellors and ministers, and he himself would not move from his promise.

Seeing that he would not repudiate the vow, Bharata sorrowfully prepared to return, taking with him a pair of Rāma's sandals as a token of kingship. It is said that these sandals, placed in the Council Chamber, showed their appreciation of right action, and warning of wrong action, by flapping! Bharata refused to live as a king, but said for fourteen years he would wear the hermit's dress and live on hermit's wild fruit. If, at the end of the fourteen years, Rāma did not return, he would die on the pyre!

When Bharata had returned to the kingdom Rāma, Lakshmana and Sitā moved further into the forest, for now that they had been found, countless visitors would disturb their quiet. Also the presence of the soldiers had made the place unfit for quiet meditation and worship. One other reason decided them: evil Rākshasas had begun to worry the other hermits nearby. If they retired deeper into the forest the Rākshasas would leave. Accordingly they travelled south to the Deccan, to the hermitage of Agastya, and built a home for themselves near the source of the Godāvari river, a hundred miles from Bombay, and there they spent the next thirteen and a half years in peace and happiness.

It was towards the end of this period that an evil Rākshasi, Surpa-nakhā, (a word meaning "basket nails," or "having nails like winnowing fans"), sister of Rāvana king of Lankā on her evil work in the forest saw the royal exiles sitting outside their huts. Seeing the beauty of Rāma she immediately fell in love with him, and, changing her ugly form into that of a young and beautiful woman, approached him. She asked him to marry her and go back with her to Lankā where every delight of life would be his. Rāma pointed to Sitā and told her he was already married. But, he added, his brother had no wife with him and if she sought his love she would have no rival to fear. As she turned her eye on Lakshmana he said in "merry, mocking accents," "I am slave of royal Rāma, would'st thou be a vassal's bride!" Torn by her passion and infuriated by "these mocking accents," she tried to kill Sitā, and she warned the brothers to "beware a Rākshas' fury and an injured female's wrath." Rāma protected Sitā from her and told Lakshmana to fight her. And he added:

> Brother, we have acted wrongly, for with those of savage breed,
>
> Word in jest is courting danger,—this the penance of our deed.

In the fight, Lakshmana cut off the Rākshasi's nose and ears, and she fled shrieking into the forest depths to her brothers. When Khara, her eldest brother, heard her story he sent fourteen Rākshasas to destroy the exiles, but they were all killed. He then sent his brother with fourteen thousand Rākshasas to destroy them. When Rāma saw this army he told Lakshmana to take Sitā to a safe place, and he then destroyed the brother and all the Rākshasas with his celestial weapons. Then Khara himself came and fought with Rāma single-handed, but was destroyed in an instant by Rāma's arrow of fire.

Only one Rākshasa remained, and Surpa-nakhā, in anger and fear returned to Lankā to tell Rāvana all that had happened and to beg him to send more men to destroy Rāma. Rāvana, however, in his pleasure-loving life, was not very concerned with the disaster, so, in order to arouse him, she spoke strongly of the beauty of Sitā. This inflamed his passion so that he planned to capture her as his bride. Before starting on his mission he sent for Māricha, a Rākshasa hermit, in his employ. Māricha was a son of Tārakā, and had by many austerities gained many peculiar powers, one being the capacity to change his form at will. It was he who had been disturbing Viswāmitra in his hermitage when the young Rāma shot him with a peculiar weapon, driving him many miles out to sea. Now, Rāvana told him to change into a wonderful deer and play near Sitā so that she would see his beauty and would want to possess him. Indeed, when Sitā saw the deer, "golden necked," with "silver-white" flank, and "sapphire on his antlers," she asked Rāma to capture it for her alive, so that it could be her companion in the forest, and the loved playmate when she returned to the palace. If he could not capture it alive, then he should kill it and bring its beautiful skin which she could use as a carpet in their home, a memento of their forest stay.

Lakshmana told her that he thought it was a Rākshasa and not a deer, for often these evil demons took on such forms to mislead the hunters. But Sitā would not listen, and Rāma, leaving Lakshmana to guard her, went into the forest after the deer. He shot it deep in the forest, and as it died it called out, imitating Rāma's voice, "Speed, my faithful brother Lakshmana, helpless in the woods I die!"

Sitā and Lakshmana heard the cry, and Sitā begged Lakshmana to go to Rāma's rescue. He again warned her that this might be a Rākshasa's deceit, for Rāma knew no equal and would never thus call for help. Also he had bade him stay by her. Overcome by fear and anguish, Sitā upbraided him with disloyalty to his brother, and seared to the heart by the words she used, he called the unseen dwellers of the forest to witness that he broke his promise to guard her at her own command, and turning away, disappeared into the forest in search of Rāma.

No sooner had he gone than Rāvana, in the guise of a Brāhman, approached Sitā as she sat "lighting up the lonely cottage.... as the Moon with streaks of silver fills the lovely midnight sky." He asked her who she was, and "wherefore then this dismal forest doth thy fairy face adorn?" Thinking he was a Brāhman she told her story and, as was the custom of the time, asked him to stay until Rāma returned. She asked him why he was in the forest alone, and who he was. And he replied he was neither a Brāhman nor a righteous Rishi but was:

"Leader of the wrathful Rākshas, Lankā's lord and king am

He gave her a wonderful description of his kingdom and asked her to share it with him as his foremost queen. With her eyes blazing with anger she told him scornfully of the greatness of Rāma, and her pride in being his wedded wife. She scorned his palace and kingdom, calling them a dungeon's hold. It would be easier to snatch the sun and moon from the heavens, she said, than to take Rāma's wife without punishment for:

> "Deed of sin, unrighteous Rāvan, brings in time its dreadful
> mead,"

and she added:

> "For this deed of insult Rāvan, in thy heedless folly done,
> Death of all thy race and kindred thou shalt reap from
> Raghu's son!"

But she spoke in vain. Neither threat nor entreaty availed, and he lifted the struggling royal princess into his celestial car, "yoked with asses winged with speed." It rose into the air and passed on the way to Lankā over forest and hill and vale. As she went, Sitā called to Rāma, to Lakshmana, and to the unseen things of the forest, asking their aid. She asked Lakshmana for forgiveness for her insults, for now she saw his warning had been true. But there was no answer. Soon they passed over the mountain peak where the king of the vultures, Jatāyu, was sleeping. He awoke, and rising swiftly into the air with the speed of Indra's thunderbolt, destroyed Rāvana's car. But Rāvana got above him and, pierced and bleeding, the bird fell to earth. Rāvana clasped Sitā in his arms, and in his own horrid shape, with ten heads and a body scarred with the tusks of Airāvata, Indra's elephant, and the discus of Vishnu, they sped south to Lankā. On the way they passed the monkeys' hill, and Sitā dropped her scarf and jewels, hoping they would see that a princess was being carried away.

At last they arrived at Lankā, "the emerald island, girdled by the sapphire wave," and Rāvana gave Sitā to the women of the palace telling them to guard her night and day. Sometimes they did this with pleasant service, sometimes with tortures, but in spite of suffering and inducement she refused Rāvana's advances.

The descriptions of Rāvana's palace are vivid. There were crystal floors and gold and silver stairs. Beauty shone from every angle, and nothing that a luxury-loving person could wish for was missing. It was the perfection of earthly delight. It was set in a perfection of surroundings, with coloured blossoms, richly fruited trees, and gloriously green grass.* The palace rose "snowy-white like fair Kailāsa cleaving through the azure sky." As the palace of Dasa-ratha and his Court glowed with austere perfection, so Rāvana's palace and Court shone with sensuous delights.

Here, in an Asoka grove, guarded by Rākshasis Sitā was imprisoned until she should yield to Rāvana's demands.

When Rāma and Lakshmana realised the deception, they hurried back to their huts, but they were too late. In their agony of grief they called Sitā's name as they wandered in the forest, seeking her. Sometimes they seemed to be cheated by the shadows cast by the trees and saw her face there, or lurking among the lotus blooms in the lakes. But though they called there was no answer. The first news they received was from the dying Jatāyu. This great-hearted bird told them with his last breath about his fight with Rāvana and added that Sitā had been taken southwards.

As they went south they met a monster who tried to stop them, but they killed him. As he lay dying he begged them to cremate his body and, when this last service had been performed, out of the ashes rose Kabandha, a Gandharva, who had been forced

---

* This description "green grass" is eloquent, for the contrast of the barren dry earth of the Deccan and the lush vegetation of Ceylon strikes every traveller from India to Ceylon.

into the monster body by a spell. Now, freed, he was able to tell them that Rāvana had taken Sitā to Lankā. But, he added, they would need help to conquer him and advised them to enlist the aid of Su-griva, the king of the monkeys, who dwelt on a mountain in the Nilgiri Hills.

Accordingly the brothers proceeded south to the Nilgiris. Hanumān, son of Vāyu god of the wind, in the service of Su-griva, saw them as they neared the mountain, and told his master who went out to meet them. When Rāma asked for his aid he said he well knew of "righteous Rāma, soul of piety and love," and thought himself very fortunate to meet him. Willingly would he give all the help he could to bring Sitā back but, first, he would like to be aided in his own trouble. This was very similar to Rāma's, for his wife had been stolen by his half-brother Bāli, son of Indra, who had also usurped his kingdom. Rāma agreed to this condition and in a short time he shot a weapon which destroyed Bāli, and Su-griva was again installed in his kingdom and re-united with his wife. In honour of this victory geat festivities took place, but before any further move was made towards the rescue of Sitā, the monsoon came, and Rāma and Lakshmana had to retire to the caves and await weather more suitable for their journey.

When the monsoon abated they were tired of waiting and, as Su-griva made no move, messengers were sent to him to ask if help could now be forthcoming. Su-griva then gathered together his divisions, and soon a large army of monkeys and bears were ready, and they started out, north, south, east and west, in the search for Sitā. (These monkeys, it must be remembered, were those created by the gods at the time of Rāma's birth so that they would be able to help at this time. Also they were not true monkeys or bears, but aboriginals who appear to have belonged to Aryan culture from the descriptions there are of their cities and political and artistic institutions, though the drawings of them certainly show them with tails!)

One of the armies was commanded by Hanumān. On his journey he found Sampāti, brother of Jatāyu, on a mountain top. Legend says that these two great birds were brothers, sons of Vishnu's Garuda. They lived happily together until one day Jatāyu, the younger, wanted to rise up to the sun. Sampāti knew this would be too hot for them but, as Jatāyu was determined, he decided to go with him on the condition that Jatāyu would carry him on his back. Jatāyu agreed, and they flew up so near to the sun that the heat scorched Sampāti's wings. When they came down to earth again the wings were useless and he could fly no more. But Jatāyu was happy and proud because he had flown to the sun, not knowing the price paid by his brother. Sampāti told Hanumān that he had seen Rāvana with Sitā on the way to Lankā, and for this information he was rewarded. His wings began to grow again and in a short time he was able to enjoy his rapid flights through the air as before.

As they neared Lankā, Hanumān thought he would hop over to the land, and having the power to become enormous, and to fly with the speed of his father, the wind, he made himself grow to such proportions that, with only one flying leap, he landed in Lankā, the mountains rocking with the force of his leap. He had a few adventures on the way for the air tried to stop him. Then the mother of the serpents said he would have to pass through her mouth before he could go on. But he made himself grow larger and larger and the serpent's mouth grew larger and larger too. Then, suddenly, he began to shrink, and when he was no bigger than a thumb he rushed into her throat and out of her right ear. Later Sinhikā, a Rākshasi, tried to seize his shadow. This was her method of procuring food, for she was able to drag those she wanted to eat into her mouth by their shadows. Hanumān allowed her to eat him and then began to grow so large that she burst, and he escaped to continue his journey.

At last he arrived at Rāvana's palace and changed himself into the form of a cat so that he could wander at will in the rooms, courtyards and grounds. He was much impressed by the wonders he saw, and, as he walked through the sleeping quarters of the

ladies of the court, he thought they were so lovely that they
looked like lotus blooms. But Sitā was not to be found in the
palace, and he began to search the grounds. At last, in the
Asoka grove, he saw her, "like a star in the midnight sky,"
surrounded by women of dreadful shapes. He dared not approach
or make any sign but sat and watched. In the morning Rāvana
came and tried with all kinds of entreaties to persuade her to
marry him, but in vain.

After the king had left, Hanumān caught her attention and,
though at first she thought it was another deception of Rāvana,
he was able to convince her of his genuineness by showing her
one of Rāma's rings. Her heart overflowed with happiness when
she saw this, and Hanumān offered to carry her back with him to
Rāma. She refused however, for she did not think it was seemly
that Rāma's wife should be carried by a monkey. Instead she
gave him a jewel from her hair to give to Rāma and told him to
tell him that Rāvana had threatened that if she did not marry him
in two month's time she would be killed.

We cannot help asking why Rāvana did not take her by force,
but, it appears, that once he had carried off a nymph from Indra's
court by force, and Brahmā was so angry that he said if Rāvana
ever took anyone else by force his head would be struck off!

As Hanumān left to fly back to Rāma, he thought he would do
all the harm he could to Lankā and, making himself large again,
and acting as a hurricane, he demolished houses and tore up
trees until Indra-jit, son of Rāvana, shot him, bound him with a
noose and took him to Rāvana. Rāvana treated him as an
ambassador from Rāma, and sent him back, but before letting
him go they tied a rag soaked in oil to his tail and set it alight. As
he sped on through the air the wind fanned the flames and
Hanumān jumped from housetop to housetop setting them alight
so that much of Lankā's city was destroyed. As Sitā saw the
flames she prayed that Hanumān would not be hurt.

When Hanumān returned to Rāma's camp, there was great

rejoicing, and preparations began for the rescue. The army assembled on the coast where sixty miles of water divides the mainland from Lankā. Here Vibhishana, the younger brother of Rāvana, joined them. He had been banished by his brother because he had told him he ought to send Sitā back to her husband and make peace, for Rāma was no ordinary foe, and "righteousness becomes the brave." He had also added that his brother should "cherish peace and cherish virtue." But Rāvana would not listen. After the banishment he had gone to Siva who told him to join forces with Rāma. Rāma was glad to welcome him for he knew him as a virtuous man who would never do an unworthy action.

The preparations for battle did not go very well for there was one seemingly insurmountable obstacle:—How could the army get across the water. Rāma performed sacrifices with no result: he sent his celestial weapons through the waters, even to the bottom of the ocean, causing great earthquakes and thunder and lightning, and the mountains began to fall to pieces. But the waters remained. He then threatened to dry them up. At this threat the king of the ocean rose up, majestic and unperturbed, and explained that by immutable natural law the ocean waters could not be crossed on foot. They might be crossed by means of a bridge over them, and he advised them to seek those who could build such a bridge. Then he slowly disappeared once more and the ocean remained as before.

Rāma now sent for Nala, son of the divine architect Viswakarmā and according to his directions huge boulders of rock were thrown into the sea so that the monkey army could jump from rock to rock. The bridge thus made is called to-day Rāma's bridge, (or Adam's bridge). In thankfulness Rāma set up the *lingam* and worshipped Siva, making the rock island a holy island, called Rāmeswaram.

When all was ready Hanumān took Rāma with him and flew across to Lankā, and Angada, son of Bāli, grandson of Indra took Lakshman. The apes and bears jumped from rock to rock, and in due time the whole army reached the island.

It was a strange looking army for the apes were of various colours. The leaders were most striking: Su-griva shone like silver, Angada was like a lotus, pure white, Hanumān yellow like gold. One leader had a black body, yellow tail and red face. Another was green, another yellow. The whole array looked somewhat like a rainbow.

When Rāvana saw the forces surrounding his city he ordered the gates to be opened and his army went forth to combat the enemy. It, too, was a strange looking army for the soldiers rode on elephants, lions, camels, asses, hogs, hyaenas and wolves, and carried all kinds of weapons. As they marched out they made all kinds of noises in the hope of frightening the monkeys. Rāma's army, on the other hand, had no real weapons but tore up trees and rocks, and used their own sharp nails and teeth. For days the battle raged without any decided victory. Once Indra-jit, Rāvana's son, tried to destroy Rāma and Lakshmana by binding them with a noose of serpents, and he would have succeeded had not Vāyu, god of the wind, sent Garuda to their aid. The serpents were so terrified of the serpent-killer that they fled, and the two princes were freed.

When Rāvana tried to kill him, Rāma shot off his ten crowns, making him so ashamed that he retired from the battle. With success so delayed Rāvana sought the aid of his brother Kumbha-karna who, at the council of war before the battle started, had, like his younger brother told him he ought to make peace and give Sitā to her husband. But, unlike Vibhishana he said he would fight on his side for "faithful Kumbha-karna will his loyal duty know, he shall fight his monarch's battle, he shall face his brother's foe! True to brother and to monarch, be he right or be he wrong, Kumbha-karna fights for Lankā 'gainst her foemen fierce and strong."

Kumbha-karna was a strange creature. He suffered from a curse of Brahmā which made him sleep for six months, wake for one day, when he ate a prodigiously large meal, and then fall asleep for the next six months! It was difficult to arouse him at this time because he was in the middle of his sleep, but at last the messengers from Rāvana succeeded, and, after his meal, he went into battle. After a short struggle Rāma cut off his head and he fell into the water, his weight and size causing great disturbance.

Indra-jit made another attempt against Rāma and Lakshmana, this time using magic and, becoming invisible, rose in the air and shot his arrows at them. They could not shoot back for they could not see him and they fell, apparently lifeless, to the ground. When Rāvana heard of this he was delighted and praised his son. But his evil nature very quickly rose up and he ordered that Sitā should be taken to see her dead husband. When she saw the two beloved princes lying dead she wept:

> Anguish woke in Sitā's bosom and a dimness filled her eye,
> And a widow's nameless sorrow burst in widow's mournful cry:

> "Rāma, lord and king and husband! didst thou cross the billowy sea,
> Didst thou challenge death and danger, court thy fate to rescue me,

> Didst thou hurl a fitting vengeance on the cruel Rāksha force,
> Till the hand of hidden foeman checked thy all resistless course?......

> But I weep not for my Rāma nor for Lakshman young and brave,
> They have done a warrior's duty and have found a warrior's grave,

> And I weep not for my sorrows,—sorrow marked me from my birth,—
> Child of Earth I seek in suffering bosom of my mother Earth!

But I grieve for dear Kausalyā, sonless mother, widowed
   queen,
How she reckons days and seasons in her anguish ever
   green."

The "silent stars of midnight wept to witness Sitā's woe," and
the heart of her companion, though a Rākshasi, was touched.
She told her that the princes were not dead for had they been the
war would have ended. Also she saw that friends of Rāma were
watching his face, and she was sure that he would soon awake.

With the coming of night the fighting always stopped, and
Hanumān and Vibhishana took torches and went over the
battlefield to look for the wounded and the dead. At first they had
been sad that so many monkeys were destroyed, but the
monkey physician told Hanumān to fly to one of the Himālayan
mountains where certain herbs grew and bring some to him.
Hastily making himself huge in size, he flew off. He found the
mountain but not the herbs so, using his great strength, he
uprooted it and carried it to the physician who quickly found what
he wanted and revived the mounkeys. In this way Rāma and
Lakshmana were also revived. Hanumān flew back with the
mountain and put it in its place.

With the dawn of day the battle started again. Indra-jit soon
fell, killed by an arrow shot by Lakshmana, an arrow given by
Indra himself. When Rāvana heard this he wept for him—
"greatest of my gallant warriors, dearest to thy father's heart,"
and "tears of sorrow, slow and silent, fell upon the monarch's
breast." His sorrow soon turned to anger, and he went to Sitā
determined to destroy her. The Rākshasa women with her
prevented this great crime by hiding her, and Rāvana mounted
his chariot and rode into the battle.

He shot a great weapon at his brother Vibhishana, but
Lakshmana destroyed it while it was still in flight, and Rāvana
was so angry at this that he shot at Lakshmana and he fell,
pierced to the heart and fastened to the earth. But at night the

mountain herbs revived him and he rose alive and well.

During the night the monkeys raided the city and destroyed a sacrifice Rāvana was making to try and compel the gods to help him.

Finally the last day of battle dawned and Rāvana, "mighty in his vengeance," with a "new and glorious car" met Rāma in single combat for the last time. For this great day Indra had sent Rāma his own arms and chariot, telling his charioteer to hasten, for, "Gods assist the brave and true."

> "Take this car," so said Mātali, "which the helping Gods provide,
> Rāma, take these steeds celestial, INDRA'S golden chariot ride,

> Take this royal bow and quiver, wear this falchion dread and dire,
> VISWA-KARMAN forged this armour in the flames of heavenly fire,

> I shall be thy chariot driver and shall speed the thund'ring car,
> Slay the sin-polluted Rāvan in this last and fatal war!"

The contest was watched by gods and mortals. Clouds of arrows hid the sky as the battle raged. But success did not come. Arrows gave place to the mace, club, trident and spear, and the struggle was so fierce that the winds "were hushed in voiceless terror and the livid sun was pale." One arrow sent by Rāma cut off one of Rāvana's ten heads, but another grew immediately and the contest continued. At last Rāma took the dreadful Brahmā weapon given him by Brahmā, and threw it at Rāvan. It pierced his heart and, coming out of his back, rushed to the ocean, and then back to Rāma's quiver.

Now all Nature seemed to rejoice, for heavenly flowers fell on the field of battle, heavenly music filled the air, the ocean "heaved" in gladness, and the sunlit sky seemed brighter. Soft breezes blew in from the forest, and "sweetest scent and fragrant odours wafted from celestial trees."

When the Rākshasas heard of Rāvana's death they became demoralised and Rāma was able to enter the city. Rāvana's widow, Mandodari, wept for her husband, and Rāma, "tender, tearful, true," ordered that the funeral rites and honours due to a fallen foeman should be performed. Vibhishana lighted the funeral pyre, and "the zephyrs gently blowing fanned the bright and blazing fire."

Rāma laid aside his weapons for all was over. He appointed Vibhishana king, who according to custom, married Mandodari his brother's widow.

Rāma now sent for Sitā, and as she walked to greet him, her eyes downcast, her hands folded on her breast, her heart was full of joy. But Rāma's "brow was clouded." He told her he had destroyed the enemy and rescued her, but he did not want to see her again for she had "dwelt in Rāvan's dwelling," and "rumours cloud a woman's fame." In her distress she asked him why he had come across the sea with an army to free her if he thought she was a fallen woman? She reminded him of the years they had spent so happily together when she went with him into the forest; she reminded him of her birth and stainless character. But, "a woman pleadeth vainly when suspicion clouds her name," and she turned to Lakshmana saying "if thou lov'st thy sister, light for me the funeral flame," for when "the shadow of dishonour darkens o'er a woman's life, Death alone is friend and refuge of a true and trustful wife."

Rāma remained silent, and "drooped his tortured head" while the pyre was being built, and remained so through Sitā's appeal to Agni, god of fire, that, if in act or thought she had sinned, then she would perish in the fire, but:

*"If in life-long loving duty I am free from sin and blame,*
*Witness of our sins and virtues, may this Fire protect my*
*fame!"*

So saying, "fearless in her faith and valour, Sitā stepped upon the pyre" and vanished in the flames.

The people wept, the air was full of celestial beings, devarishis, gandharvas and gods and all nature watched the ordeal. Then the flames parted and Agni himself came forth holding her with "not a curl upon her tresses or a fibre of her mantle" tarnished, and to the people assembled, and to Rāma, he proclaimed her innocence:

"Pure is she in thought and action, pure and stainless, true and meek,
I, the witness of all actions, thus my sacred mandate speak!"

Rāma's eye was radiant and he spoke gladly to Agni and to the people. He said he had never doubted her, never doubted her virtue or her truth, for he knew her, but for the sake of the people he had brought on this ordeal so that her virtue was proclaimed.

"Be the wide world now a witness,—pure and stainless is my dame,
Rāma shall not leave his consort till he leaves his righteous fame!"

In his tears the contrite Rāma clasped her in a soft embrace, And the fond forgiving Sitā in his bosom hid her face!

Preparations now began for the homeward journey and Vibhishana brought his car, Pushpaka, for them. This was an aerial car of two storeys which moved by itself, making a musical sound as it flew through the air. It had belonged to Kuvera, the half-brother of Rāvana, given to him by Brahmā, but Rāvana had stolen it for his own use. Just as they were taking off, the monkey army clamoured to go too, and when Rāma gave permission they crowded in, or clung to the outside. At last they were all there and the car rose into the air and proceeded over the Nilgiris *en route* to Ayodhyā. When they were about to pass Su-griva's home, Sitā asked if they could stop and pick up his wife Tārā and the wives of the other monkey chiefs so that they could join in the festivities at Ayodhyā. Rāma gladly consented. Throughout the journey he described the country to Sitā, pointing out the woods and lakes and hermitages where they had lived. Legend has it that Rāma called the Nilgiri mountains, Ootacamundala, a word meaning camel's back, for they reminded him of the round humps on the back of that animal, and it is from this that the lovely hill station Ootacamund takes its name.

Meanwhile messengers told Bharata the glorious news. He ordered the city to be decked with flags and banners and garlands; minstrels sang the ancient songs, the priests made offerings to the gods, and the chieftains, with their forces, gathered round the city gate. From every turret and tower the flags flew and the city shone like gold.

And five days after the end of the fourteenth year of banishment, Rāma, Sitā and Lakshmana returned home.

A huge procession met them. There were elephants with their golden trappings, chariots, cars, horses; troops of soldiers with their banners proudly held; the queens Kausalyā and Sumitrā in their gilded litters, and Bharata himself with the faithful sandals and the silver-white umbrella of state. All eyes were turned to the sky as Pushpaka flew in, borne by its silver swans, and Bharata waved a greeting to his brother. Rāma ordered the swans to descend to earth and, as the huge chariot landed, Bharata mounted it and greeted his long-lost brother. He placed the sandals at his feet and said:

"Bharat's life is joy and gladness, for returned from distant shore,

Thou shalt rule thy spacious kingdom and thy loyal men
  once more,

Thou shalt hold thy rightful empire and assume thy royal
  crown,
Faithful to his trust and duty, Bharat renders back thine
  own!

When they had all left, Pushpaka obeyed Rāma's command,
and returned to its home.

During the consecration Rāma was annointed with the sacred
water and placed on the throne. The gods assisted at the
ceremony, Vāyu giving a golden garland, Indra a wreath of
pearls, Gandharvas played celestial music and all the world
rejoiced. Rāma gave many gifts to the priests and to the heroes
of the fight. To Sitā he gave a matchless string of pearls. As she
held them in her hand she looked at Hanumān and then at
Rāma. He caught her thought and agreed, and she placed the
string round Hanumān's neck like a garland. The monkey god's
heart overflowed and his happiness shone until he looked "like
a mountain illumined by the moon and fleecy clouds."

The monkey visitors stayed for a time, feasting on the good
things of the earth for, in reward for their services, all kinds of fruit
ripened no matter what the season. But at last the time came for
them to go home and they bade Rāma farewell. More gifts were
given, and each monkey touched Rāma's feet as he passed on.
When it came to Hanumān's turn for a gift he asked for a special
one. He asked that he should be remembered for as long as men
recounted the deeds of Rāma. This gift was certainly given, for
all who read of Rāma read of Hanumān and remember the ever
faithful loving service of the great-hearted son of Vāyu!

Rāma's reign is looked upon as the time of the most perfect
prosperity: the rains came in their due season; the earth produced
the most marvellous crops; no one was sick or ill; the moral life
of the people was all that could be desired. The rules of life and

of government which were laid down stand even today as models of perfection. There is advice on taxation, "A light and well-distributed taxation is one of the primary essentials of a well-governed State." The king's revenue was obtained by one-sixth of the produce of agriculture one-fourth of the *tapas* gifts given to the sages, together with royalties on mines and tributes from feudatory kings. The ideal State is described as one where there is "no poverty or wretchedness or squalor, no ignorance or unrighteousness or unholy greed." No one should be without sufficient food, clothing and shelter, and each one must receive a proper education. Possessions were not equalized, but no one had less than a sufficient amount. The hermitages which abounded in the forests were looked upon as "centres of austerity and holiness," and also as "great power-houses of altruism and spiritual force." Kingship did not mean autocracy, for the ruler carried the people with him in his ideas and undertakings, as, for instance, when Dasa-ratha asked the people's advice before proclaiming Rāma as heir-apparent. Anarchy and unrighteous rule were said to be evil, for neither industry nor agriculture, trade, commerce or the arts could survive.

Rāma himself possessed the five basic virtues: non-injury, truth, non-covetousness, purity and sense-control, and the people said of him:

> As a father to his children to his loving men he came,
> Blessed our homes and maids and matrons till our infants
>     lisped his name,
>
> For our humble woes and troubles Rāma hath the ready
>     tear,
> To our humble tales of suffering Rāma lends a willing ear!

For ten thousand years these conditions lasted, and with this description, the *Rāmāyana* ends. A supplement, however was written which describes the events leading to Sitā's death.

After a time, happy and contented, Sitā conceived, and Rāma

asked her if there was any wish she had which he could fulfil. She asked if she might visit the sages who dwelt by the sacred Ganges, and he agreed. But it so happened that at this time he noticed that there was a little tension among the people, and he called his counsellors and asked the cause. At first they would not tell him, but at length he learnt that the people were wondering why he had taken Sitā back, for if he could overlook her indiscretions, then they could be more lenient with those of their own wives. This was not good, for if a ruler is not above reproach the tone of the country is lowered, and Rāma was greatly distressed. Although he knew Sitā was above reproach, and although she had been proved by the ordeal of fire, if the people were not satisfied she would have to be sent away. He spoke to Lakshmana and told him to take Sitā on her way to the hermits, but when they had arrived, he should tell her his decision.

Heavy at heart Lakshmana set out with the happy Sitā. When they had crossed the Ganges and were near Vālmiki's hermitage he could not restrain his tears. Sitā upbraided him, for, she said, he had only just left Rāma and would be seeing him again in another day or two so why did he grieve ? Then he told her, and she meekly accepted the order. With the gentleness always associated with her, she sent a message back to Rāma stating her innocence and bowing to his decree. She said she did not grieve for her own suffering but for the people who had so misjudged her, and then, weeping bitterly, she left Lakshmana and went towards the hermitage. Soon she met Vālmiki's sons, and then Vālmiki himself, who took her to his hermitage and placed her in the care of the hermits' wives.

In due time she gave birth to twins, Kusa and Lava. They were brought up by Vālmiki and he composed the *Rāmāyana* which they learnt by heart. But he did not tell them Rāma was their father.

Many more years passed, and though the country was peaceful and happy, Rāma was sad and lonely.

One year he decided to make the Aswa-medha sacrifice, and a black horse in the charge of Lakshmana was sent out to roam where it wished for a year. During this time great festivities were held, and visiting kings, including Vibhishana, princes and sages came to the Court, awaiting the return of the horse and the completion of the sacrifice. Valmiki went too, taking with him the two boys. He told them to sing the song of Rama all day long, everywhere, to Brahmans, to the warriors, and to all in the streets; to Rama himself and to the royal ladies. For this they were not to accept gifts or ask alms, but only to eat the fruit and berries he gave them. If Rama should ask who they were they should answer, "Valmiki is our Teacher and our Sire on earth below."

Mixing with the crowds and other minstrels the boys sang their song. Rama heard of them and asked to hear them. As he listened he began to wonder. He offered the boys gold but they refused. When he asked who had written the story they told him it was Valmiki. Slowly it began to dawn on him that these must be his own sons, and he greeted them with tears of happiness. His heart craved for Sita and he sent a messenger to Valmiki asking if Sita could come and once more prove her innocence for the sake of the people.

The following morning Valmiki and Sita came, a Sita full of sorrow, a banished wife, a weeping mother. Valmiki vouched for her innocence, Rama re-affirmed that he had never doubted her, and he asked forgiveness for bowing to his peoples's wishes and disowning her. "Help me, Gods," he cried "to wipe out this error and this deed of sinful pride. May my Sita prove her virtue; be again my loving bride!"

In the vast Assembly Hall filled with gods and spirits as well as with men of every race, and perfumed with the fragrance of heavenly flowers, Sita saw her husband, "bright as heaven-ascending star, saw her sons as hermit-minstrels beaming with a radiance high." With her eyes filled with tears she thought how could Rama's queen and Janaka's daughter stoop to plead her cause, for, "Witness of her truth and virtue can a loving woman need?"

Oh! her woman's heart is bursting, and her day on earth is
    done,
And she pressed her heaving bosom, slow and sadly thus
    begun:

"If unstained in thought and action I have lived from day of
    birth,
Spare a daughter's shame and anguish and receive her,
    Mother Earth!........

*If in truth unto my husband I have proved a faithful wife,*
*Mother Earth! relieve thy Sitā from the burden of this life!"*

Then the earth was rent and parted, and a golden throne
    arose,
Held aloft by jewelled *Nāgas* as the leaves enfold the rose,

And the Mother in embraces held her spotless sinless
    Child,
Saintly Janak's saintly daughter, pure and true and undefiled,

Gods and men proclaim her virtue! But fair Sitā is no more,
Lone is Rāma's loveless bosom and his days of bliss are
    o'er!

Prostrated with grief Rāma had to face life alone again. Brahmā himself came to comfort him and reminded him of his purpose in life, and with this in mind he carried on his kingly duties as before. For his private religious ceremonies, in which Sitā used to join him, he had made a golden figure of her.

A thousand years passed and the time came for him to leave the earth. Lakshmana went first, but soon everyone knew that Rāma was about to go, and men and monkeys came to greet him and some to follow him in death. Hanumān came too, but he had the boon of living for ever while the tale of Rāma should be told and could not die with him. Brahmā came, accompanied by other gods, and all who were to die ascended to heaven in golden cars. Rāma entered as Vishnu himself whom he really was, and there he was reunited with Sitā who was none other than Lakshmi, wife of Vishnu.

And so the *Rāmāyana,* the Tale of Rāma, comes to an end. But it is still alive in the heart of India, and every year at the festival of Divāli, or Deepāvali, it is especially remembered, for that season of "lights" is said to refer to the homecoming of Rāma and Sitā and the beginning of his reign. As the city was decorated then, so it is decorated today. Thousands of little wicks are placed in small jars of oil, set alight, and placed in the courtyards of the houses, on the steps and in the windows. Coloured electric lights often replace the older form and in early autumn every town and city, is truly "alight." The story is alive too in the dances that are performed all over India, and Rāvana is perpetually destroyed while Hanumān keeps alive the very spirit of devoted joyful service.

Near Bombay on the sea shore is a temple of Rāma. It is said that when he stayed at this spot on his way to Lankā, Hanumān used to bring him fresh water from the Ganges for his daily bath. One day he forgot. Rāma struck the ground, causing water to rise and make a pool in which he could bathe. The pool is still there, and the water is always fresh and pure. Only comparatively recently was it discovered that the water comes from an underground river.

# CHAPTER IX

# THE MAHĀ-BHĀRATA

The *Mahā-bhārata* gives the history of the *mahā,* great, *Bharata,* family, from its origin to the great war between its two branches which culminated in the battle on the field of Kuru-kshetra five thousand or so years ago.

It is a record not only of actual happenings, but also of their causes. The battle of Kuru-kshetra did not start with the enmity and hatred of Dur-yodhana for the Pandus, but with the action of Sāntanu whose love for Saty-avati deprived Bhìshma of the throne and resulted in the birth of two heirs and their descendants, the Kurus and the Pāndavas.

Karna's hatred, brought to a head by the insults of Draupadi and Arjuna, began with Prithā's initial mistake in bearing him and refusing to acknowledge him as her son: its result is summed up by Yudhishthira's sorrowful comment after the battle when he learnt that the dead Karna had been his elder brother:

> All that wish can shape and utter, all that nourish hope and
> pride,
> All were ours, O noble Karna, hadst thou rested by our side,
>
> And this carnage of the Kurus these sad eyes had never
> seen,
> Peace had graced our blessed empire, happy would the
> earth have been!

Bhishma is one of the most majestic characters in history, yet his great sacrifice, when he vowed never to marry or to take the throne, was surely misplaced: not all personal sacrifices bear good fruit. His wonderful strength of purpose, firm judgment and perfect performance of duty or *Dharma* stand out clearly throughout the Epic. It was because of his rigid yet perfect self-sacrifice that he was able, when dying on the bed of arrows, to give advice to those around him which stands crystal clear today, and is summed up in those memorable words of his, "Exertion is greater than Destiny."

Krishna walks through much of the Epic as prince, friend, teacher and the divine Avatāra. The lament of Prithā, the fight and death of Abhimanyu, Arjuna's vow of vengeance and his graphic ride to battle that day, stand out as gems of great literature.

There are light touches too, as when the boy prince was too frightened to take down from the tree the weapons of the Pandus because they were wrapped up and looked like corpses! Also in his fear of the conch blowing of Arjuna and his wish to escape from the battle.

Prithā is a much-tried woman who does not show anger at her fate but follows her duty to her sons—a stern, exacting duty, making her often lonely and sad. But she is strong in her despair. She comes on their scene without much notice except in her anguish at parting with her first-born Karna as she watched him, in his basket of rushes, float away on the river—to what fate she did not know. She is in the background all the time, suffering with her sons when they are banished, and later for herself when she is not allowed to accompany them. Even the ladies of the rival court try and comfort her. We see her also at the end of the battle looking at the field of the dying and the dead, and at last admitting Karna as her son. At the close of her life she does not share for long the blessings of peace with her sons but retires into the forest with the old king and queen, to die in a forest fire. We see her as a symbol of mother earth bearing sons supporting them and suffering with them but demanding nothing.

Draupadi is of different metal. She is certainly much tried also, but her complaints are more selfish and petty, and she earns from Krishna the rebuke that the sorrows of Prithā are greater than her own.

We are carried from the lightness of touch of the marriage of Sāntanu and the goddess Gangā to the heavy-laden atmosphere of war, with the resulting deaths of almost all the characters. Some period of relative happiness, relative because so tinged with the memory of the war, comes between the end of the war and the deaths of the Pandus and of Krishna. In the deep search for the "why?" of each death the answer is given, and as death is not the end, we are given a glimpse of the heaven-condition of the Pandus, and Kurus just as in the vision at the close of the battle we have the comfort of seeing the happiness of those who had been slain.

But life goes on. Kings and princes rule and die, but kingship continues, and we leave the fate of Hastinā-pura in the hands of Parikshit, grandson of Arjuna and Su-bhadrā, son of the hero Abhimanyu, and Indra-prastha in the hands of Yuyutsu, half-brother of Dur-yodhana.

The story starts in the reign of King Dushyanta, who was descended from Soma and Atri (one of the ten Prajā-patis created by Brahmā). One day, while hunting deer in the forest, the king outstripped his retinue and came to a hermitage. Here he had to give up the chase as the space around a hermitage was traditionally considered a sanctuary for animals. While seeking to discover to whom it belonged, he saw a very beautiful young girl, wearing the bark garments of a hermit. Dushyanta fell in love with her at once and asked her who she was. She told him her name was Sakuntalā. Her birth had been a strange one. Indra, worried about the great austerities of the sage Viswāmitra, had sent Menakā, one of his most beautiful Apsarās, down to earth to distract him. This she had done so successfully that she bore him a baby girl who was looked after by the birds of the forest (hence her name, which means "the nursling of the birds"). One day the sage Kanwa found her and brought her to his hermitage where she grew up as his daughter.

In those days what was called a Gāndharva marriage, i.e., a marriage by mutual consent, was legal, no ceremony being necessary. Accordingly, Dushyanta and Sakuntalā took their marriage vows to one another, Sakuntalā insisting that if she bore a son the king must acknowledge him as his heir.

Soon afterwards Dushyanta left, promising to send for her later on. Sakuntalā, awaiting the return of Kanwa with fear, hid herself for some time. But when he found her the sage assured her that all would be well: being of a noble race the king would keep his word.

In due time an exceedingly beautiful baby boy was born, bearing all the marks that proclaimed him to be of royal birth. When he was six years old Sakuntalā took him to his father so that he could declare him his heir. At first the king did not recognise her. But he heard a voice from heaven telling him that the child was, in fact, his own, and he acknowledged him as his heir. The son was called Bhārata, and from him the great Bharata family sprang. During his reign he extended the kingdom until it covered all Hindustan, then called Bhārata-varsha, and in time that name was given to the whole of India. His son built the city of Hastinā-pura near the present Delhi and his grandson was Santanu.

One day when Santanu was walking on the bank of the river Ganges he saw a beautiful maiden sitting on the water's edge, looking like a mermaid with her long, loose hair. She seemed as beautiful as a lotus bloom, and her laugh was like the pleasant rippling of waters. Santanu fell in love with her and asked her to marry him. She agreed at once, but extracted from him two promises: he was never to speak harshly to her and he should never try to stop her from doing anything she wished to do. He readily agreed, and asked her when he could arrange for the wedding ceremony. Saying that she would marry him the following day, she vanished from his sight.

Santanu was so convinced of the reality of this that he went back to his palace and ordered the most elaborate preparations to be made for his wedding, but when the courtiers asked whom he was marrying he could not answer. All day the people toiled to make the city festive and beautiful while Santanu waited impatiently, but trustfully. Just at the right moment the maiden arrived. As the sun was slowly sinking to rest in the west, from the north, where the Ganges has its source, came the most wonderful procession that has ever been seen! Down what looked like a golden road of light came swans, coloured fishes of all sizes and shapes, wild geese holding chains of gold with golden baskets filled with amber, red flamingoes with filigree silver baskets filled with coral, cranes with baskets of jasper and pearls, herons trumpeting loudly, red carp, blue carp and white carp. Finally, two white carp decorated with pink lotus buds came into view, drawing a mother-of-pearl shell covered with the flimsy multicoloured wings of the dragon fly. And in the shell was the bride.

In a year's time the people heard of the birth of a son and heir and were overjoyed. But when Santanu, full of pride and happiness, went into the nursery to look at the baby and drew back the curtains of butterfly wings which formed part of the mother-of-pearl cradle, he found it empty. Not even the most strenuous search brought the baby back to them.

The birth and disappearance of six children took place in this way, but the king dared not ask his wife what was happening because of the betrothal promises. When, however, she was about to bear another child he kept watch, and one day he saw her take the new infant in her arms and walk towards the balcony which stretched out over the Ganges. Then she paused, hugged the child, and cast it into the river.

The king resolved to say nothing of what he had seen, but when the next child was born he thought he would watch more carefully. In due time another child was born and when he saw the queen take the new baby in her arms, without giving her time to reach the balcony, he spoke to her and upbraided her. She burst into tears, for now that he had spoken angrily to her he had broken his vow, and she would have to leave him. Before going she told him the reason for her former behaviour, and, strange though it seems nowadays, it was not strange at that time, for people then believed they had to spend more than one life on earth, and freedom from rebirth was the goal to be striven after. She said that she had destroyed the other children in order to help seven holy men. These men were so pure that they were almost perfect, but for some slight fault committed in the past they had to be reborn once more. The birth itself removed the last obstacle from their path to perfection, and she, the goddess of the Ganges, had agreed to give them birth herself and then throw them into the water immediately. This duty done, any other child would be her own and therefore she would not have to destroy it. Now, however, she could not stay but must leave, and in great sorrow she took the child and disappeared, saying that she would bring him up fit in all ways to take his part in the world, and would then return him. She gave him the name of Sāntavana which means 'the gift of the gods'.

She fulfilled her promise and when he had grown to manhood she brought him to his father and then departed for ever.

Santanu had lived a lonely life and the return of his son did not fully satisfy him. One day as he was walking by the banks of the Yamunā he saw a beautiful girl around whom there seemed to be a delightful perfume, and he asked her who she was. She told him she was Satyavati, daughter of a fisherman, and that she ferried people across the river. The fisherman was not her real father, but he had brought her up as his daughter. One day, it appears, he had caught a fish which had swallowed two unborn babies, a boy and a girl, belonging to a rajah. The boy he sent to the rajah but the girl he kept for himself. As she grew her beauty increased, but unhappily she was always surrounded by a fishy smell.

One day a Brāhman was struck by her beauty as she ferried him across the water, and told her that if she would consent to be the mother of his son she would lose her fishy smell and have, instead, a most delightful perfume. She consented, a cloud covered the boat, the boat vanished, and the girl gave birth to a son who at once grew up, said goodbye to her, and went to the forest to spend his life in meditations. His name was Vyāsa. Before leaving he told her that if she ever needed him she had but to think of him and he would come to her aid.

Santanu fell in love with Satyavatì and wanted to marry her. The fisherman father agreed on condition that any child of hers should be acknowledged heir to the throne. This Santanu could not promise, for his heir was Sāntavana, and he grew more and more melancholy. Sāntavana asked him many times what was wrong, and when at last he learnt the truth he at once renounced the heirship to the throne and made a vow never to marry, so that any child of Satyavati would be heir. At this great sacrifice—great because in those days it was a bounden duty for a man to marry and have a son thus bringing beneficent consequences in the after life—the heavens rejoiced and flowers fell all around him. From this time on he was called Bhishma, a word meaning, "one who undertakes a terrible vow and fulfils it."

Satyavati married the king and gave birth to two sons, Chitrāngada and Vichitra-virya. Soon afterwards Santanu died, and Bhishma took care of the queen and her sons. He formally renounced the throne and Chitrāngada became king. After a short rule he was killed in battle during a war with a tribe in the north-west of India and Vichitra-virya became king. He was only a boy, and Bhishma was therefore made regent.

Under Bhishma's regency the country flourished. When the time came for the young king to marry, Bhishma went to a neighbouring kingdom where there were three daughters of marriageable age. In those days it was lawful for a bride to be abducted, and without waiting for any tournament or permission, Bhishma abducted the three girls and rode away with them. The queen was glad to receive them, but the girls were very disappointed to find that it was not Bhishma they were to marry, but a young boy. The eldest girl, Ambā, told them she was already betrothed to the rajah of Sālwa and Bhishma sent her to him. He, however, returned her, saying that as she had stayed at another man's house he did not want her. She begged Bhishma to marry her but he could not. For some time she stayed in the country and then on Bhishma's advice made one more attempt to get the rajah to marry her. When he refused again she left for the forest, anger burning in her heart against Bhishma. She performed the usual austerities and won from Kārttikeya a garland made of never-fading lotuses. Anyone who wore this garland would become an enemy of Bhishma. She approached warrior after warrior but none would wear the garland and at last she hung it up on the palace gates of king Drupada and went into the forest again to perform more austerities. In the forest she met some ascetics who told her to go to Parasu-rāma and implore his help. This she did and he fought Bhishma for her but without avail. Then he advised her to make her peace with Bhishma but she refused and went instead to the Himālayas to try and win a boon from Siva. This she achieved and he promised that in her next birth she should be the slayer of Bhishma. Delighted with the news she built a pyre so that she could die at once and in a short time she was born as a daughter of Drupada. When a young child she saw the ever-fresh garland and put it round her neck. Drupada fearing the wrath of Bhishma sent the child into the forest where again she practised austerities and was transformed into a male, known as Sikhandin. She fought in the great battle and was the cause of Bhishma's death.

The other sisters, Ambikā and Ambālikā, settled down in their new home with their husband, but after a short time he died, leaving no heir.

Satyavati asked Bhishma to break his vow and marry the girls in order to ensure an heir, but he refused. Then she asked him to marry her, but again he refused to break his vow. Then she thought of her first son, Vyāsa, and as she thought of him he appeared as he had promised. She explained the situation and he consented to marry the young queens. His years of austerities in the forest, however, had made him so ugly and deformed that when Ambikā saw him she closed her eyes and was filled with horror, and when her son Dhrita-rāshtra was born he was blind.

Ambālikā was terrified when she saw him and turned pale, and when her son was born he was so light in colour that he was called Pāndu.

The queen mother was not satisfied with these children, and asked Ambikā if she would have another child. She consented, but her heart failed her and she made her servant take her place. In time a child was born to the servant and was called Vidura. Now it happened at this time that the god of justice, Dharma, had to be born a man because a Rishi had laid a magic spell on him, and so he entered the body of the baby Vidura.

The story says that one day when a great sage was sitting in his hermitage in a deep trance some robbers came and hid their spoils in the hermitage. Soon the soldiers of the king came and asked him if he had seen the robbers, but as he was in a trance he did not hear them. Incensed, especially as the soldiers found the treasures, the officer drove a spear into the sage. As he was in a trance he did not die and in time many sages visited him. When they asked why he suffered so he answered that it was through the king's soldiers. The king was horrified and went to him, ordered that the spear should be removed, and fell at his feet asking for forgiveness. When the sage went to the god Dharma and asked why he had deserved to suffer in this way he was told that it was because he had tortured birds and bees when a child. All deeds, whether good or bad, must inevitably bring about their results he was told. Thinking that it was very unfair that a child's evil deeds should be so rewarded he cursed the god to be reborn as a human being.

Vyāsa, having fulfilled his task, now returned to the forest.

The three boys were brought up by Bhishma, and when they were old enough for one of them to become king, Pāndu was chosen, for a blind king would not have been suitable, and Vidura, because of his humble mother, could not be offered the throne.

Pāndu was a good king and a brave warrior. He had two wives, Prithā, the chief, and Mādri, the favourite. Prithā's mother was a nymph, and her father a Brāhman. She was also called Kunti, because she had been brought up by Kunti-Bhoja, the king of the Kuntis. Her brother was Vasu-deva, the father of Krishna.

As a young woman she had waited on the sage Durvāsa when he was on a visit to the palace, and had pleased him so much that he had given her a *mantra* which would enable her to make any celestial being fall in love with her. She used this power one day when the Sun was shining, and he came to her, dressed as a king, but wearing the celestial earrings. In due time she bore him a son, born with golden armour and celestial earrings. She dared not let this birth be known and put the baby in a basket which she placed on a river, a tributary of the Ganges, praying to the gods to shelter him and make all people love him. The basket floated on to the Ganges, where it was seen by Rādhā, the wife of Dhrita-rāshtra's charioteer, Shantānanda. This couple had no children, so Rādhā took the baby and brought him up as their own. He was called Karna.

But Kunti did not know where he was, and Karna knew no other mother than Rādhā.

Mādri, the favourite wife, came from Madra—probably the present Kashmir—and Bhishma had bought her for Pāndu with many horses and elephants, jewels and much gold.

Kunti became the mother of three sons and Mādri of two, but as Pāndu, under a curse, could not beget any offspring, he asked Kunti and Mādri to use the sacred *mantra*. Kunti's sons, Yudhi-shthira, Bhima and Arjuna, had Dharma, Vāyu and Indra respectively as fathers; Mādri's sons, the twins Nakula and Sahadeva, had the twin Aswins as fathers. As was to be expected from their parentage, the boys grew up to be distinguished in one way or another. Yudhi-shthira was a good warrior with a keen sense of righteousness and duty, for Dharma is the god of justice and duty: Bhima was known as the terrible, and being the son of Vāyu, the wind god, was strong, courageous and daring, easy to anger, coarse in many ways, and very fond of his food; Arjuna, bright and silvery, having Indra, chief of gods, as father, was brave, high-minded, generous and devoted. Nakula and Sahadeva were noble and brave, but do not play as great a part in the Epic as the others.

Some say that Pāndu might have had a touch of leprosy, which would account for his paleness and for his inability to have children; others that the inability was the result of a hunting mishap. It appears that he once shot at two deer while they were playing together, and killed the male. Before it died it told him that they were a Brāhman and his wife in the guise of deer, and as the result of this act Pāndu would himself die in the arms of his wife. This so frightened him that he remained celibate, gave his kingdom to Dhrita-rāshtra and went to the forest with his wives.

After some years he died there—in the arms of Mādri having for a moment forgotten his vow of celibacy and a discussion began as to who should be burnt with his body, each wife claiming it as her right to die with him. At last it was decided that Mādri should die. She gladly mounted the pyre, and Kunti, with the five sons, (Yudhi-shthira being 16 years old) returned to Hastinā-pura, the city of Dhrita-rāshtra, where they lived for many years. The boys called the Pāndavas were brought up with their cousins, Dhrita-rāshtra's sons.

Dhrita-rāshtra had married Gāndhāri, daughter of the king of Gāndhāra and was the father of one hundred sons. Gāndhāri had, it appears, once been very kind to Vyāsa and he had offered her a boon. She asked that she should be the mother of one hundred sons, and after a pregnancy lasting two years, she gave birth to a lump of flesh. Vyāsa took this and divided it into one hundred and one pieces and placed them in different jars to develop and grow. In due time Duryodhana appeared first, but the portents were so terrible that people asked his father to leave him to die, but he would not do so. Later ninety-nine other sons were born, and then one daughter. The sons were known as the Kauravas, or Kurus.

Gāndhāri never appeared in public with her husband unless her eyes were bandaged; some say that she had them bandaged all the time from the day of her marriage in sympathy with her blind husband—a terrible sacrifice and one which made her a symbol of courage and steadfastness.

As the youths grew up together they often quarrelled, and the seeds were sown of that jealousy which was to result in the Great War.

Once the Kauravas plotted to kill Bhima who outdid them in skill at games. After his death they intended to kill the other brothers and their mother. So when the Pāndavas went to stay at a palace on the banks of the Ganges, they poisoned Bhima's food. While the others were at a party enjoying themselves, Bhima was eating great quantities of food which the cousins offered him. Feeling sleepy, he went to a room overlooking the Ganges to lie down, and the cousins plied him with sweets which had been poisoned with a narcotic. Bhima therefore fell into a deep sleep and the cousins threw him into the river. His brothers did not worry when he did not appear at the end of the festivities, for they were told he was asleep, and they went home without him, leaving the Kauravas full of joy at the success of their plan.

As for Bhima, as soon as he was in the water, snakes attacked him, and their poison worked on the narcotic he had taken so that he recovered, burst his bonds, and fought them off. Then he found himself in the underworld city of the serpents, where Vāsuki was king, and where Bhima's great-great-grandfather, Aryaka, lived. Vāsuki greeted him warmly and offered him a boon. Aryaka suggested that he might be given a liquid which contained the strength of a thousand serpents, and after drinking eight bowls full, he fell asleep for eight days. When he awoke, the serpents fed him well, and he returned to his mother and brothers. They were overjoyed to see him but decided to keep his return secret till the next day when they all went to the Assembly Hall together, much to the consternation of the Kauravas. Bhima greeted his cousins and thanked them for his dip in the river, saying that he had had a marvellous time and had gained enormously in strength. He was now ready to fight them all, singly or together, at once or in the future!

But Bhishma pleaded with them not to quarrel and to leave all important questions until they were older. So for a time peace reigned at the Court.

When Bhishma decided it was time the cousins began their training in the use of weapons, he looked about for a good teacher.

One day, when the boys were playing with a ball, it fell down a disused well, and they could not retrieve it. While they were discussing its loss, they happened to see a Brāhman resting as if tired after his meditations, and they asked him if he could tell them how to get the ball. He got up and, going to the well, threw a ring from his finger into it and said that he would get them back their ball, and also his own ring, with just a few blades of grass. Before the astonished eyes of the young princes, he took blades of strong grass pointed at the end, and threw them down the well one after another until they reached the top. Then, as he began to pull them up, it was seen that the point of each blade had pierced the stem of another, so that they formed a plaited rope, at the end of which was the ball. The Brāhman now shot another arrow of grass into the well, and it came back to him with his ring. The boys were delighted and asked him who he was. He told them to go to their grandfather and say that Drona was here, and *he* would understand.

When Bhishma heard this he was delighted and sent for Drona, greeting him warmly. He asked him if he would undertake the training of the boys, for no one could surpass him in the use of weapons. Drona agreed, but on one condition, *viz.,* that when he had trained them thoroughly, they should help him to fight Drupada, King of Pānchāla, once his friend, now his enemy. This was agreed, and Drona with his wife and his son Aswatthāmā settled in Hastinā-pura, his son taking his training with the princes. The nobles of the land also came to him for training, and so did Karna, the reputed son of the charioteer, who soon began to equal Arjuna in the use of arms. Thus began the rivalry that grew into hatred between the two, and caused Karna to become a friend of Dur-yodhana, fighting on his side in the battle of Kuru-kshetra and being slain by Arjuna.

Who was Drona? His birth was miraculous, for his mother was a beautiful nymph and his father a Brāhman. As a youth he had been very friendly with Drupada, a rajah's son, for both boys were brought up by the Brāhman Bhāradwāja, in his *ashrama* in the Himālayas near the source of the Ganges. When Drupada's father died, he returned to rule the kingdom, but Drona continued with his austerities after the death of his father, and won many celestial weapons from the gods. He married Kripā, half-sister of Bhishma, and their son was Aswatthāmā.

After a time he decided to revisit his old friend Drupada—some say because he wanted to share the great knowledge and power he had gained with his friend; others say because he realised that he was too poor to do all he would have liked to do for his son, having only his wisdom and knowledge of weapons to give. Whatever the reason, he went to Drupada, but, to his surprise, was turned away and called a beggar, Drupada saying it was impossible for a beggar and a warrior to be friends. Drona left, but began to hate Drupada and plan his revenge. Hence the condition he made to Bhishma.

After a time Drona arranged a trial of skill for his pupils. An artificial bird of wood was set up on a tree, and the cousins were asked to shoot their arrows at the bird's head. As each youth stepped forward, Drona asked him what he saw. All of them saw the bird, and some saw Drona also, or the tree, or the people around, and to them Drona said they need not shoot. At last it was Arjuna's turn. When asked what he saw, he replied that he saw the bird. When Drona asked what else he saw, he said he did not see anything else. When asked further what the bird was like, he replied he did not know, for he only saw its head. Then Drona told him to shoot, and his arrow cut off the birds's head.

And jealousy grew stronger in the hearts of the Kurus.

When Drona considered his pupils were fully trained he asked if a tournament could be held in which they would show their proficiency in the use of all weapons, and Dhrita-rāshtra readily consented. A suitable place, near a "crystal fountain," was made ready, and a day, auspicious according to the stars, was chosen. The rules for the tournament were spread abroad, huge stands round the great open centre were erected for the onlookers, white mansions, "gay and glittering, gold-encased" and with jewels and ropes of pearls, were built for the King and the royal ladies, each with the appropriate coat of arms. And when the nobles came they set up their white tents. The day arrived, and thousands of spectators from towns, villages and hamlets filled the stands. At the appointed hour, Dhrita-rāshtra took his place, followed by Gāndhāri with her eyes bandaged, Bhishma and the royal tutors, Prithā and other royal ladies, all arrayed in their most gorgeous silks, making the scene more wonderful still in the brightness of the sun. Last of all came Drona, all in white—white clothes, white garland, white sacrificial cord, white sandals—for, as a Brāhman, he had also become the priest of the royal household. Attended by his son he approached the altar set up for the sacrifices, which were then performed, and holy hymns were chanted.

Then the heralds' trumpets proclaimed the beginning of the contest, and warrior after warrior showed his skill at archery and other methods of war. Sometimes the air was so full of swiftly flying arrows that the spectators were terrified, but none of the arrows missed its appointed mark.

Then chariots filled the arena with noise and speed. Great horsemanship was displayed, and many single combats took place with sword and shield. Bhima and Dur-yodhana fought with the mace, but they soon forgot this was merely a tournament and began to fight in earnest. When Drona saw this he stopped them by entering the lists himself, and called for the trumpets to announce the entry of Arjuna.

Arjuna, in golden armour, "gauntleted and jewel-girdled," carrying a great bow, now entered the arena and walked proudly round, looking like "the sunlit cloud of evening with the golden rainbow graced," and the crowd roared its welcome. Dhrita-rāshtra asked Vidura, who was explaining everything to him, the reason for this tremendous cheering, and Vidura answered. "It is Prithā's gallant boy,.... god-like in golden armour, and the people shout for joy!" Dhrita-rāshtra was pleased, for he said the Pāndus "sanctified" the kingdom.

Arjuna then performed marvellous feats, until with the coming of evening, the festivities were over and the spectators began to leave. Suddenly "like welkin-shaking thunder wakes a deep and deadly sound, Clank and din of warlike weapons burst upon the tented ground," and Karna entered the arena, "in his golden mail accoutred and his rings of yellow gold,.... lion-like in build and muscle, stately as a golden palm, Blessed with every manly virtue, peerless warrior, proud and calm." And "In a voice of pealing thunder spake fair Prithā's eldest son, Unto Arjun, Prithā's youngest, each, alas! to each unknown!"

> "All thy feats of weapons, Arjun, done with vain and
>    needless boast,
>
> These and greater I accomplish—witness be this mighty
>    host."

Dur-yodhana was delighted at this, but Arjuna was filled with anger. Prithā, by a secret sign, had recognised her first-born whom she had abandoned in the little boat of rushes, but she dared not acknowledge him, and, "by an equal love divided.... swoned in grief." Vidura brought her round with sandal wood and water and she watched in silence while the enmity of the brothers grew, and she heard the insults flung at Karna for his supposed low birth.

After Karna had shown his proficiency to be equal to that of Arjuna, Dur-yodhana welcomed him and said he had won the "victor's honours," and offered him a boon. "Answered Karna to Dur-yodhana, 'Prince! thy word is good as deed, but I seek to combat Arjuna and to win the victor's meed!'"

Angry words were spoken by Arjuna and Karna, lightning flashed over the arena as Indra, father of Arjuna, sent his dark clouds to cover his son, and Surya, the sun god, father of Karna, radiated his bright beams on his son. Dur-yodhana and his brothers stood by Karna, Drona and Bhishma by Arjuna, as the heralds began to proclaim the name and lineage of the contestants. When they turned to Karna to know his lineage he, "like a raindrop-pelted lotus bent his humble head in shame."

As, according to the rules of tournament, Arjuna could not fight against a "base and nameless foe," Dur-yodhana called the priests and, with various rites, made Karna king of a small state called Anga so that the contest could go on. While Karna's head was still wet from the anointing with water, an old man, in the clothes of a charioteer, came forward to greet him as his son, and Karna bowed his head in reverence to him, thus acknowledging his lowly birth. But by this time night was falling and the tournament had to end, and everyone departed. Karna, now a fast friend of Dur-yodhana, left with the Kauravas and remained with them until his death.

No one quite knew who had won the contest—some said Arjuna, some Karna; and even Yudhi-shthira wondered in his heart if Arjuna was really the better of the two.

This tournament marked the end of Drona's instruction to the princes and he demanded his fee, *i.e.,* that they should go with him and conquer King Drupada. When all was ready they started out for Pānchāla, the city of Drupada, performing on the way, many valiant deeds. Owing to the jealousy between the cousins, the Kauravas went into the city first, but they were driven back. Then the Pāndavas went in and, owing to the great warriorship of Arjuna, Drupada, fighting valiantly in his white chariot, was taken prisoner and led to Drona. The Kurus wanted to continue the fight and destroy the city, but the Pāndavas refused for it was only Drupada whom Drona wanted to conquer.

Drupada was not taken to Drona as a conquered enemy for Drona wanted him as a friend. When they met, Drona reminded Drupada that he had said there could not be friendship between people who were not of equal rank and, as he wanted his friendship, he would divide the conquered kingdom, keeping half for himself. In this way, he thought, their youthful friendship might be resumed.

But Drupada thought otherwise and began to hate Drona and plot his revenge.

Dhrita-rāshtra now thought it was time to proclaim Yudhi-shthira heir-apparent, and the popularity of the Pāndus grew, while the jealousy of the Kurus became so great that Dur-yodhana began to plan the destruction of his cousins.

When the festivities of Siva were taking place in the city of Vāranāvata, Dhrita-rāshtra told the Pāndus that this was a wonderful city and well worth seeing, adding that they might go there on a visit. The Pāndus, well knowing that this amounted to banishment, could do nothing but express joy at the prospect and in due time they set out, accompanied by their mother. They had one friend at court however,—Vidura, whose father, it will be remembered, was the god of justice. He had the power to read people's minds and knew what Dhrita-rāshtra and Dur-yodhana were thinking. He therefore warned Yudhi-shthira to be very watchful, and told him to learn the pathways through the forests, and how to travel by the stars. He also warned him that it was good to have many exits from a house, and that a deep hole was a good refuge. To this advice Yudhi-shthira listened attentively.

Word had meanwhile been sent to Sakuni, brother of Gāndhāri, that the Pāndus should be destroyed, and when they arrived, they found that a special house had been built for them, beautiful to look at, but made of highly inflammable material. Yudhi-shthira discovered this through the strong smell of the oil used in the structure, and he told Bhima of his suspicions. They decided not to say anything about it, for if they showed dissatisfaction with the house, some other method to destroy them would be sought. They therefore settled down and waited. A few days later, a man came to them, saying Vidura had sent him. He was a miner, and he began to dig a passage under the floor by which they could escape if the house caught fire.

A year went by, and it seemed to Bhima that they could turn the tables on Purochana, the agent of Duryodhana, whose house adjoined theirs. They arranged a great feast, and in the night Bhima set fire to Purochana's house so that the flames, blown by the wind to the inflammable house, burnt both to the ground. Prithā and her five sons escaped through the underground passage into the forest. They did not know that a beggar woman and her five sons had been asleep in the house and were burnt to death, so that when their charred remains were found, it was thought that Prithā and her five sons had perished, and the Kurus rejoiced. The miner returned to the ruins and destroyed all evidence of the underground passage.

Meanwhile the Pāndus and Prithā went quickly through the forest. It was a hard journey, and some times Bhima, the strong, had to carry his mother or one of his brothers, but at last they came to the river Ganges. There they found a ship waiting for them, whose captain said he was there at the request of Vidura to take them across the river. When he had done so, he sailed away, saluting them with the word "Victory!"

In time the travellers reached the town of Ekachakrā, where they stayed for some time, living in the house of a Brāhman, wearing Brāhman clothes, and begging their food. Often visitors came to see them, and one day they heard that Drupada's daughter, Draupadì, was to hold her Swayam-vara ceremony. This news disturbed the brothers, so their mother suggested they should go to Drupada's palace. They gladly set out, and on the way joined a party of Brāhmans.

Draupadi was dark, and so beautiful that she seemed to have come from the city of the gods with her soft curling hair, graceful body, and eyes like lotus-petals. True it was in any case that her birth was miraculous; for when her father had been conquered by Drona, he vowed vengeance on him, and for this purpose made many sacrifices in the hope of obtaining a son. At last he made a specially great sacrifice and sent for his queen to come and partake of it. Unfortunately she had just eaten and perfumed her body—both conditions rendering her unfit to participate in a religious ceremony, and she sent a message to the king saying she could not come. But sacrifices will not wait on mortals, and immediately a youth, clothed in armour and with bow and arrows, a jewel burning brightly in the middle of his forehead, sprang out of the sacrificial fire, and a voice from heaven proclaimed that he had come to destroy Drona. This was Dhrishta-dyumna. Then a girl, Draupadi, dark and with curling hair, came out of the fire, filling the place with a sweet perfume. The heavenly voice spoke again, saying that she would be the greatest among women and cause the death of many warriors, bringing suffering to the Kurus.

Draupadi was now of marriageable age, and, according to custom, she would give her garland to the favoured suitor from among the kings and princes who had come to compete for her hand. Drupada remembered the feats of Arjuna during the battle with Drona, and he hoped that he would come and win his daughter. He therefore ordered that a strong bow be made.

And he made a whirling discus, hung it 'neath the open sky,

And beyond the whirling discus placed a target far and high.

"Whoso strings this bow," said Draupad, "hits the target in
    his pride
Through the high and curling discus, wins Pānchāla's
    princely bride."

On the appointed day the Pāndus, still in Brāhman dress, took
their place with the Brāhmans. Among the princes present were
the Kurus and Karna, Krishna and his brother. Gods in their
"cloud-borne chariots" came to watch; Ādityas and Maruts,
Gandharvas and Apsarās filled the sky, and the contest began.
One after another kings and princes failed, for the strong bow
sprang back at them, felling them to the ground. Then came
Karna. He stood like "SURYA in his splendour," drew the bow to
a circle, fixed the arrow, and would have won, had not Draupadi
called out proudly that she would not marry the son of a
charioteer: "Monarch's daughter, born a Kshatra, Suta's son I
will not wed." Karna heard this, and

"... with crimsoned forehead, left the emprise almost done,
Left the bow already circled, silent gazed upon the Sun!"

Others tried and failed.

Then Arjuna rose, serene and holy, "fair as INDRA'S rainbow
bright," and walked towards the bow. Three times he walked
round it, then, breathing a prayer,

Bent the wondrous bow of Drupad, fixed the shining darts
    aright,

Through the disc the shining arrows fly with strange and
    hissing sound,
Hit and pierce the distant target, bring it thundering on the
    ground!

Draupadi's eyes shone with approval, and she placed her

garland round his neck. Her father was also pleased, for he had recognised Arjuna, but the nobles were very angry that a mere Brāhman had been chosen, and for a time it looked as if there would be a fight. Arjuna and Bhima rushed to Drupada's rescue, Bhima tearing up a tree to act as a club. But order was soon restored, for Krishna spoke to the disappointed suitors and peace reigned once more.

Meanwhile, Yudhi-shthira and the twins left the arena lest anyone should connect them with Arjuna and Bhima and remember the five Pāndus.

Later when the five brothers with Draupadi reached the hut which was their dwelling place, they called out to their mother in jest, "Look what we have brought as alms to-day"; and Prithā, without turning round, said that whatever it was they must all share it. Thus Draupadi became the wife of the five brothers, and the promise Siva had made to her was fulfilled, for in a previous incarnation she had prayed to him five times for a husband and he had granted her wish; but as she had prayed five times, she would have five husbands. According to some, however, she was the wife of Yudhi-shthira, the eldest, as there is no other reference to polyandry in Hindu legend and tradition. There may, however, be a psychological meaning to this.

The same evening Krishna and his brother visited them, and greeted them with pleasure, congratulating them on their escape from the fire. Drupada's son also went to find out how his sister was faring, and thus learnt that it was indeed Arjuna who had won her that day.

The news reached Dhrita-rāshtra, and he called his counsellors together to consider the best plan of action under the circumstances. Karna wanted to fight them; Dur-yodhana wanted to try and separate them by fraud; Bhishma, Vidura and Drona suggested that they should be given back at least half the kingdom. This last advice was taken. One half, including the capital, was to remain with Dhrita-rāshtra and his family, and the other half, on the bank of the Yamunā, was given to the Pāndus. This part was poor—mostly desert and forest—but the Pāndus set to work, cleared the ground, built a city, Indra-prastha, near the present Delhi, and, through Yudhi-shthira's good government, it soon became a prosperous kingdom.

It was, however, difficult for five men to have one wife, even if she spent two days with each in turn; and, benefitting from a tale which Nārada told them on a visit, they decided that when Draupadi was with any brother, the others would not intrude. If they did, the punishment was banishment for twelve years. This befell Arjuna alone, for one day, when Draupadi was with Yudhi-shthira, some Brāhmans called on Arjuna and asked for his help against thieves who were stealing their goods. Arjuna could not refuse to help, but unfortunately his weapons were in the room where Yudhi-shthira and Draupadi were. He decided that the Brāhmans' need was great, and went for his weapons.

When, after helping the Brāhmans, Arjuna returned ready to accept his punishment, Yudhi-shthira tried to persuade him that such an entry as his did not necessitate banishment. But Arjuna insisted that a vow was inviolable.

Arjuna started on his banishment, travelling from city to city and visiting many holy places. One day, while bathing in the Ganges, he saw Ulupi, daughter of Vāsuki, king of the serpents. She was very beautiful, and he fell in love with her. They lived together very happily at her father's palace until she bore him a son, Irāvat.*

Soon after the birth of Irāvat, Arjuna left and went southwards until he reached Manipura. There he met Chitrāngadā, the daughter of the king, and she too was beautiful. Her father consented to their marriage on condition that if a son was born he should stay in the kingdom and be his heir. It appears that the

---

* Some say that this refers to a visit to America, the land of the serpents, and that Ulupi was a Mexican or Inca princess.

king could not have any more children owing to a decree of Siva that every ruler of that kingdom should have only one child, and he already had his daughter Chitrāngadā. Arjuna agreed to this condition, and in time a boy was born called Babhru-vāhana.

After a time, Arjuna set out once more and arrived at Dwārakā, where Krishna welcomed him gladly and arranged a feast. Here Arjuna saw Subhadrā, Krishna's sister, and wanted to marry her. Krishna agreed, but his brother, Bala-rāma, thought she ought to marry Dur-yodhana. So, as a solution to the problem, Krishna advised Arjuna to elope with her. When Bala-rāma heard of this he wanted to pursue them and bring her back, but Krishna pointed out that no one else would marry her now, and the best thing to do was to make the marriage official. A great wedding ceremony was then arranged and the marriage took place. Arjuna stayed with Krishna until his exile was over and then, with Subhadrā, returned to Indraprastha. At first, Draupadi did not take kindly to the new wife. But, after a time Subhadrā's goodness and willingness to serve overcame her jealousy, and the families lived happily together.

Subhadrā had one son, Abhimanyu, who became a hero in the battle of Kuru-kshetra.

Draupadi had five children,—one, it is said, by each husband. They do not appear much in the story, except for their death at Kuru-kshetra, where they were murdered through a misunderstanding.

It was during this period of banishment that Arjuna won the bow Gāndiva which was one of the celestial bows mentioned in the *Mahā-bhārata.* The two other bows were Vijaya belonging to Rukmi, Krishna's brother-in-law, and Shrangā the bow of Krishna himself. Gāndiva is said to have been of many colours, smooth, without knot or stain. It was first in the possession of Brahmā, then after a thousand years it was held by Prajā-pati for five hundred years, then by Sakra for five hundred and eight years. Soma next had it for five hundred years, then Varuna for one hundred years. Agni procured it from Varuna and gave it to Arjuna who, together with Krishna, helped him to burn the Khāndava forest in his war against Indra. Arjuna was so proud of Gāndiva that one day he was about to show it to his brothers when the sage Nārada suddenly appeared and told him he was never to use the bow unless he was "sorely pressed," for heavenly gifts must be used only in case of great need. With the bow, Arjuna was given two quivers of arrows, and no matter how many arrows were shot the quivers were always full.

In this forest fire struggle the Pāndus had helped a Daitya to escape and in return he built them a wonder-palace.

Yudhi-shthira now thought the time had come for the Rāja-suya sacrifice—the assumption of sovereignty over all other kings. In this there was a large element of danger, and it was never undertaken lightly for many kings would be invited to the ceremony and then the host would be proclaimed lord of them all. It was not always successful and happy for often quarrels and dissensions arose.

Before making the decision, the Pāndus asked Krishna's advice, and he, too, thought the time was ripe, but suggested it would first be necessary to fight and conquer the king of Magadha. This would be no easy task, for he could only be killed by a man fighting with his bare hands, but Krishna said that if Arjuna and Bhima went with him they could overcome him. Disguised as Brāhmans, they set out for his palace and on arrival they asked for an audience.

The king asked them who they were and what they wanted, to which Krishna replied that his companions were under a vow of silence until midnight. The king then gave them the sacrificial room to stay in until midnight when he would visit them again. When midnight came and the king went to see them, Krishna suddenly appeared in all his glory, and told him that he had committed so many wicked acts in his life (for the kings he took in battle he had offered in sacrifice of Siva) that his only hope for the next world was to die in battle. He offered him a choice: either to set free the kings he was holding in his dungeons, or to fight either of Krishna's two companions now. The king refused to forego his vow to Siva, and decided to fight Bhima. The fight with bare hands, before a huge multitude of spectators, lasted thirteen days. In the end Bhima threw the king into the air and, as he landed, he broke his back. Krishna immediately set free the imprisoned kings, and placed the dead king's son on the throne.

The way was now clear for the Rāja-suya ceremony and Yudhi-shthira sent out his invitations to the neighbouring kings. Some paid tributes; others, who refused, were fought and conquered.

Great preparations were made for the festival which was to take place round Yudhi-shthira's palace on the bank of the Yamunā, whose "dark and limpid waters laved" its walls. "Milky white" pavilions were built, "like the peaks of famed Kailāsa lifting proud their snowy height," and "nets of gold belaced the casements, gems bedecked the shining walls," so that from a distance the scene which "caught the ravished gazer's eye" was one of shining turrets, colourful and gay, arising from the swan-white purity of the tents. Inside, the walls were studded with jewels, rich carpets were laid, and garlands filled every room with their perfume.

As the appointed day drew near the kings and nobles began to arrive: Dhrita-rāshtra and his sons, accompanied by Karna, Bhishma, Drona and Ashwatthāmā; Drupada and his sons; and Vasu-deva, Krishna's father, with Bala-rāma among them.

> *Deva-rishi* saintly Nārad, marked the sacrificial rite,
> Sanctifying by its lustre Yudhi-shthira's royal might.

With his divine vision he saw that the assembled kings were "gods incarnate," and in "lotus-eyed Krishna saw the Highest of the High." He saw the gods had been sent to uphold righteousness, and though they would perish in the righteous war they would rise to heavenly mansions after their death.

But in the hearts of some, jealousy began to grow as they saw the prosperity of the Pāndus, and it flared up when it was time for the offering of flowers and fruits to the wisest and best among them.

Bhishma spoke first and said that Krishna was the greatest, for he was the origin of all and the incarnation of the Creator of the universe. But Sisu-pāla, king of Chedi, (who hated Krishna because he had run away with Rukminì to whom he had been betrothed), declared that offerings should not be given except to a crowned king. He said he thought there were others older, wiser and far better than Krishna, the "cowherd," and compared the Pāndus to the Kurus disparagingly.

Hearing this, Krishna recounted to the assembly some of the evil things Sisu-pāla had done—how he had sacked Dwārakā in Krishna's absence, and seized the queen by force; had deceived a pure princess by pretending to be her husband; had broken faith with another king, and so on. Before this moment, Krishna said, he had taken no action against him, because he had promised Sisu-pāla's mother that he would forgive her son for a hundred offences. He had done so, but with this insult, the hundred and first, he would act and fulfil his destiny, as he was born to kill him. It appears that when Sisu-pāla was born he was deformed. His father and mother were told that by holding a certain baby in their lap the deformity would go, but in later life the baby would be the cause of Sisu-pāla's death. When Krishna was taken in the lap of the queen, the deformity vanished, and the queen exacted the promise from Krishna.

Sisu-pāla laughed at Krishna and threatened him saying "Sisu-pāla seeks no mercy, nor does Krishna's anger dread."

But Krishna thought of his discus and it came from behind him whirling straight at Sisu-pāla, cleaving his head. Then a strange

thing happened: out of the dead body, Sisu-pāla's pure soul
arose, advanced towards Krishna like a flame, and, in reverence,
entered into his being.

The sacrifice could now be completed, and afterwards the
guests left, the chief monarchs being attended to the borders of
the kingdom by one of the Pāndus, Arjuna escorting Drupada,
Bhima, Dhrita-rāshtra and Bhishma, and Sahadeva, Drona.

Krishna, dearest, best beloved friend, was the last to leave for
"Dwārakā's dear-loved shore." Before going, he visited Prithā,
saying:

> "Regal fame and righteous glory crown thy sons, revered
>     dame,
> Joy thee in their peerless prowess, in their holy, spotless
>     fame.
>
> May thy sons' success and triumph cheer a widowed
>     mother's heart,
> Grant me leave, O noble lady ! for to Dwārakā I depart."

He took farewell of Draupadi and his own sister Subhadrā,
and finally,

> . . . his faithful chariot-driver brings his falcon-bannered car,
> Like the clouds in massive splendour and resistless in the
>     war, . . . .

The brothers followed him for a time, for they could not bear
to see him go, and at last Krishna stopped the chariot and spoke
to them:

> "King of men ! with sleepless watching ever guard thy
>     kingdom fair,
> Like a father tend thy subjects with a father's love and care,
>
> Be unto them like the rain-drop nourishing the thirsty

ground,
Be unto them tree of shelter shading them from heat
around,

Like the blue sky ever bending be unto them ever kind,
Free from pride and free from passion rule them with a
virtuous mind."

Dur-yodhana returned home full of envy and hatred. He hated
the cousins for their beautiful city and palace, and for the honour
they had won from all. His pride, too, was hurt, for once when
walking in the palace grounds he had seen what looked like a
lake, and had drawn his robe away so that it would not get wet,
but it turned out to be a stretch of crystal, and those who saw him
laughed. On another day he saw what looked like a lake, and,
thinking it must be crystal, and not wishing to be deceived again,
he walked on. But it *was* water this time, and he fell in. In the
palace there were crystal doors which he tried to walk through,
and empty doorways which he thought were crystal doors. He
was envious, too, of the riches of Indra-prastha, and the jewels
which covered the palace walls, and he brooded on his revenge.

In those days gambling with dice was a favourite pastime and
Sakuni, Queen Gāndhāri's brother, was a well-known player. He
invariably won as he played with loaded dice, saying that if you
played to win it was lawful to do so by foul means or fair.

Yudhi-shthira was also fond of the game, but had given it up
for once he began playing he became so intoxicated with it that
he was unable to stop. To make matters worse, he was a poor
player.

As Dur-yodhana was brooding on revenge, he thought of all
this, and, with the reluctant consent of his father, sent messages
to the Pāndus asking them to come to a festival bringing with
them Draupadi and Prithā. Vidura protested, but they retaliated
by sending him as messenger, and there was nothing he could
do to prevent it.

When the Pāndus heard that there was to be gambling and that Sakuni was to be their opponent, they did not want to go; but a challenge must be accepted, and they prepared for the journey to Hastinā-pura.

Meantime the city was made festive. In the palace a wonderful pavilion was built, with a roof of crystal, walls of gold and deep blue lapis lazuli, the roof supported by a thousand magnificent pillars. In this pavilion the Pāndus were welcomed by their cousins. Prithā and Draupadi were greeted by the ladies of the court but Draupadi's peerless beauty and magnificent clothes soon aroused their jealousy.

The fatal day arrived, the stakes were decided upon, and play was about to begin when Yudhi-shthira asked who was going to pay the stakes for Sakuni, for he obviously could not. Dur-yodhana replied that he was accepting the stakes. This was against all the rules of the game, and Yudhi-shthira realised, even more clearly than before, that the whole game would be unfair. But it was impossible to withdraw. As was to be expected, he lost every throw, and one possession after another was staked—his elephants, chariots, money, jewels and kingdom; finally his brothers one by one. Then himself.

He was now the slave of Dur-yodhana!

But he was offered one more throw to regain all he had lost, and the stake was Draupadi.

There was nothing to be done. Apart from the impossibility of refusing a challenge, Yudhi-shthira was intoxicated by the game. He threw, and lost. His brothers, being already staked and lost, could only watch helplessly.

Dur-yodhana's revenge was now complete, and with joy he sent a servant to fetch Draupadi and to tell her she was now a slave of the house, and as such he ordered her to come to the pavilion.

Draupadi was resting when the servant brought the news and she refused to leave her chamber, saying that as her husband had lost her *after* he had become a slave, she was not lost, for a slave had no possessions to lose.

Dur-yodhana then sent his brother Duh-sāsana to fetch her, telling him to have no fear now that the Pāndus were slaves! Still she would not go, attired as she was for rest , and tried to escape. But Duh-sāsana took hold of her hair and dragged her to the pavilion, mocking her: "Loosely clad or devoid of clothing—to the council hall you go!"

Standing there, dishevelled, before the whole court, she cried out, "Is there no one who can help me?" and Bhishma and Drona hid their faces in shame at the great wrong done. She called on her husbands, but none could help.

Lip nor eye did move Yudhi-shthir, hateful truth would not
    deny,
Karna laughed, but saintly Bhishma wiped his old and
    manly eye.

Then Dur-yodhana called to her to come and sit on his thigh, and at this outrage Bhima vowed to kill him. Then Duh-sāsana, with rude remarks, tried to tear off her clothes, and, at this last indignity she called on Krishna. In his compassion he made new clothes appear each time they were torn off.

All this time the old blind king Dhrita-rāshtra was unaware of what was happening. But the noise of "jackal's wailing and the raven's ominous cry" was heard and Vidura and queen Gāndhāri knew these omens. Bhishma and Drona and Kripa muttered the holy word "Svasti" and Vidura went to tell Dhrita-rāshtra. He was terrified at the great wrong that had been done, and hurried to the pavilion.

Slow and gently to Draupadi was the sightless monarch
    led,

And in kind and gentle accents unto her the old man said:

"Noblest empress, dearest daughter, good Yudhi-shthir's
    stainless wife.
Purest of the Kuru ladies, nearest to my heart and life,

Pardon wrong and cruel insult and avert the wrath of
    Heaven,
Voice thy wish and ask for blessing, be my son's misdeed
    forgiven!"

She asked that Yudhi-shthira be freed, and he gladly granted
her wish; then she asked that his brothers should be freed, and
this too was granted. Asked if there was anything more, she
answered "No"—for as the Pāndus were free men they could
make their fortunes again!

The king left, and the others began to depart.

But Dur-yodhana was angry at what his father had done, and
begged for one more throw of the dice—the loser to be banished
to the forest for twelve years and then to remain unknown for one
more year. The Pāndus were recalled, the loaded dice were
again thrown, and the result was as before. The Pāndus were
now banished for thirteen years.

Draupadi went to Prithā to say goodbye:—

In the inner palace chambers where the royal ladies dwell,
Unto Prithā came Draupadi, came to speak her sad farewell,

Monarch's daughter, monarch's consort, as an exile she
    must go,
Prithā wept and in the chambers rose the wailing voice of
    woe!

Heaving sobs convulsed her bosom as a silent prayer she
    prayed,
And in accents choked by anguish thus her parting words
    she said:

"Grieve not, child, if bitter fortune so ordains that we must
    part,
Virtue hath her consolations for the true and loving heart;

And I need not tell thee, daughter, duties of a faithful wife,
Drupad's and thy husband's mansions thou hast brightened
    by thy life!"…..

"May thy blessings help me, mother" so the fair Draupadi
    said,
"Safe in righteous truth and virtue, forest paths we fearless
    tread!"

The brothers also went to say farewell. Prithā wanted to go
with them into exile, but was now too old, and Vidura suggested
that she remained with him as a loved and respected guest in his
own palace at Hastinā-pura. Prithā's lament is very powerfully
described, for she bewailed the fate that made her lose her
husband and remain alive while the favourite wife died with him
to comfort him in heaven. Now her earthly treasure of five sons
and a daughter-in-law were also to be taken from her. She
prayed for an end to her life of woe, and begged that even one
child should remain with her.

"Part not, leave me not, my children, seek ye not the
    trackless way,
Stay but one, if one child only, as your mother's hope and
    stay;

Youngest, gentlest, Sahadeva, dearest to this widowed
    heart,
Wilt thou watch beside thy mother, while thy cruel brothers
    part?"

Whispering words of consolation, Pritha's children wiped
    her tear,
Then unto the pathless jungle turned their foot-steps lone
    and drear!

Kuru dames with fainting Prithā to Vidura's palace hie,
Kuru queens for weeping Prithā raise their voice in answering
cry,

Kuru maids for fair Draupad fortune's fitful will upbraid,
And their tear-dewed lotus-faces with their streaming fingers
shade;

Dhrita-rāshtra, ancient monarch, is by sad misgivings pained,
Questions oft with anxious bosom what the cruel fates
ordained.

The Pāndus and Draupadi now began their thirteen years'
exile, visiting many of the shrines scattered over the country and
studying the sacred scriptures. Sometimes they dwelt in pleasant
places where the sun shone and flowers and fruits were in
abundance; at other times the monsoon rains came and they
had to endure the heavy storms that accompany that season of
the year in India. Draupadi did not take kindly to the new life for
"insult rankled in her bosom and her tresses were unbound."
This did not make life any easier for the others, and one day
Yudhi-shthira asked a sage whether he knew of any true and
faithful wife who had suffered as severely as Draupadi was
suffering. In reply the sage told them the story of Nala and
Damayanti.

During this period many sages including Vyāsa and Krishna,
visited them and gave good advice. Krishna told them not to
worry, for they would regain their kingdom in time, and Vyāsa,
who knew that Yudhi-shthira was worrying because they were
alone while Dur-yodhana had a large army, told them it was time
to begin planning for their return. As part of the plan he advised
Arjuna to visit the gods and win merit from them.

Arjuna followed this advice and went to a mountain in the
Himālayas where he took the vow of an ascetic. He worshipped
daily at a clay model of Siva, eating little and performing all kinds
of austerities until his progress was so great that the gods and

the earth itself were disturbed. One morning a large boar rushed at him and he shot it. But at the very moment his arrow struck it so did another, and looking round in astonishment, Arjuna saw a huntsman and his laughing wife, attended by many followers. Both archers claimed the boar and a fight took place. First they fought with arrows, but Arjuna saw that though all his arrows mysteriously disappeared into the body of the huntsman he remained uninjured. He therefore asked if they could fight by wrestling. The huntsman agreed, and after a short while Arjuna fell senseless to the ground. When he recovered he continued his devotions, which had been disturbed by this incident, and placed his garland on the clay image of Siva. When he had finished he turned round and saw that the huntsman was still there and the garland was round his neck. Then he realised that he had been wrestling with Siva himself and throwing himself at his feet he worshipped him. Siva gave him his blessing. He also gave him Pāsu-pata a divine weapon of great power. Immediately a storm arose, shaking the foundations of the earth, and the spirit of the weapon appeared and promised to do Arjuna's bidding.

Indra, Arjuna's divine father, came to see him, so did Yama and Kuvera, god of wealth, and they all gave him divine weapons, the mountain becoming bathed in glory by the presence of the gods. Indra took him back with him to his palace where he stayed five years, listening to the songs and music of the Gandharvas and watching the dancing of the lovely Apsarās, one of whom tried to beguile him, and failed. In her annoyance she cursed him telling him he would for a time have to live an obscure life as a woman dancer and musician himself. Indra heard this and told him not to worry, for, though this would indeed happen, it would work for his good. Arjuna continued to practise with his new weapons and gained great proficiency in them.

One day he went to fight some of Indra's foes, the demons who lived below the earth. Travelling in his father's great car he reached the ocean whose waves rose up and appeared to swallow him. In them he saw such marvellous sights that he was almost lured from his object. But he went on, chanting his divine *mantras* and using his divine weapons, so that he was able to withstand fire and rock and water, and drove the demons back. The demon women tried to frighten him with their ugliness, but he drove straight on and finally arrived at the demon city, Hiranya-pura, where he saw many strange things, including chariots so large that they needed thousands of horses to draw them. He destroyed the whole city and then returned to Indra's palace. Indra gave him jewels and a conch or war-shell, Deva-datta, the sound of which filled the hearts of all who heard it with fear, and afterwards frightened the young prince Uttara.

At the end of the five years Indra and his Apsarās and Gandharvas escorted him back to his brothers, filling the sky with divine radiance. Indra told Yudhi-shthira that he could take heart for he would regain his kingdom.

While Arjuna had been away Yudhi-shthira had won from a god the art of throwing dice—an art which was to serve him well in later years. During this period many sages visited the brothers telling them ancient tales and legends. They also visited many places. Once, going towards the Himālayas, they saw in the distance the palace of Kuvera, god of wealth. It glittered with gold, jewels and crystal. The gardens were full of flowers whose perfume was wafted to them by the gentle breeze, and as the trees swayed they gave out melodious sounds like the song of birds. Kuvera himself went out to greet them and told Yudhi-shthira to be patient and to wait for the right moment before attempting to win back his kingdom.

Bhima had an adventure on his own. One day when he was hurrying along, swift as the wind, destroying everything that stood in his path—even large elephants—he met Hanumān. Hanumān was also a son of Vāyu, and when he saw Bhima, he made himself as small as an ordinary monkey, but he let his tail swell to such proportions that Bhima had to stop. These two sons of Vāyu talked, and Hanumān told Bhima the tale of the *Rāmāyana*. Then he took him to Mount Kailāsa where he picked some beautiful flowers which could give youth back to the old and take away all sorrow. These Bhima took to Draupadi to help her in her grief.

One incident brought tragedy—a tragedy which came to a final close in the great battle. Jayad-ratha, king of Sindhu, the husband of Dhrita-rāshtra's only daughter, was hunting in the forest one day, accompanied by his six brothers and with a large following, and they came to the dwelling of the Pāndus. Only Draupadi was there for the brothers were out hunting. She gave refreshments to them all from the inexhaustible cauldron which Yudhi-shthira had won from the sun. Jayad-ratha was so impressed by this and by the beauty of Draupadi that he asked her to elope with him. When she refused he carried her off by force. The Pāndus, discovering this on their return, went in pursuit and rescued her and Bhima captured the fleeing king. He could not kill him because he was a relative, but he cut off most of his hair and compelled him to make obeisance to Yudhi-shthira. Then he was sent home.

It was about this time that Karna suggested to Dur-yodhana that they should go to the forest to see how the Pāndus were faring, and to mock at them. They therefore followed the cattle at branding time and reached the forest home of the exiles. Nearby some Gandharvas and nymphs were feasting and sporting together and they would not let them pass. A fight ensued and the Kurus were defeated and taken prisoners. A few, however, escaped and found their way to the Pāndus. Arjuna, with Bhima and the twins, immediately started out to free their cousins and brought Dur-yodhana back to Yudhi-shthira who prepared a feast of welcome. But Dur-yodhana hated them all the more and tried to kill himself for he would rather die than accept this kindness, but he failed in his attempt. When he returned to his palace he decided to make a sacrifice, and with deceit in his heart, he invited the Pāndus. They refused because their time of exile was not yet over, but Bhima sent a haughty message saying that when their exile *was* over *they* would make a sacrifice and burn all the family of Dhrita-rāshtra!

It was at this time that Indra decided to take away the armour and earrings with which Karna had been born and which rendered him invincible. Surya knew of this and told his son, adding that he could ask Indra for a boon in exchange. So, when Indra, disguised as a Brāhman, came for the armour and earrings, Karna could not refuse but he demanded in exchange a divine weapon. He was given a javelin or lance, which would kill anyone at which it was hurled, but if it was used except in dire necessity it would act as a boomerang. Indeed divine gifts cannot be bartered for! (Bhima's son Ghatotkacha, whose mother was a Rākshasi, was killed by this lance during the battle of Kuru-kshetra. Though he was so strong that as he was dying he grew to such an enormous size that in falling he killed hundreds of soldiers.)

What Karna's golden armour and earrings were is not clear but they seemed to be part of his body for they had to be cut away.

Karna also learnt a Brahmā-sastra from Parasu-rāma to whom he had gone for help. Knowing that Parasu-rāma was a deadly foe of all *kshatriyas* Karna had represented himself as a Brāhman and had become a favourite with the warrior. One day, however, he had remained unmoved while in great pain, and when Parasu-rāma saw this he knew that he was a *kshatriya* for none but men of that caste could bear pain in that way. He then cursed him for the deceit he had practised and told him that the Brahmā-sastra would fail him at the critical moment for he would be unable to remember it. This happened during the Great War.

As the end of the twelfth year of exile drew near the Pāndus began to prepare for the last year, during which they had to be among people, but unrecognised.

One day while a Brāhman was preparing his sacrifice a deer carried off the sacred sticks with which, by friction, he was making his fire, and the Pāndus started in pursuit. After a long chase they stopped, tired and thirsty. They could not see any water nearby, so one of them climbed a tree for a wider view of the surroundings, and from the greater height he saw a stream. Nakula reached it first, but a voice told him to answer a question before he drank. The youth, however, being very thirsty paid no attention and drank. Immediately he fell to the ground dead. The same thing happened to the other brothers, until it was Yudhi-shthira's turn to drink. Seeing the dead bodies of his brothers, he thought it better to answer the question before drinking! The voice asked him many questions, which he answered. Then it said it was the voice of the god Dharma, his own father, and offered him some wishes. Yudhi-shthira first asked that all his brothers should become alive again, and this was granted. Then he asked that all of them should remain unrecognised during the coming year. This, too, was granted. His last wish was that Pārvati should grant them her blessing and protect them.

When all was ready for their journey they made their way to the neighbouring kingdom of Virāta, king of the Matsyas, (near the present Jaipur), intending to offer him their services. Knowing that they would be recognised if their weapons were seen, they hid them before reaching the city. Choosing a Sami* tree in the nearby forest, Arjuna loosened Gāndiva's string, and they all made their weapons ready to leave, wrapping them up to preserve them from the weather. Then they hung them on the tree. The bundles looked like corpses, and as such, would be free from theft. They said one was the corpse of their mother.

Further to prevent recognition, they grew beards (except Arjuna), and, wan and weary, at last arrived at their destination and offered their services. Yudhi-shthira, who had learnt the secret of the dice, was welcomed by Virāta who was notoriously unlucky at gambling; Bhima went to the kitchen as cook—which was to be expected because of his love of food; Nakula looked after the royal stables and his twin brother after the cows. Draupadi became a serving maid to the royal princess, and Arjuna who, to disguise himself even more fully, had plaited his

*A sacred tree—Sami deva.

hair, put on bangles, and dressed as an eunuch, took service in the inner chambers where he taught dancing and music to the ladies of the Court. Thus the curse of the nymph of Indra's heaven was fulfilled! Draupadi made two conditions: she would not eat left-over food and she would not wash anyone's feet. The queen had a slight misgiving about taking her into service because of her great beauty, but for a time all went well.

Trouble came towards the end of the year when the queen's brother tried to run away with Draupadi. Bhima heard her cry for help and killed the would-be abductor. The courtiers tried to burn Draupadi on his funeral pyre, but Bhima prevented this by uprooting a large tree and killing many of them.

The death of the queen's brother was a national disaster for it left the army without a general. Seizing the opportunity a neighbouring rajah raided the country from the north to steal cattle and Dur-yodhana raided from the south.

In this crisis every man was called to help, and Yudhi-shthira, Bhima and the twins, took arms. Soon the Kurus were driven back, and Virāta turned to the invaders at the north, leaving the city defenceless. Dur-yodhana immediately returned, stealing sixty thousand head of cattle.

Learning this Arjuna thought it was time to act, and hearing that the king's son, Uttara, a mere boy, had said he could not fight because he had no charioteer, told Draupadi to let it be known in the royal chambers that he had often driven Arjuna's chariot. The princess Uttarā, sister of Uttara (the accent on the a makes the word feminine) took armour to him and after pretending he did not know how to put it on, he was finally dressed and ready, and with the young prince set out for the Kuru army. When they saw it on the horizon Uttara became terrified and begged Arjuna to turn back. Arjuna refused and the boy jumped down. But Arjuna soon picked him up again and told him to drive the chariot while he himself fought. But to fight means possessing weapons, and he directed the prince towards the Sami tree where the weapons had been hidden. There, he told him, was a bow which, "strongest warriors scarce can in the battle bend," and he asked him to fetch it. Seeing the corpse-like bundles the boy was afraid, but was reassured when Arjuna said the "tree conceals no dead. Warriors' weapons cased like corpses lurk within its gloomy shade." Encouraged, Uttara climbed the tree and brought the bundles down. He watched with amazement as they were undone and the wonderful weapons came into view. He asked to whom they belonged and:

> Joyously responded Arjun: "Mark this bow embossed with
> gold,
> 'Tis the wondrous bow, *Gāndiva*, worthy of a Warrior bold,
>
> Gift of heaven! to archer Arjun kindly gods this weapon
> sent,
> And the confines of a kingdom widen when the bow is bent,
>
> Next, this mighty ponderous weapon worked with elephants
> of gold,
> With this bow the stalwart Bhima hath the tide of conquests
> rolled,
>
> And the third with golden insects by a cunning hand inlaid,
> 'Tis Yudhi-shthir's royal weapon by the noblest artists
> made,
>
> Next the bow with solar lustre brave Nakula wields in fight,
> And the fifth is Sahadeva's decked with gems and jewels
> bright!
>
> Mark again these thousand arrows, unto Arjun they belong,
> And the darts whose blades are crescent unto Bhima brave
> and strong,
>
> Boar-ear shafts are young Nakula's, in the tiger-quiver
> cased,
> Sahadeva owns the arrows with the parrot's feather graced,

These three-knotted shining arrows, thick and yellow vulture-
    plumed.
They belong to King Yudhi-shthir, with their heads by gold
    illumed!

Listen more, if of those sabres, prince of Matsya, thou
    wouldst know,
Arjuna's sword is toad-engraven, ever dreaded by the foe,

And the sword in tiger-scabbard, massive and of mighty
    strength,
None save tiger-waisted Bhima wields that sword of wondrous
    length,

Next the sabre golden-hilted, sable and with gold embossed,
Brave Yudhi-shthir kept that sabre when the king his
    kingdom lost,

Yonder sword with goat-skin scabbard grave Nakula wields
    in war,
In the  cowhide Sahadeva keeps his shining scimitar!"

Arjuna's whole bearing had so changed that Uttara said:
"Strange thy accents.... stranger are the weapons bright; Are
they arms of sons of Pāndu famed on earth for matchless
might?" Where, he asked, were the Pāndus and Draupadi?

Proudly answered valiant Arjun, and a smile was on his
    face,
"Not in distant lands the brothers do their wandering
    footsteps trace,

In thy father's court disguiséd lives Yudhi-shthir just and
    good,
Bhima in thy father's palace as a cook prepares the food,

Brave Nakula guards the horses, Sahadeva tends the kine,
As thy sister's waiting woman doth the fair Draupadi shine!

Pardon, prince, these rings and bangles, pardon strange
    unmanly guise.
'Tis no poor and sexless crature,—Arjun greets thy wondering
    eyes!"

Quickly taking the weapons and armour, Arjuna and Uttara
drove towards the enemy. As they neared them Arjuna blew on
his famous conch, creating such a terrible noise that Uttara
begged him not to blow it again! But Arjuna told him to hold on
tightly for he would certainly use it again.

Drona, in the enemy ranks, heard it, and he knew Arjuna was
near; Bhishma heard it, and asked the Kurus to make peace;
Karna heard it and refused to consider peace. While they were
discussing this, an arrow, long and pointed, with golden feathers,
fell lightly down and rested gently on Bhishma's foot. Another
came and touched Drona's foot. Then all knew for certain that
Arjuna was showing his reverence for his grandfather and his
instructor before he started to fight.

In the battle which followed the air was so thick with arrows,
that the day seemed darkened, and the Kuru army, "struck with
panic, neither stood and fought, nor fled," but "gazed upon the
distant Arjun" as the sound of his great conch and the twanging
of the arrows "filled the air like distant thunder," and "shook the
firm and solid ground." Once Arjuna and Karna met in single
combat, so well matched that neither won until Karna was struck
on the breast and retired. Then Arjuna and Bhishma met, and
fought with celestial weapons. One such brought the whole army
under a spell so that none could move, and Arjuna, remembering
that the young princess had asked him to bring back clothes for
her dolls, sent Uttara to the unresisting Dur-yodhana and Karna,
telling him to bring back their clothes. But he warned him not to
touch Bhishma for he was not entirely under the spell. Then they
retired and started for home, taking with them the rescued cattle.

When Dur-yodhana came out of the spell he railed against
Bhishma, asking why he had not used his celestial weapons to

prevent this last insult of Arjuna? But Bhishma rebuked him, saying he ought to feel gratitude to so chivalrous a foe as Arjuna, for he could as easily have killed him as taken his clothes.

As the Kuru army turned back, Arjuna sent more arrows towards them; one landed lightly at Bhishma's feet and one at Drona's but another shot Dur-yodhana's crown off and shattered it to pieces.

Back at Virāta's court Arjuna told Uttara to take all the credit for the day's activities. For a while he did so, but at last could not bear his father's praise any longer and told him that he had only been the charioteer; a celestial visitor had fought the battle.

As the time had now come for the Pāndus to declare themselves, they went to the Assembly Hall the following morning, dressed as warriors, and took their rightful places. At first Virāta was angry, but when Uttara told him Arjuna was the celestial warrior of the battle he recognised them and acknowledged their services with gratitude. He offered Uttarā to Arjuna as his bride, but Arjuna asked if she might marry his son Abhimanyu instead. This was agreed to and preparations for the ceremony began. Many neighbouring kings and nobles attended and Krishna and Bala-rāma came, for it will be remembered that Abhimanyu's mother was their sister Subhadrā.

Afterwards the Pāndus began to plan how to regain their lost kingdom, and they received offers of help from many of the neighbouring kings and nobles.

Taking the advice of Krishna and the friendly kings Yudhi-shthira sent a priest of Drupada's court to Dhrita-rāshtra asking for the return of his kingdom, or, at least, for five villages.

Dhrita-rāshtra received the message in his full Court and the old story was repeated: Bhishma counselled for peace, Dur-yodhana and Karna stood for war. Dhrita-rāshtra, unable to decide, sent Sanjaya his charioteer to the Pāndus asking them to return in peace and he would see that justice was done. But, profiting from past experience, Yudhi-shthira replied that though he knew Dhrita-rāshtra meant well, he also knew he had not the power to control Dur-yodhana, and therefore they could not return in peace. Krishna, who was still with the Pāndus, told Sanjaya to tell the Kurus that if they wanted peace they could have peace, but if they wanted war then war was inevitable.

For many days no news came. Then Krishna decided he would go to Hastinā-pura and speak with Dhrita-rāshtra himself. When the Kurus heard of his coming they wanted to meet him with due honours and Dur-yodhana agreed. But, he added, it was only by war that he would let the Pāndus have any part of the kingdom, and if Krishna interfered he ought to be put in prison. This so horrified Bhishma and Vidura that they left the Chamber.

On his arrival Krishna went first to Prithā in Vidura's palace where she had stayed the last thirteen years, and gave her news of her sons and Draupadi. He also told her that it was now time for them to come back to their kingdom.

Afterwards in the Council Chamber he pleaded for peace in the only way it could come, *i.e.,* by giving the Pāndus what was theirs by right. Drona and Vidura supported him. Dhrita-rāshtra added his plea:

"Listen, dearest son, Dur-yodhan, shun this dark and fatal strife,
Cast not grief and death's black shadow on thy parents' closing life!

Krishna's heart is pure and spotless, true and wise the words he said,
We may win a world-wide empire with the noble Krishna's aid,

Seek the friendship of Yudhi-shthir loved of righteous gods

above,
And unite the scattered Kurus by the lasting tie of love!

Now at full is tide of fortune, never may it come again,
Strive and win, or ever after all repentance may be vain,

Peace is righteous Krishna's counsel and he comes to offer
    peace,
Take the offered boon, Dur-yodhan! Let all strife and hatred
    cease!"

Gāndhāri added her plea, but to no avail. Dur-yodhana
answered proudly:

"Take my message to my kinsmen, for Dur-yodhan's words
    are plain,
Portion of the Kuru empire son of Pāndu seek in vain,

Town nor village, mart nor hamlet, help us righteous gods
    in heaven,
Spot that needle's point can cover shall not unto them be
    given!"

Saying which he left the Chamber followed by Karna and
Sakuni.

In the consternation which followed, Krishna told Dhrita-
rāshtra he ought to arrest the princes, and the old king sent
Vidura to bring Dur-yodhana back. Meanwhile Karna, Sakuni
and Duh-sāsana plotted among themselves how to take Krishna
prisoner as he left the Hall. Krishna saw this and for a brief
moment showed himself in his real nature, radiant, glorious,
surrounded by gods and celestial beings, amazing everyone by
his splendour.

But to Dur-yodhana there was no vision.

Before Krishna left the city he saw Karna and offered him the chance of coming with him on the side of the Pāndus, but Karna felt his loyalty must go to the Kurus who had befriended him in the past. Also he felt that he must meet Arjuna in a final test in order to prove which of them was, in fact, the greater. Accordingly he bade Krishna farewell, saying he hoped they would meet again on earth, but if not, then they would in heaven.

Prithā made a last attempt to win Karna over for she sent for him and told him he was her eldest son, born of Surya the sungod, and therefore he was Arjuna's brother. But this information came too late, he said, for his loyalty was pledged to the Kurus. He promised her, however, that he would spare all her sons save Arjuna; with him it must be a fight to the death.

Preparations for war were carried on by both sides. Duryodhana's divisions were at least a hundred thousand strong, men, horses, cars and elephants. Yudhi-shthira's forces were less in number, said to be about seventy thousand. In the early days of preparations both Arjuna and Dur-yodhana went to Krishna to ask for his help. They found him sleeping and Arjuna sat down at his feet, Dur-yodhana at his head. When Krishna awoke he saw Arjuna first and offered him the choice of the whole of his armies or of himself. Dur-yodhana said he had come first and should have the first choice, but Krishna reminded him he had seen Arjuna first! However, there was no discussion for Dur-yodhana wanted all Krishna's armies while Arjuna wanted Krishna himself.

Neighbouring kings helped one side or the other and the stage was set for what must have been one of the most terrible battles of history. Bhishma led the Kuru army; Draupadi's brother Dhrista-dyumna, the Pāndus, and they finally faced one another on the great plain of Kuru-kshetra (the plain of the Kurus), near the modern Delhi:

Ushas* with her crimson fingers oped the portals of the day,

* Ushas is the dawn.

Nations armed for mortal combat in the field of battle lay,

Beat of drum and blare of trumpet and the *sankha's* lofty
    sound,
By the answering cloud repeated, shook the hills and
    tented ground,

And the voice of sounding weapons which the warlike
    archers drew,
And the neigh of battle chargers as the arméd horsemen
    flew,

Mingled with the rolling thunder of each swiftly-speeding
    car,
And with pealing bells proclaiming mighty elephants of war!

Bhishma's standard of a palm tree and five stars, Arjuna's of
Hanumān, and thousands of pennants floated in the wind as the
armies faced each other. While they remained thus Yudhi-
shthira stepped out from the Pāndus ranks and walked towards
the Kurus. They thought he was going to sue for peace, but he
went to his grandfather Bhishma, saluted him and asked his
permission to begin the fight. Then he turned to Drona, his old
preceptor, and asked his permission. Turning away, he called
out loudly that if any of that host wanted to follow him they were
very welcome. One chieftain only responded, Yuyutsu, half-
brother of Dur-yodhana, who with all his men joined the Pāndus.
(When Yudhi-shthira gave up his kingdom shortly before his
death he appointed Yuyutsu king of Indra-prastha.)

It was when the arrows had started to fly, that Arjuna asked
Krishna who was his charioteer to drive his chariot into the midst
of the field so that he could see who were in the opposite ranks.
There he saw his friends, relations and teachers, and his heart
sank. He sat down in his chariot saying he would not fight. How
could he enjoy the fruits of victory, he asked, if he had slain all
his friends? Surely it would be better to die, unresisting in the
fight! In his despondency his bow, Gāndiva, slipped from his

hands. It was now that Krishna delivered to him the discourses known as the *Bhagavad-Gitā,* in which the various systems of philosophy with which Arjuna was familiar were brought back to his mind. He was shown the difference between the spirit and matter-forms, between the immortality of the spirit and the destruction of forms. He was told that: "Those who are wise in spiritual things grieve neither for the dead nor for the living. I myself never was not, nor thou, nor all the princes of the earth; nor shall we ever hereafter cease to be. As the lord of this mortal frame experienceth therein infancy, youth, and old age, so in future incarnations will it meet the same. One who is confirmed in this belief is not disturbed by anything that may come to pass.... As a man throweth away old garments and putteth on new, even so the dweller in the body, having quitted its old mortal frames, entereth into others which are new. The weapon divideth it not, the fire burneth it not, the water corrupteth it not, the wind drieth it not away; for it is indivisible, inconsumable, incorruptible, and is not to be dried away; it is eternal, universal, permanent, immovable; it is invisible inconceivable, and unalterable; therefore, knowing it to be thus thou shouldst not grieve.... Death is certain to all things which are born, and rebirth to all mortals; wherefore it doth not behove thee to grieve about the inevitable.... This spirit can never be destroyed in the mortal frame which it inhabiteth, hence it is unworthy for thee to be troubled for all these mortals."

He was given an insight into the hidden side of Nature and of the wonder of Krishna as Lord of the World. At the conclusion he was told to decide for himself, in view of all that had been said, what course of action he should pursue. His despondency left him and he rose up ready to fight.

The battle raged for eighteen days.

During the first ten days Bhishma held his own and destroyed many of the Pāndus' forces. All the enemies of the past met face to face in combat, Dur-yodhana and Bhima, Duh-sāsana and Nakula, Drona and Drupada, Abhimanyu and Jayad-ratha,

Yudhi-shthira and Salya (king of Madras, brother of Mādri, the favourite wife of Pāndu), who had left the side of the Pāndus and gone over to the Kurus. In the dreadful battle "no mortal tongue can tell what unnumbered chieftains perished and what countless soldiers fell." "Son knew not his father, and the sire knew not his son," and "brother fought against his brother." Once Abhimanyu struck down Bhìshma's standard, arousing him to such fury that nothing stayed his onslaught until evening came and, "friendly night and gathering darkness closed the slaughter of the day."

One day brought great disaster, and the Pāndus retired at nightfall, almost defeated. Once Arjuna thought it was hopeless to continue, but Krishna jumped from the chariot and said he would continue the fight with his discus. These words so stung Arjuna that he rushed after him and put him again in the chariot saying that while *he* was alive *he* would do the fighting!

Irāvat, Arjuna's son by the serpent princess, was slain after a terrible struggle and lay "like a lotus rudely severed." In his grief Arjuna vowed vengeance and killed many of Dur-yodhana's brothers.

When each day's carnage brought no decisive victory Dur-yodhana went to Bhishma and told him he thought he was favouring the Pāndus in his heart, and he asked him to give the lead of the army to Karna. The ancient Bhishma reminded him that the Pāndu's cause was just and, "gods nor men can face these heroes in the field of righteous war." But, he added, he would do his duty as leader of the army. The next day brought another furious battle with Bhishma fighting so valiantly that in the evening Yudhi-shthira held a conference. Fighting against Bhishma, the Pāndus felt, was hopeless, for the battle would always go with him, and they decided to ask him what they could do. Bhishma greeted them warmly and told them that they knew he loved them but they also knew his loyalty was pledged to the Kurus. There was only one way out of the dilemma; they should remember he would not fight against a woman or against one who was wounded.

Disheartened, the Pāndus and Krishna returned to their tents. On the way back Krishna whispered to Arjuna that Sikhandin, Drupada's son, was born a woman and now fought as a man beside Yudhi-shthira. If Arjuna had him in front of him in his chariot, Bhishma would not fight, and Arjuna could kill him. At first Arjuna refused either to fight his old guardian or to hide behind a woman, but when the next day's battle began the Pāndus set out ruthlessly to reach Bhishma's chariot, driving through the ranks until they met him coming towards them "god-like in his might." Then Sikhandin was sent forward so that Bhìshma could only see him and, remembering his vow, he dropped his arms, his standard was struck and fell across his car, and he fell pierced by arrows.

When night came the Pāndus, full of sorrow, visited him. They found him resting on the arrows with which he had been pierced, but his head hung down and he was not comfortable. He asked Arjuna to make him a pillow for his head and Arjuna shot more arrows in such a way that the dying chief could rest his head on them. In that position he lay for fifty eight days waiting for an auspicious time before casting off his body in death.

Many people visited him as he lay dying, among them Dur-yodhana and Karna and he again asked Dur-yodhana to make peace. After the war was over Yudhi-shthira went to visit Krishna. He found him deep in meditation. Seated on a couch shining with gold and jewels, dressed in yellow silk and blazing with jewels, the famous jewel Kaustubha which came from the Churning of the Ocean on his breast he looked "like the Udaya Mountain bathed by the rising sun."

When Krishna awoke he asked him whether all was well with the three worlds as he was meditating thus in his glory and Krishna told him that soon Bhishma would disappear from the world and with him would disappear every kind of knowledge. Therefore if Yudhi-shthira were wise he would go to him and ask him any questions that worried him. Yudhi-shthira answered that if Krishna would be gracious enough to go with him as leader he would go to Bhishma at once, and Krishna's car was yoked and together they went. When they arrived they were sad for the aged grandsire looked "like a fire about to go out." Krishna asked him to give of his great knowledge to those around. At first he did not want to, for how could he speak when the Master Krishna was there himself! But Krishna told him he had just inspired him with wisdom so that he could speak as a father, to his sons words of truth and morality, especially to Yudhi-shthira whose mind was clouded by his grief for the death of so many of his kinsmen. Bhishma then spoke as recorded in the *Sānti-parva* book of the *Mahā-bhārata.*

When Bhishma could not longer lead the army Drona took over, and for five days many great combats took place, ending with the death of Abhimanyu and of Drona himself.

The description of the fight and death of Abhimanyu, the "peerless son of peerless Arjuna" forms one of the most graphic parts of the Epic. Throughout the day he had fought valiantly and had killed Duh-sāsana and also Dur-yodhana's son Lakshman, but at last Jayad-ratha king of Sindhu, with six car-borne warriors, circled him and fell on him together—against all the laws of combat. His peacock standard was struck down, his car was broken, his bow and sabre destroyed and his driver killed, but, undaunted, and against these tremendous odds he seized his mace and, heedless of death and danger, misty with the loss of blood, he wiped the blood from his forehead and rushed at the foe. The odds were too great and he fell, "like a tusker of the forest by surrounding hunters slain."

> Like the moon serene and beauteous quenched in eclipse dark and pale,
> Lifeless slumbered Abhimanyu when the softened starlight fell !

When Arjuna returned to his tent in the evening he was obsessed with fears and sorrow; the Camp was quiet, his brothers were pale, and he missed the greeting of his son, his "pride and hope and love." Yudhi-shthira told him of the day's tragedy and his "bosom felt the cruel cureless wound." His wrath rose because of the unwarlike attitude of Jayad-ratha and he vowed to avenge his son's death.

"Didst thou say that Sindhu's monarch on my Abhimanyu
     bore,—
He alone,—and Jayadratha leagued with six marauders
     more,

Didst thou say the impious Kurus stooped unto this deed of
     shame,
Outrage on the laws of honour, stain upon a warrior's fame?

Father's curse and warrior's hatred sting them to their dying
     breath,
For they feared my boy in battle, hunted him to cruel death,

Hear my vow, benign Yudhi-shthir, hear me, Krishna righteous
     lord,
Arjun's hand shall slay the slayer, Arjun plights his solemn
     word ! . . .

Jayadratha dies tomorrow, victim to my vengefull ire,
Arjun else shall yield his weapons, perish on the flaming
     pyre !"

His mother, Krishna's sister, mourned him in gentle tones:

"Dost thou lie on field of battle, smeared with dust and
     foeman's gore,
Child of light and love and sweetness whom thy hapless
     mother bore.

Soft thine eye as budding lotus, sweet and gentle was thy
     face,
Are those soft eyes closed in slumber, faded is that peerless
     grace? . . .

Earth to me is void and cheerless, joyless is my hearth and
   home,
Dreary without Abhimanyu is this weary world to roam !

And oh! cheerless is that young heart, Abhimanyu's princess-
   wife,
What can sad Subhadrā offer to her joyless, sonless life?

Close our life in equal darkness, for our day on earth is
   done,
For our love and light and treasure, Abhimanyu, he is
   gone!"

Long bewailed the anguished mother, fair Draupadi tore
   her hair,
Matsya's princess early widowed shed her young heart's
   blood in tear!

When morning came the wrathful Arjuna blew his *sankha* and
the Kurus knew of his vow.

"Speed, my Krishna," out spake Arjun, as he held aloft his
   bow,
"For to-day my task is dreadful, cruel is my mighty vow!"

The horses "urged by Krishna flew with lightning's rapid
course" through the lines of the Kurus, scattering elephants and
men. Drona tried to stop him, but Arjuna would not fight with him
for he was only fighting Abhimanyu's slayer that day. On and on
the horses went towards Jayad-ratha and his friends.

At last Krishna asked that the horses might rest for, "thy
foaming coursers falter and they need a moment's rest."

"Be it so," brave Arjun answered, "from our chariot we
   alight,
Rest awhile the weary horses, Krishna, I will watch the
   fight!"

Then on again, until at length he reached the inner circle surrounding his foe, five great chieftains and Karna. First he took on Karna in single combat. The sun was nearing the end of its journey, and at a moment of danger—for Arjuna and Karna were so well matched—Krishna caused a cloud to cover the sun so that all thought it had gone and night had fallen. The Kurus relaxed in joy for now the battle would have to end and Arjuna would have to die because of his vow, but, taking advantage of this, Arjuna rushed forward and killed Jayad-ratha. The cloud lifted and it was seen to be still day.

Once again Dur-yodhana attempted to change his battle leader, and with the same excuse as before. He asked Drona if his heart was in the fight against the Pāndus whom he had taught. Drona's answer was the same as Bhishma's—he would do his duty. But on the following day he fell in battle, not at the hands of Arjuna who refused to fight him, but by the arrow of Drupada's son Dhrishta-dyumna, who thus avenged his father's death at Drona's hands. But it was not a fair combat for Drona was told his son Aswatthāmān had been killed and he faltered in the fight. He asked Yudhi-shthira if this was true, for he knew Yudhi-shthira would never tell a lie. Yudhi-shthira answered, "Lordly tusker, Aswatthāmān named is dead"—referring to an elephant of that name.* But Drona did not hear all the words, and thinking his son dead, "feebly drooped his sinking head" and was killed.

Karna then led the Kuru forces for two days.

At last the fateful combat between Arjuna and Karna took place, their hatred made greater by Karna's victory over Yudhi-shthira whose standard and car he had destroyed and whom he had wounded severely, but whose life he had spared for :

---

* It is said that whereas before he told, or implied, this untruth, the wheels of his chariot never actually touched the earth but passed over it, four inches above, now, as he sank to the level of ordinary men so his chariot wheels sank until they touched the earth and henceforth travelled as other chariots.

"Speed, thou timid man of penance! thus insulting Karna said,
"Famed for virtue not for valour! blood of thine I will not shed;

"Speed and chant thy wonted *mantra*, do the rites that sages know,
Bid the helmed warrior Arjun come and meet his warlike foe!"

During the combat Arjuna's bow string broke and, according to the laws of combat he called to Karna to cease while he mended it. But Karna refused and showered his arrows on him. Later on Karna's car was struck in the earth and he called to Arjuna to stop fighting, but Krishna answered, asking him if he had taken the path of virtue when he aided in the dice match, or the path of honour when he heard the insults heaped on Draupadi, or his duty when Yudhi-shthira's exile was over, or when he joined six warriors against Abhimanyu?

The combat went on until Arjuna fell fainting to the ground. But he roused himself by the memory of his son's death, and taking aim with Gāndiva shot an arrow which killed his foe.

Salya then led the Kurus. The last day of battle dawned and the slaughter continued till nearly all the Kurus were slain. Dur-yodhana fled to the shores of a lake in which he hid as he had the power of staying under water. Here the Pāndus found him and a struggle with Bhima took place. The two were evenly matched, but suddenly Bhima remembered his vow to break Dur-yodhana's thigh because of his insult to Draupadi, and though it was against the rules of combat, he struck him, breaking his thigh so that he fell to the ground.

After the Pāndus had left him to die Aswatthāmān came. He told him to go to the camp and kill all the Pāndus. Aswatthāmān went, but he did not know that the camp was deserted as the war was over and the Pāndus had gone to the Kuru camp. There only remained Draupadi's five sons, whom he killed, and Sikhandin, and Dhrishta-dyumna whom he stamped to death as they lay asleep. When he returned to tell Dur-yodhana, he cursed him, for he had killed the five young sons and not the five hated Pāndus! Then he died.

The war was over. There remained only the aftermath of victory, bathed in sorrow for the slain. During that first morning Draupadi went to the field mourning for her lost sons, and in her anger she demanded that the head of Aswatthāmān should be brought to her. When this could not be done, for as a Brāhman, he could not be killed, she asked for the great jewel he wore which had the power to protect the wearer and Krishna and Arjuna went after him and brought it back to her. She then gave it to Yudhi-shthira.

Dhrita-rāshtra, "sonless and sorrow-stricken," with Queen Gāndhāri, "sorrow-laden," and the "ancient Prithā" with the ladies of the Court, "now by common sorrow-laden," visited the battlefield. The "men from stall and loom and anvil" left the city to follow, and "a universal sorrow filled the air . . . as when ends the mortal's *Yuga* and the end of world is nigh!" Queen Gāndhāri "Stainless Queen and stainless woman, ever righteous ever good," saw her dead son lying on the field and wept for him and for her grandson. She railed against Krishna as she saw the widows of her many sons in their sorrow; she described the horrors of the field so full of matchless heroes, kings and youths, now the prey to the creatures of the forest and air. The battlefield was strewn with "shining mail and costly "jewels," golden garlands rich and burnished." Do the dead "still the life-pulse feel?" she asked. She "clasped her dead Dur-yodhana," while tears "like rain of summer fell," and remembering her plea to him, all unheeded, before the war started, her words are specially poignant:

"Mother!" said my dear Duryodhan when he went unto the war,

Wish me joy and wish me triumph as I mount the battle-car,

'Son!' I said to dear Duryodhan, 'Heaven avert a cruel fate,
*Yato dharma stato jayah!* Triumph doth on Virtue wait!'

But he set his heart on battle, by his valour wiped his sins,
Now he dwells in realms celestial which the faithful warrior
 wins,

Kuru owns another master and Duryodhan's day is fled,
And I live to be a witness! Krishna, O that I were dead!

Mark Duryodhan's noble widow, mother proud of Lakshman
 bold,
Queenly in her youth and beauty, like an altar of bright gold,

Torn from husband's sweet embraces, from her son's
 entwining arms,
Doomed to life long woe and anguish in her youth and in her
 charms,

Rend my hard and stony bosom crushed beneath this cruel
 pain,
Should Gāndhāri live to witness noble son and grandson
 slain?

Mark again Duryodhan's widow, how she hugs his gory
 head,
How with gentle hands and tender softly holds him on his
 bed,

How from dear departed husband turns she to her dearer
 son,
And the tear-drops of the mother choke the widow's bitter
 groan,

Like the fibre of the lotus tender-golden is her frame,
O my lotus! O my daughter! Bharat's pride and Kuru's fame!

If the truth resides in *Vedas,* brave Duryodhan dwells
   above,
Wherefore linger we in sadness severed from his cherished
   love,

If the truth resides in *Sastras,* dwells in sky my hero son,
Wherefore linger we in sorrow since their earthly task is
   done!"

Yudhi-shthira approached the old king and bowed to him in reverence and Dhrita-rāshtra embraced him. Bhima came too to show his respects but Krishna saw that Dhrita-rāshtra's anger against him was so great that he would destroy him and placed a metal statue in the old king's arms when he tried to embrace Bhima. The statue was crushed to pieces but Bhima was saved.

Yudhi-shthira ordered full sacrificial rites to be performed for all the slain. Vidura who had comforted the mourners performed the last ceremony and the field was full of "sandalwood and scented aloes, fragrant oil and perfumes . . . dry wood from the thorny jungle, perfume from the scented grove." The broken cars and lances were piled, and the warriors laid in their respective ranks. When the vast funeral pyres were lighted they blazed :-

. . . with wonderous radiance by the rich libations fed,
Sanctifying and consuming mortal remnants of the dead.

Sacred songs of *rick* and *sāma* rose with women's piercing
   wail,
And the creatures of the wide earth heard the sound
   subdued and pale,

Smokeless and with radiant lustre shone each red and
   lighted pyre,
Like the planets of the bright sky throbbing with celestial
   fire!

Countless myriads, nameless, friendless, from each court

and camp afar,
From the east and west collected, fell in Kuru-kshetra's war,

Thousand fires for them were lighted, they received the
    pious rite,
Such was good Yudhishthir's mandate, such was wise
    Vidura's might,

All the dead were burned to ashes and the sacred rite was
    o'er,
Dhritarāshtra and Yudhishthir slowly walked to Gangā's
    shore!

But none were comforted.

As for Prithā, her sorrow had a keener edge for she told her
sons: "Karna was your honoured elder and the Sun inspired his
birth."

The horrified brothers spoke of Karna's wonderful prowess,
but

Woe to us! our eldest brother we have in the battle slain,
And our nearest dearest elder fell upon the gory plain,

Not the death of Abhimanyu from the fair Subhadrā torn,
Not the slaughter of the princes by the proud Draupadi
    borne,

Not the fall of friends and kinsmen and Panchāla's mighty
    host,
Like thy death afflicts my bosom, noble Karna loved and
    lost ! . . .

Long bewailed the sad Yudhishthir for his elder loved and
    dead,
And oblation of the water to the noble Karna made . . . .

Done the rites to the departed, done oblations to the dead,
Slowly then the sad survivors on the river's margin spread,

For along the shore and sandbank of the sacred sealike
  stream,
Maid and matron lave their bodies 'neath the morning's holy
  beam,

And ablutions done, the Kurus slow and sad and cheerless
  part,
Wend their way to far Hastina with a void and vacant heart.

Yudhi-shthira reigned as king and Dhrita-rāshtra and Gāndhāri lived with the Pāndus. Yudhi-shthira asked the old king for advice on all occasions, trying to make him feel that the only difference was that he had Yudhi-shthira for a son instead of Dur-yodhana.

Fifteen years passed in this manner. All the Pāndus tried to help the defeated ones to forget their sorrow, save Bhima. He had also tried but at times he could not resist reproaches or insults and Dhrita-rāshtra was upset. He decided that it was time to go to the forest and prepare for death and appealed to Yudhi-shthira to let him go. Obtaining consent he set out, accompanied by Gāndhāri and Kunti. Yudhi-shthira was very sad that Kunti went with them but she said that it was time she too prepared for death. All through her life the wonderful Kunti or Prithi had been a comfort and help to those she had been with for she was, as it was said, the very embodiment of *dharma* and forbearance.

Soon after they had arrived in the forest Vyāsa promised all who were there a gift of divine sight so that they could see again those whom they had lost. When evening came everyone sat by the shore of the holy river and waited. Soon a sound was heard, and from the smooth waters of the river came a great procession of men, elephants, horses and chariots. The war trumpets sounded again and all the splendour of the war hosts seemed to radiate over the water. The dead came and mingled with the living in joyful reunion, and there was no enmity between them. Karna greeted his mother, the cousins were friendly to each other, Abhimanyu came to Arjuna and gladdened his heart. Wives joined their husbands, mothers and fathers their sons, in thankful joy. The scene was made gay by hundreds of dancing girls and heavenly musicians who sang of the great deeds of courage that had been performed by each on the field of battle, and all sorrow went from the hearts of the living.

The meeting lasted throughout the night and then, as dawn began to show its first pale light in the sky, the procession silently made its way back to the waters. Some warriors mounted their elephants, some rode in their chariots, and some took to their horses, and all, with arms raised in salute, and with smiling faces, slowly slipped from sight. And, as was the custom of that time, the ladies of the court kissed the feet of Dhrita-rāshtra and his queen, and disappeared into the river to join their departing husbands. Dhrita-rāshtra's sight, which had returned to him during this vision enabling him to see his sons for the first time, began to fade, and he was once more blind.

Three years passed. Then the sage Nārada came to Yudhi-shthira and told him there had been a great forest fire and Dhrita-rāshtra, Gāndhāri and Prithā, had perished, together with all who were with them. This was said to be an auspicious way to die.

For some time all was peaceful, but another tragedy was coming and began to cast its shadow before it. Krishna's city Dwārakā was about to be destroyed, and with it his whole tribe, the Yādavas. Dreadful convulsions shook the earth, the moon was eclipsed, rats seemed to fill the city, and Krishna sent a message to his people telling them not to drink wine but to go to the seashore and perform religious devotions. The time of Krishna's earthly life was also drawing to a close and his chariot and horses and his *chakra* or discus went before him to heaven. One day the people were told to go to the seashore where they found a feast prepared, and for that day they were allowed to drink wine. But they became quarrelsome and soon all was in an uproar. Indiscriminate killing took place till everyone was slain and the Yādavas completely destroyed.

Krishna and Bala-rāma left for the forest after sending a message to Arjuna asking him to come quickly. As Krishna rested in the forest with his legs crossed and one foot exposed, a hunter shot him thinking the jewel in the ring he wore on the big toe was part of a deer. He blessed the hunter and died.

The story of the arrow which killed Krishna is a graphic one. One of Krishna's sons, Sāmba, whose mother was Rukmini, was a bad son. At the *swayam-vara* which Draupadi held he actually ran away with her but she was brought back by Dur-yodhana and his followers who kept Sāmba in prison. Bala-rāma went to rescue him and when he threatened to destroy the town if the prisoner was not released Dur-yodhana gave him up and he was taken to Dwārakā.

Sāmba continued in his bad ways and laughed at everything good, especially at the sages Viswāmitra, Dur-vāsa and Nārada. One day his friends dressed him up as a woman with child and asked the sages if the child would be a boy or a girl. They knew what was happening and said that it was not a woman who was before them but Sāmba, and he would give birth to an iron club which would destroy their whole race. When the club was born they pounded it to dust and threw it into the sea. There it grew into rushes that bordered the land, and when they were picked they turned into clubs or sharp reeds which could be used as swords. One piece of the iron could not be reduced to powder and a fish swallowed it. When the fish was caught the iron was used to make the tip of an arrow, and this was the arrow which entered Krishna's foot as he lay resting.

Later on Sāmba became a leper having been cursed by Dur-vāsa, but he made many penances and worshipped the sun and was cured. He then built a city to the sun.

When Arjuna arrived at Dwārakā he arranged for the funeral rites for the slain and asked all who would to go back with him to Indra-prastha. On the journey back robbers tried to stop them and Arjuna found to his dismay that Gāndiva his bow had lost its celestial quality and was of no more real use to him.

Seven days after the death of Krishna the sea rose and covered the city. But some say that at times it can still be seen within the water and one day it will rise again. Who can tell?

When Arjuna told Vyāsa all that had happened the sage said it was now time for all the Pāndus to close their earthly life which had contained so much sorrow and suffering. Yudhi-shthira though so too, and placing Abhimanyu's son, Parikshit,* on the throne of Hastinā-pura, and Yuyutsu on the throne of Indra-prastha he, with his brothers and Draupadi, now old and grey, set out on their last pilgrimage. As they started a dog joined them and followed Yudhi-shthira to the end.

First they travelled towards the east and met Agni god of fire. He told Arjuna it was now time to give Gāndiva back to its rightful owner, Varuna, and Arjuna threw it into the sea. As they passed on towards the Himālayas one by one they fell to the ground and died till only Yudhi-shthira was left with the faithful dog. At last he too met death for, with the roaring of thunder, Indra came in his chariot to take him home. As he was about to mount the chariot, the dog tried to follow, but Indra said it could not go with him and must be left behind. Yudhi-shthira's great sense of duty would not allow him to leave the dog, and as nothing would change his mind, Indra showed him who the dog really was. It changed into the god Dharma, who thanked Yudhi-shthira for all he had done in life—Dharma it will be remembered was Yudhi-shthira's father—and they all entered the car and rose up to heaven where they were greeted by the gods and sages. There he was

* Parikshit had been born dead, killed in the womb by Aswatthaman but had been brought to life by Krishna.

told to remain in happiness and peace.

But Yudhi-shthira could not see his brothers and asked for them. He was shown many heavens, in one which Dur-yodhana and his brothers were sitting, full of happiness, but nowhere could he find his own brothers or Draupadi. As he would not rest he was sent with a messenger to visit the various hells. He passed through most horrible scenes and heard the pitiful cries of his brothers as though they were in torment. His guide told him to leave them to their fate and to enjoy the heaven he had earned, but he refused, saying he would stay with them no matter how bad their condition was.

Then he was shown that this was only a *māyā* or illusion to test him and he learnt that his brothers and Draupadi were already dwelling in bliss where he could join them. And entering *Swarga* (heaven) he dwelt in company with Krishna and all the gods. There, too, he saw Krishna as he really was, the great Lord of the Universe.

And with this the *great epic* ends.

## PART IV

Nala and Damayanti

Sāvitri and Satyavān

Vasishtha and Viswāmitra

Puru-Ravas and Urvasi

Dhruva, the Pole Star

Nachiketas and Yama

Rohita

# CHAPTER X

## NALA AND DAMAYANTI

This story is one of trial and suffering, but in the end love and steadfastness win through. Its beginning is fragrant in its loveliness, the middle is of torment, and the end quiet bliss, strengthened by suffering. It is told in the *Mahā-bhārata* to show Draupadi that another woman had suffered more than she.

There were two kings, Nala, king of Nishadha, and Bhima, king of Vidarbha. The former was handsome, clever, popular, and "like the sun in his splendour," and his kingdom was happy and prosperous. He had one fault, however, and that was his love of gambling with dice.

Bhima was also brave and virtuous. He was married but childless, and he performed many rites to try and obtain favour of the gods. One day through his kindness to a Brāhman named Damana he was promised a child, and the queen gave birth in due course to a girl and to three sons, Dama, Danta and Dhamana. The girl was called Damayanti.

As Damayanti grew up she became very very beautiful and it was said that she shone among all her handmaidens, themselves beautiful, as though she was the goddess of beauty herself. Her fame reached the ears of Nala, and his fame reached her ears, so both of them began to fall in love with one another though they had not met.

One day when Nala was in his garden he saw a flock of graceful swans playing together, and he caught one of them. To his surprise, it began to speak to him with a human voice saying, that if its life was spared, it would go to Damayanti and tell her how handsome and wonderful Nala was. Nala let it go and it flew away and found Damayanti in her garden. It explained to her what had happened, and her love for Nala grew, so that she told it to go back to Nala and take her love to him.

But unfulfilled love makes the sufferers despondent, and the father of Damayanti, seeing how silent she had become, thought it was time for her to be married and arranged her *swayam-vara.* All the neighbouring kings and princes, including Nala, were invited and great preparations were made at the palace.

The gods heard of this, for two sages, Nārada and Parvata, sons of Brahmā, had gone to the heavenly court of Indra. There they had been asked how the world was getting on, and why there were no wars, with soldiers dying and going to heaven. The sages answered that the world was in a good condition and all was peaceful. They also told the gods of the approaching *swayam-vara,* and Agni, god of fire, Indra, god of thunder, Varuna, god of water, and Yama, god of death, decided they would go down to earth and compete for Damayanti's hand.

When they arrived they met Nala, looking so handsome and happy that he might have been the god of love himself, and they asked him to take a message to Damayanti for them. He was to tell her that they, Indra, Agni, Varuna and Yama, were about to ask for her garland, and she was to choose her husband from among them. Nala begged to be excused, for owing to his own love for her, how could he tell her this? Also, he asked, how could he reach her for the palace would be guarded? But the gods told him it would be all right and he must do their bidding, and suddenly he found himself standing before her. Seeing her for the first time, he was struck by her great and tender beauty, just as she was by his grace, and their love deepened. When she asked him how he had got in the Palace he told her of his mission.

Damayanti said her love was his, and begged for his in return. She said she belonged to him, and all she had was his, so how could she choose one of the gods? He was overcome with joy and asked her how she could prefer him to one of the gods? Damayanti answered that though she worshipped the gods, she wanted him for her husband, and if he entered the Assembly Hall the next day with the gods she would choose him.

Nala returned and told the gods.

When the great day dawned and all was ready, Nala and the gods entered the Assembly Hall together, but as the gods had made themselves look and dress like Nala, Damayanti saw five Nalas as she stood before them! In desperation she begged the gods to show themselves as gods, which meant that they would keep their eyes open and not wink, their skin would look dry, their feet would not quite touch the earth, and their garlands would remain fresh and free from dust. The gods granted her request, and seeing which was Nala, she placed her garland round his neck. Though all the other suitors were disappointed the gods were pleased with her constancy, and when Nala and she did homage to them, they gave Nala eight gifts. Indra's gift was to walk as a god and the power to see the god in every sacrifice; Agni gave him the right to call on fire at his will and to hold dominion over the three worlds; Varuna gave him power to call on water at his will and made his garlands remain always fresh; Yama gave him power to remain ever constant in all virtue, and also supreme taste in food and the preparation of food.

After a short stay Nala and Damayanti went to Nala's country and for twelve years they lived in great harmony and happiness.

When the gods were leaving the *swayam-vara* they met Kali, god of evil, with Dwāpara, an evil spirit coming through the air, and when they asked them where they were going Kali answered to the *swayam-vara* because he wanted Damayanti for his bride. When he heard that she had chosen a mere mortal he was so angry that he determined to be revenged, and for a long time kept watch to see what he could do. The gods, however, said that as they had approved of her choice if anyone cursed Nala that curse would rebound on the curser!

But Kali planned for an opportunity to enter the body of Nala and take control of it.

All through the twelve years of happiness during which two children were born, a son and a daughter, Kali waited. At last an opportunity came. Before taking part in any sacrifice it was necessary to sip holy water and wash the feet, but one day Nala sipped the water and neglected to wash his feet. This gave Kali the opening he required and he took charge of Nala's body. Then he called for Pushkara, Nala's brother, and told him to play dice with his brother. He added that he would see that he won, for Dwāpara had entered into the dice so that they would do what he wanted. And in this way, in the presence of Damayanti, Nala pledged his kingdom, his riches, his all, for the play went on for many months. When the counsellors of state and the people heard what was happening they begged Damayanti to try and stop him, but nothing could move him, for Kali in him was urging him on.

At length the time came when Damayanti sent for the charioteer and told him to take the two children quickly to her father, and when he had done this she said he was free to go wherever he wanted. After taking the children he went into service with another king.

When only one last throw remained—the pledging of Damayanti herself—the king awoke to his senses and left the chamber. With Damayanti, possessing but one cloth each, he went into the forest, poor, homeless, and under a ban of his brother that no one was to give them food or drink.

For three days they wandered, drinking from the pools and rivers, and eating wild fruit, and they became more and more hungry and weary. Then Nala saw a flock of golden winged birds and he tried to catch one by throwing his garment on it. But the birds flew away with the cloth saying that they were the dice, and that while he had even one thing to call his own they had been unsatisfied. Now naked, and with nothing, the king told Damayanti that she must go down one of the paths in the forest which led to a dwelling of hermits. There she would find plenty of food, and could go on to her father's kingdom. He himself, would go another way. Damayanti would not do this for she wanted to remain with him. Was it not true, she said, that the wife was a comforter to her husband and should be with him in times of grief? Why, she asked, did he not go with her to her father's kingdom? But Nala, in his disgrace, felt that was impossible, and so, together, they went on their way, dividing Damayanti's garment into two so that they both had some covering.

One night when Damayanti had fallen asleep through sheer fatigue, Nala, urged by Kali, decided to leave her, for only thus would she go to her father's kingdom and be safe. He got up and began to move away, but time and again he came back to look at her, unable to tear himself away. But at last he rushed into the deeper forest.

When Damayanti awoke she was frightened and ran about calling for him to come. But her cries remained unanswered. As she ran, a serpent rose up in her path, and coiled itself round her body. She cried louder for help, thinking of her husband and wondering who would comfort him if she died. Her cry was heard by a huntsman who shot the serpent, released her, washed her and gave her food. As she rested, he saw how lovely she was and tried to make love to her, but she cursed him so vividly and potently that he fell dead at her feet.

On she wandered, sometimes in lovely parts of the forest, shady and with fresh streams, sometimes she saw buffaloes and wild boar, sometimes serpents or demons and giants, sometimes lions and tigers and robbers, while the whole forest seemed full of the noise of the cricket. As she went she called to a mountain and asked if he had seen Nala, and if she would ever hear him speaking to her again and filling her heart with joy? Once she came upon some hermits who told her to keep on, for one day she would be reunited with her husband. And having said this the hermits and their huts suddenly disappeared and she was alone once more.

Further on she came to a caravan of merchants who, with their elephants and camels, horses and carts, were fording a river the banks of which were covered with undergrowth and stout canes. When the men saw her they were astonished that a young woman of beautiful form, dusty and dirty and clad only in half a garment, should be wandering in the forest. Some of them were frightened of her; others asked if she were a goddess. She told them her true story, and when the caravan departed she went with them. At night they camped by a lake full of lotus blossoms, and both men and animals were glad to bathe in the cool water. Then they rested. At midnight a herd of wild elephants went to drink at the pool, and when they smelt the tame elephants of the caravan they rushed like a torrent on them and overthrew the whole camp. Some men were killed, others hurt themselves in their efforts to escape, and the whole caravan was wrecked.

Damayanti was not hurt, and ran into the forest where she found some of the men who had escaped. They were discussing the calamity, and wondering what they had done to cause it. (It must be remembered that in these stories the causes of all happenings were traced to some action in the past.) Some said it might be because of the woman they had taken the day before, and suggested that she should be killed. When she heard this she fled deeper into the forest, saying to herself that misfortune seemed to haunt her wherever she went! In the morning she met some Brāhmans who had been with the caravan and had escaped, and she went with them to Chedi where Subadhu was king.

As they passed through the city everyone stared at her for she looked so unkempt, so weary and starved. Fortunately the queen-mother saw her as she passed the palace, and sent her nurse to fetch her, for she saw, in spite of her dishevelled appearance, that she was very beautiful. Damayanti told the gentle queen-mother all that had happened except who she was, and she was asked to stay in the palace and be a friend to Su-nandā the queen-mother's daughter. Meanwhile servants searched for her husband.

When he had left her Nala went on through the forest. One day he saw a great fire and went towards it. When he got nearer he heard a voice saying, "Nala, come hither !" As Agni had given him power over fire as a wedding gift, Nala rushed into the midst of the fire and, in the centre, saw the serpent king, Karkotaka, who had a serpent body with a human face and hands. Karkotaka asked Nala to lift him up, for he had been cursed by Nārada to remain in the centre of the fire until Nala should rescue him, and to make this possible he shrunk himself till he became as small as a man's finger. When Nala placed him in the cool air outside the fire Karkotaka told him to leave him and walk on, counting his steps, and good fortune would come to him. Nala did so, but on the tenth step, the serpent bit him, and he was transformed into an ugly dwarf. Then the serpent spoke to him. He told him he had made him into a dwarf so that he would not be recognised, and he should go to Ayodhyā and take service with king Rituparna as his charioteer, calling himself Bāhuka. He said he had bitten him so that the poison in his blood would be anguish to the evil demon who was inhabiting him, but would cause him no harm, and in time the evil demon would leave him. He also gave him power over the wild boar and over any human being or priest or sage. He gave him a garment which he was to put on, thinking of him, when he wanted to appear as he used to be as Nala the king. Finally he advised him not to grieve, for in time all would be well.

So Nala went towards Rituparna's palace. When he arrived he told him that he was good with horses, and knew all about the preparation of food, and the king took him into his service. He had as companions Vārshneya, who had once been in his own service, and Jivala. Every night he sang the same song :

Where is she all worn but faithful, weary, thirsty, hungering too?

Thinks she of her foolish husband? . . . doth another man her woo?

Once Jivala asked him who he was mourning for, and he said for a great lady whose husband had a weak will and left her in the forest, and now, overcome with grief he constantly sang this song.

Hearing of his daughter's disappearance king Bhima had sent out one hundred Brāhmans to try and find her and her husband, and he had offered great reward to anyone who could give him news.

One day a Brāhman, Sudeva, happened to be in Chedi during a holiday and saw Damayanti standing by the Princess Sunandā and the queen-mother. He went to her and told her he had recognised her, and that her father and mother and the children were well. He told her also that her father had sent everywhere searching for them, and she wept with joy. Hearing this Sunandā told her mother and the Brāhman was sent for. He told the queen-mother the story, and as proof, said that she had a dark spot like a lotus between her eyebrows. This could not be seen at the moment because it was covered by dust, but when the dust was removed it shone again with the quiet radiant beauty of the moon.

The royal ladies were glad, for the queen-mother said that Damayanti must be her sister's daughter whom she had once seen when she was a little child, and now, whatever she wanted, she would try and give her.

Damayanti said she would like to go home and meet her mother, father and children, and an army was given to her to take her and protect her on the journey. When she arrived her mother greeted her with joy and her father gave Sudeva a thousand cattle and a village in gratitude.

Now all that remained was to find Nala, and so Brāhmans were again sent out to seek for him. Damayanti told them to say wherever they went:

Whither art thou gone, O gambler, who didst sever my garment in twain? Thou didst leave thy loved one as she lay slumbering in the savage wood. Lo! she is awaiting thy return: by day and by night she sitteth alone, consumed by her grief. Oh hear her prayer and have compassion, thou noble hero, because that she ever weepeth for thee in the depths of her despair!

Many Brāhmans returned home without hearing of Nala, but one, Parnāda, who had been to Ayodhyā, came back and told her that the king's charioteer, Bāhuka, had given him a message. Then Damayanti knew that Bāhuka was Nala, and without saying anything to her father, she and her mother spoke secretly to Sudeva. They asked him to go to Ayodhyā and say to the king that the daughter of king Bhima was to hold another *swayam-vara* for no one knew whether Nala her husband was alive or not, and she wished to choose another husband. If Rituparna wanted to win her he would have to travel swiftly for the *swayam-vara* was to be held the next day. When Rituparna heard this he sent for his charioteer and they set out. Nala wondered why Damayanti was doing this but he urged the horses forward so swiftly that the king wondered who he could be, for only Nala had the power to drive so swiftly.

On the way two incidents happened: first the king's robe flew off and he wanted the chariot to stop while his servant went back for it, but Bāhuka would not stop. Then they passed a fruit tree. The king said he knew all about numbers and that he knew the number of berries on a branch. Bāhuka said he did not know if that was correct but he would break off a branch and count them. Rituparna did not want the chariot to stop, but Bāhuka said he was going to stop, and the king could either stop with him or go on with the chariot driven by Vārshneya. So they stopped and Nala counted the berries and found the king had been correct. He then asked him for his secret, and Rituparna told him he knew the secret of the dice. Nala told him if he would teach him that secret he would give him the knowledge of horses. So it was agreed.

When Nala knew the secret of the dice Kali left his body, and Nala vomited the poison of the serpent, and Kali resumed his own evil form. Seeing him, Nala started to curse him, but he begged him not to, for Damayanti had already cursed him when he left her in the forest, and he had since then been in great pain. So Nala stopped, and Kali went into the fruit tree and the chariot went on its way.

As they reached the city of Bhima, all nature seemed to rejoice, peacocks on the palace roofs danced, elephants trumpeted, and Damayanti said that surely the sound of a chariot driven so swiftly heralded the return of Nala, and she went to the palace roof to watch its arrival in the courtyard.

When Bhima saw who had come he greeted him royally but wondered why he had come, for he did not know of his daughter's plan. Rituparna, in his turn, was astonished, for he did not see any signs of a *swayam-vara,* and so said he had just come on a visit.

Damayanti sent her handmaid to speak with the charioteer and to bring back news of him, and from what he said she felt he must be her lost husband. She sent the girl back to watch him. When it was time for him to prepare food for Rituparna the order was given that neither fire nor water should be given to him, and the girl watched. She went back to Damayanti and told her that he just looked at the pans and they became full of water and when he held up dry grass to the sun it caught fire and the fire did not burn his hands. Also he picked up some flowers which had lost their freshness and they immediately became fresh.

Damayanti was now sure that he was Nala, and she sent the maid to the kitchen to bring up a portion of the food he was cooking, and when she tasted it then she knew for certain that the hunchbacked charioteer was in truth Nala.

She then sent her two children to the kitchen, and when their father saw them, he greeted them tenderly, and tears came to his eyes. He told the maid they reminded him of his own children and he could not restrain himself.

Damayanti now was so sure that she sent word to her mother saying she would like to see him, with or without her father's permission. They decided to tell Bhima and the charioteer was sent for.

When he came Damayanti asked him if he had ever heard of the man who had left his sleeping wife in the forest. She asked what offence she had ever committed that made him leave her. The charioteer answered that he had indeed lost his kingdom by the dice, but that it was because the evil demon Kali had entered him that he had forsaken her in the forest. He reminded her that she had cursed Kali, but he still remained in his body, and he had only won through because of his sufferings and devotion. Now that the evil one had departed he had come at once to see her. But, he asked, how could she think of marrying again! However, she told him of her ruse and swore she had been faithful to him all the three years of their parting. She called the wind and the sun and the moon to vouch for her faithfulness. The wind told Nala she had proved her faithfulness, and they should now be reunited. Flowers fell round them from the sky, and the sound of the music of the gods filled the room. Then Nala put on the magic robe given to him and thought of the king of serpents, and Damayanti saw her husband as he had been before all the sorrowful years.

All night long husband and wife recounted to one another the story of their wanderings, and when the next day came they were reunited and the whole world rejoiced.

When Rituparna heard the news he was very pleased and asked forgiveness if he had at any time been unjust to his charioteer. But Nala told him he had been happy in his service and he would give him the power over horses which he had promised. Rituparna fulfilled his promise in return, and gave Nala full knowledge of the dice, and then departed to his palace.

A month passed. Then Nala said goodbye to his father-in-law and went to his own kingdom where he met his brother. He told him he had come to play yet one more game of dice, and that he had gained enough riches to play. He reminded him that he could not refuse to play, for no one having won a kingdom by dice could refuse to play the loser again. They then staked the whole kingdom on one throw. This time Nala won, but instead of turning his brother out, he made him welcome and gave him an estate and money and treated him as a friend.

The people rejoiced that they had got back their rightful king, and after a time Damayanti returned bringing great treasures from her father, and they lived together happily, the city was well ruled, and every day Nala performed due religious rites.

Hearing this story the Pāndus and Draupadi were comforted, for if Damayanti and Nala came through such sufferings, they too would in time find an end to their own.

# CHAPTER XI

# SAVITRI AND SATYAVAN

During their exile Yudhi-shthira once asked a sage if there had ever been as noble a woman as Draupadi, and in reply he was told the story of Sāvitri and Satyavān.

There was a king, Aswa-pati, who had no child, and for eighteen years he prayed to Sāvitri, wife of Brahmā, asking that he might have a child to continue his name. When at last the goddess appeared to him from the midst of his sacrificial fire, she told him she was very pleased with his devotions and would grant him a boon. He asked that he might have sons to honour him. The goddess, however, said she had spoken with Brahmā about this, and it was not possible, but he would have a daughter who would be radiantly beautiful.

The king accepted the gift with pleasure, and in a short time he became the father of a beautiful girl who, when she grew up, was indeed so beautiful that people called her a daughter of the gods. And perhaps because of her very beauty no one asked her to marry him. Her father then sent her on a visit to the surrounding countries. She travelled in a golden car, followed by well-tried servants, and in the charge of good counsellors. She visited many countries and finally made her way home again. When she arrived the sage Nārada was with her father, and when he saw her he asked to king why she was not married. Aswa-pati told him of her journey and said he could stay and listen to her story if he wished.

Sāvitri told her father she had found the one of her choice. In the forest she had seen Satyavān, son of Dyumatsena, a blind king whose kingdom had been stolen from him and who was now living with his wife and son in the forest where they had spent years in austerities. The son had grown to be a man and she wished to marry him.

Her father turned to Nārada and asked for particulars of the youth. Nārada said he was brave, wise and good—in fact he had all the virtues—but the tragedy was he had only one more year to live. Hearing this, her father asked her if she would go again into the world and make another choice. But she was firm in her resolve to marry Satyavān so he gave the marriage his blessing. Nārada then departed and went to heaven.

Preparations were made for the journey to the forest, and father and daughter set out with many gifts for Satyavān's father. When they arrived they were greeted warmly, the gifts were given, and the reason of their visit explained. Dyumatsena said he and his wife and son spent their lives in religious austerities and they could not expect the princess to share these hardships with them. But Aswa-pati told him that his daughter was determined and also he himself had always wanted an alliance with him. So in the end the marriage was arranged, neighbouring priests were sent for and, attired in her best and gorgeous clothes, Sāvitri became the wife of Satyavān. Then her father left and Sāvitri took off her royal garments, put on the hermit's dress of bark, and began her life of service to her husband and his parents. She was so dutiful, kind and helpful, that they loved her very much.

But time, inexorable, moved on until there remained only four days to the time when Satyavān would die. All through this period Sāvitri had thought of his approaching death and wondered what could be done. She had fasted for days and nights, and now she decided to fast and stand up for three days and three nights without rest. Though the king told her it was too arduous a task for her to perform, she insisted, and at the end of the period she was very weak. She spent the last night before the fateful day sorrowing and wondering what she could do.

In the morning she got up and did the usual work of the day and the usual devotional exercises, and then went to her parents-in-law. The king told her that now her vow was completed she should eat, but she put the request aside and said she would eat at nightfall. She asked if they would give her permission to go to the forest with her husband that day, for she had not been before and she would like to go. The king eagerly granted this request—the first she had made. Satyavān tried to prevent her, for he said the way was rough, but her mind was made up and they both set out to the woods where Satyavān used to gather fruit and cut down wood for their fires. As they went in the forest she saw gaily coloured peacocks, little streams, and masses of beautiful flowers, and her heart grew even more devoted to Satyavān as he pointed out the beauties they were passing. But the sorrow of the fateful moment hung heavy on her mind.

When they had obtained all the fruit that was necessary Satyavān started to cut the wood.

After a while he stopped and said his head was aching and his limbs did not seem strong enough to support him, so he would lie down and sleep for a bit. Sāvitri placed his head on her lap, and thought of Nārada's words. Then she saw the awful but majestic figure of the god Yama, with the noose of death. Quickly she laid down her husband's head and stood up to face him and asked who he was. He told her he was Yama, and as her husband's life was finished, he had come to take him away. She asked why he himself had come, for it was his messengers who sought out the dying, not he himself. Yama said that was true, but Satyavān was a virtuous and noble soul, and therefore it was not fitting that only the messengers of death came for him. As he was speaking he drew out Satyavān's soul, no bigger than a thumb, bound it fast in his noose and began to leave the lifeless body on the ground.

Then the determination and devotion of Sāvitri were stirred to their utmost and she followed him. Yama told her she should not come for it was her duty to prepare the funeral rites for her husband, but she answered it was her duty to go wherever her husband went, and that as she had performed all the domestic rites which were considered the most important, she would follow him. Yama was pleased with this answer and asked her what boon she would like. He said he would give her anything she wanted except the life of her husband.

She asked that the blind king should have his sight restored and regain his former majesty.

Yama granted this. Then he told her the journey was difficult and she must turn back.

Sāvitri, however, said she could not be weary if she was with her husband, and she would go wherever he went, for the company of the good was always desirable.

Yama, pleased with these words, granted her another boon—anything save the life of her husband.

This time she asked that the king should regain his kingdom and never lose it again.

Yama granted this, and again asked her to turn back, but with carefully guarded speech, she pleased him, and he granted her another boon.

This time she asked that her own father, who had no children but herself, should have one hundred sons.

Yama promised this too, but said she really must turn back as already she had come much further than she ought to have done. But she would not.

She asked another boon, that she should have one hundred sons and that was granted.

But even the gods get weary of constant questioning, and Yama granted her one last boon, the greatest of all. This time, then, Sāvitri said, it must be a free boon, and he agreed. So she asked for the life of her husband for, she said, without him her life was impossible, and as Yama had already granted her one hundred sons, how could he take away her husband ! She

begged that he would let Satyavān live and at last Yama
gracefully gave in.

"Have thy object," answered Yama, "and thy lord shall live
again,
He shall live to be a father, and your children too shall reign,

For a woman's troth abideth longer than the fleeting breath,
And a woman's love abideth, higher than the doom of
Death!"

Vanished then the Sable Monarch, and Sāvitri held her way
Where in dense and darksome forest still her husband
lifeless lay,

And she sat upon the greensward by the cold unconscious
dead,
On her lap with deeper kindness placed her consort's
lifeless head,

And that touch of true affection thrilled him back to waking
life,
As returned from distant regions gazed the prince upon his
wife.

"Have I lain too long and slumbered, sweet Sāvitri, faithful
spouse?
But I dreamt a Sable Person, took me in a fatal noose!"

"Pillowed on this lap," she answered, "long upon the earth
you lay,
And the Sable Person, husband, he hath come and passed
away,

Rise and leave this darksome forest if thou feelest light and
strong,
For the night is on the jungle and our way is dark and long."

Rising as from happy slumber looked the young prince on
    all around,
Saw the wide-extending jungle mantling all the darksome
    ground,

"Yes," he said, "I now remember, ever loving faithful dame,
We in search of fruit and fuel to this lonesome forest came,

As I hewed the gnarled branches, cruel anguish filled my
    brain,
And I laid me on the greensward with a throbbing piercing
    pain,

Pillowed on thy gentle bosom, solaced by thy gentle love,
I was soothed, and drowsy slumber feel on me from skies
    above.

All was dark and then I witnessed, was it but a fleeting
    dream,
God or Vision, dark and dreadful, in the deepening shadows
    gleam,

Was this dream my fair Sāvitri, dost thou of this Vision
    know,
Tell me, for before my eyesight still the Vision seems to
    glow!"

"Darkness thickens," said Sāvitri, "and the evening waxeth
    late,
When the morrow's light returneth I shall all these scenes
    narrate,

Now arise, for darkness gathers, deeper grows the gloomy
    night,
And thy loving anxious parents trembling wait thy welcome
    sight,

Hark the rangers of the forest! how their voices strike the
    ear,

Prowlers of the darksome jungle! how they fill my breast
with fear!

Forest-fire is raging yonder, for I see a distant gleam,
And the rising evening breezes help the red and radiant
beam,

Let me fetch a burning faggot and prepare a friendly light,
With these fallen withered branches chase the shadows of
the night,

And if feeble still thy footsteps,—long and weary is our way,
By the fire repose, my husband, and return by light of day."

"For my parents, fondly anxious," Satyavān thus made
reply,
"Pains my heart and yearns my bosom, let us to their
cottage hie,

When I tarried in the jungle or by day or dewy eve,
Searching in the hermitages often did my parents grieve,

And with father's soft reproaches and with mother's loving
fears,
Chide me for my tardy footsteps, dewed me with their gentle
tears !

Think then of my father's sorrow, of my mother's woeful
plight;
If afar in wood and jungle pass we now the live-long night,

Wife beloved, I may not fathom what mishap or load of care,
Unknown dangers, unseen sorrows, even now my parents
share !"

Gentle drops of filial sorrow trickled down his manly eye,
Fond Sāvitri sweetly speaking softly wiped the tear-drops
dry:

"Trust me, husband, if Sāvitri hath been faithful in her love,
If she hath with pious offerings served the righteous gods
    above,

If she hath a sister's kindness unto brother men performed,
If she hath in speech and action unto holy truth conformed,

Unknown blessings, mighty gladness, trust thy ever faithful
    wife,
And not sorrows or disasters wait this eve our parents'
    life !"

Then she rose and tied her tresses, gently helped her lord
    to rise,
Walked with him the pathless jungle, looked with love into
    his eyes,

On her neck, his clasping left arm sweetly winds in soft
    embrace,
Round his waist Sāvitri's right arm doth as sweetly interlace,

Thus they walked the darksome jungle, silent stars looked
    from above,
And the hushed and throbbing midnight watched Sāvitri's
    deathless love !

(*Mahā-bhārata,* Romesh Dutt. J. M. Dent, 1899)

# CHAPTER XII

# VASISHTHA AND VISWĀMITRA

The legend refers to a long and bitter quarrel between Vasishtha, a great sage, and Viswāmitra, born a Kshatriya (a warrior), but anxious in one life to become a Brāhman and to possess Brāhman powers.

When Viswāmitra became king after his father's death he set out on a tour of his kingdom and found himself one day at the hermitage of Vasishtha. Both he and his followers were greeted and given the simple fare of the hermits and he was pleased. The king and the sage talked for a long time on different topics until it was time for the visit to end. Vasishtha then thought he would prepare a feast suitable for a king instead of the simple hermit food. This was possible because, through his many austerities and penances, he had won Nandini, the daughter of Surabhi, the "Cow of Plenty," which had come from the Churning of the Ocean, and she could give her master anything he desired. Accordingly she now produced a feast of wonderful magnificence, so much to the amazement of Viswāmitra that he offered to buy the cow for one hundred thousand cattle. Vasishtha refused this offer, and all the other offers of stupendous amounts which the king made, for, he said, how could he part with that which enabled him to perform all his sacrifices and fed his mind and his body?

Seeing that nothing would make him part with Nandini, Viswāmitra prepared to take her away by force, but she broke loose and rushed back to her master and complained to him. He knew it would be hopeless to try and fight Viswāmitra, and he told Nandini so. She reminded him she could create anything, and why should she not create an army which would defeat Viswāmitra? This she did, but instead of Viswāmitra being defeated, the army created by the cow was routed by the great powers that Viswāmitra possessed. Nandini created again, and this time brought out a huge following of barbarians who, with horses and elephants and chariots, rushed on Viswāmitra's army at such speed that it was completely destroyed.

When Viswāmitra's one hundred sons saw this they rushed on Vasishtha to destroy him, but by his magic powers, he killed them all immediately, burning them to ashes by the fire from his breath as he made one loud cry. Viswāmitra fled, determined to gain equal powers for himself. He left his kingdom to one son who remained alive, and went to the Himālayas where, by great austerities, he hoped to gain powers, and to that end he set his heart on the worship of Siva, the great god of the ascetics.

After some time Siva, riding on his snow-white bull, came to him and asked what he desired. Viswāmitra said he wanted to have every magic weapon that gods, demons or saints could use, and to have also the magic power of the use of the bow. These things were granted to him. Joyously he went to the hermitage of Vasishtha and shot his arrows at it until it was utterly destroyed by fire. Everyone, even the birds and beasts, rushed to Vasishtha with the news, and a great battle of strength began between the two. Viswāmitra shot every weapon he had, and finally the Brahmā dart, which is the most dreaded of all arrows, frightening even the great unseen hosts of gods themselves. But Vasishtha by his greater power, took the weapon into his body, which then shone as though it was full of fire, and hot sparks seemed to come out of every pore of his skin. His friends rejoiced, but Viswāmitra knew now that no ordinary weapon, however divine, was as great as the purity of the sage.

He then retired again to continue his efforts, this time aiming at becoming a Brāhman himself. Journeying to the south with his queen he spent a thousand years in austerities. Then Brahmā came to him and said he had won the right to be a Rājarshi or Kingly Sage. This was as nothing to Viswāmitra, and he scorned it, turning once again to his austerities.

Just at this time there was a king Tri-sanku who, although good and pure in every other way, had an overpowering desire to go to heaven while in his earthly body, and he went to Vasishtha and asked him to help him. Vasishtha said he should give up such a desire for it was not a good one to have. Tri-sanku then went to the hundred sons of Vasishtha and asked them for help, but they also refused, saying how could he expect them to help if their father did not. Angry and thwarted, Tri-sanku said he would go to other sages and try for help, and this so angered the sons of Vasishtha that they turned him into an outcast, the lowest order of human being. And having done this they returned to their own meditations.

Tri-sanku then journeyed to Viswāmitra and asked for his help. This was freely given, not only for Tri-sanku's sake, but because Vasishtha was his old enemy. He therefore sent out messages to all his pupils and all the sages, asking them to come to a ceremony where he promised Tri-sanku he should ascend to the skies as he had desired. All those invited came, except Vasishtha and his sons. They sent a message instead, saying the gods would not heed a sacrifice performed by one who had not been born into the Brāhman caste. Viswāmitra was stung by this, and retaliated with a curse that for seven hundred times those hundred sons of Vasishtha should have birth in the lowest of all castes and eat the flesh of dogs. As for Vasishtha, he cursed him to be born as one who found pleasure in the death of living creatures, and be free from any king or compassionate thought.

The ceremony then began, the chanting of the holy hymns took place, and Viswāmitra called on the gods. But they did not answer. Wrathful, but determined, Viswāmitra called on all his own powers, and Tri-sanku began to ascend and reached heaven. But Indra saw him and called to him to go back to earth as he had no place there, and he began to fall down again. Viswāmitra saw this, and used all his powers to soften the fall by creating the seven stars of the southern sky, and for a time Tri-sanku hung between them.

He then created new gods who would be more obedient to him, but at this the whole universe rebelled and tried to get him to give up this mad desire. He agreed, but only on the condition that Tri-sanku was allowed to go to heaven in his body and to stay there. This the gods agreed to and there was once more peace.

Viswāmitra returned to his austerities, and for thousands of years performed all kinds of penances, and so great was his constancy that at times the gods tried to break him down. Sometimes they succeeded, but after a time he began again. In one of the attempts to disturb him the gods sent down the nymph Menakā. She succeeded, but was roundly cursed when he awoke to what he had done, and fled. She gave birth to Sakuntalā leaving her to be brought up by the birds in the forest.

One day after some of his austerities he was hungry, but before he started to eat a Brāhman came and asked him for food. Though faint from hunger himself, he gave the Brāhman all the food there was. This was his last test, and he had won through. The great power he had obtained shook the earth and the heavens, and the gods asked that his boon should be granted so that all might have peace again. So Brahmā himself went to earth and told him he had now won the full state of a Brāhman. Viswāmitra was delighted, but he wanted it confirmed by true Vedic rites, and he asked if Vasishtha could perform the ceremony. Vasishtha came, and greeted him as an equal, and friendship was resumed between them.

There are many incidents in the story of these two. One tells how Viswāmitra ordered the river Saraswati to bring Vasishtha to him so that he might kill him, but the river turned another way and took Vasishtha out of danger. So in anger Viswāmitra turned it into blood.

Another story concerns Haris-chandra.

Haris-chandra was a king whose people were specially virtuous and happy.

One day when hunting in the forest he heard a cry of distress. He thought it was a woman, but it was a cry of some of the powers that Viswāmitra was trying to control, and they were crying for help. Haris-chandra called to them not to fear, and probably all would have been well had not an evil spirit wanted to disturb Viswāmitra, and saw in the king the very person to help him. He therefore entered into the king's body and took charge of it. As Haris-chandra went towards the sound he saw that his steps led him to Viswāmitra and he begged him not to be angry as he was only going to the aid of the distressed.

Viswāmitra asked him to whom gifts should be given, and receiving the answer they should first be given to Brāhmans, he asked the king to give him a fitting gift. Haris-chandra answered that he would give him whatever he asked, whether it was the kingdom, his wife or himself. Then Viswāmitra asked for all his possessions, everything, save the queen and his son, and the king gave them without a word. Finally Viswāmitra said he would rule the kingdom himself, and Haris-chandra, with only his wife and son, clad in hermit's garb, must go into the forest away from the country.

One more fee he asked, and Haris-chandra begged for a month's grace in which to try and find the money. This was agreed to.

The people of the kingdom were much distressed to see their beloved king and queen leaving the city on foot, with no possessions, and begged them to remain. For a moment he lingered in pity for them. But Viswāmitra spoke angrily and even lifted his stick to beat the queen, and the broken-hearted king said, "I am going."

The three walked on. When they arrived at Benares, Viswāmitra was already awaiting them, demanding his fee, for the month's grace was at an end.

Haris-chandra said there yet remained half a day, and he thought earnestly how he could raise the necessary money.

There was only one way, a terrible way, but the only possible way to secure the money and escape a curse, and that was to sell his wife as a slave. She thought of it also, but when it was mentioned the king fainted with grief. The queen too was overcome, and seeing both his parents prostrate on the ground, the young prince cried bitterly. Just then Viswāmitra came, splashed cold water on Haris-chanrda to revive him, and demanded his money.

There was no hope. Haris-chandra called out that his wife was for sale, and an old Brāhman said he would buy her to help his young wife at home. He passed over the money and took the queen away. The child ran with her, and she told the Brāhman that she would work better if she had the child, and he gave the king more money and they departed.

Viswāmitra came for the money, but seeing how little it was, said it was not nearly enough, and Haris-chandra had one quarter of the day left to get more. The only thing left to sell was himself, so he sold himself as a slave to an outcast, one who stole clothes from the burning ground and was the slayer of those whom the courts had condemned to death. Nothing lower than this could be. Haris-chandra went with him and began to spend his days in the horrible work of searching corpses and taking the clothes. At night he dwelt in the hovel of his master.

One day, too tired to work, he slept. He dreamed that he had to pass many lives in anguish and in places of torment, and once he was a king again who lost his kingdom through gambling.

When he was at work one day the queen came bringing with her the dead body of her son who had been bitten by a snake. She did not recognise her own husband in the dirty attendant, but he noticed the marks of kingship on the dead body and wondered why such a case had occurred, why such an early and dreadful death should have come to him. Then the queen cried aloud in her grief, saying she could not understand what her husband had done to bring about the loss of his kingdom and the slavery of his wife and child, and Haris-chandra looked again at the body. He saw it was his own son, and the sorrowing mother was his queen. She suddenly recognised him, and together they spoke of their trials. They made the pyre for the body, and having placed the boy on it, they prepared to join him and go with him to the state of the dead.

But before they could do so, a voice spoke to them, for, hearing this last appeal, the gods, with Indra and Dharma, had come down to them. Indra told the king that they all wished him well and he was to go to heaven with his wife and child. While he was speaking the air was full of heavenly music, flowers floated down, the king's son rose up full of life, and Haris-chandra and his queen became as they had been. In this joyous moment Indra again said that they were to ascend to the heaven of bliss.

Haris-chandra however could not do this because he had a great sense of duty, and he asked if he might fulful his duty to his master who had bought him. The god Dharma was pleased with this request and told him that it was he himself who had bought him in order to test his strength and constancy. Indra again told them to ascend, but Haris-chandra thought of his people, and said if they could also ascend to heaven he would go, but if not, then he would rather be with them even if it were in hell. So word was sent to his subjects and they were all transported to heaven to the great joy of the gods, for Haris-chandra had won through by his patience and by his remembrance of his friends.

Only one was not content, and that was Vasishtha. He was still angry at what had happened, the more so as once he had been, as priest, in the service of that family, and he said he was more angry at what had been done to Haris-chandra than he was when Viswāmitra had slain all his own sons. So he cursed Viswāmitra to become a crane or heron. But Viswāmitra could curse also, and he returned the curse to Vasishtha, and both became birds, immense in size, who flew in the air and began to fight one another. So much disturbance was caused by their enormous wings that the mountains rocked, and some even fell down, the waters of the ocean were stirred from their depths and overflowed, the earth was in turmoil and the people were terrified.

Seeing all this misery and destruction Brahmā came to them and told them to stop their fight, but they would not. Then he spoke to them under their own names, and told them they were doing harm to themselves as well as to all the world and that their strife should cease. This touched their hearts and they stopped, and became fast friends, each one going back to his own hermitage while Brahmā returned to his throne.

# CHAPTER XIII

# PURU-RAVAS AND URVASI

This story of the human king and the heavenly nymph or Apsarā was used by Kālidāsa the "Indian Shakespeare," as a basis of one of his plays.

One day king Puru-ravas was hunting in the Himālayas, and hearing cries for help, went to the assistance of two Apsarās who were being carried away by Rākshasas. Both were beautiful as are all Apsarās, and one of them, Urvasi, was so beautiful that he fell in love with her at once and asked her to marry him. She consented, but only on certain conditions: she was never to see him naked, and her two rams of which she was very fond, were to be with her and never taken away. Puru-ravas agreed, and they went to his palace where for some years they lived happily together.

But her playmates were not happy for they missed her and they began to seek a way to bring her back.

One night they slipped into her room and took away one of the rams, and Urvasi called out for help. Then they came for the second ram, and again she cried could no one help her!

The king lay by her side, unable to move for he was not dressed, but on hearing this second appeal, he got up quickly in the dark and attempted to get the ram back. The Gandharvas were waiting for this, and immediately made a lightning flash light up the room, showing the king naked. Thus the compact was broken and Urvasi vanished.

Puru-ravas was disconsolate and wandered far and wide calling for her to come back. One day he reached Kuru-kshetra where swans were sporting in a lake and they, who were really Urvasi and her companions, heard Urvasi say that this was the man she had been living with. Then they all became known to the king and he begged his wife to return.

She told him she could not go back, but if he would come there a year hence she would give him his son whom she would soon bear.

This he did, entering her golden palace for the night. For some years he visited her thus until she had borne him five (some say eight) sons, and then the Gandharvas said they would grant him a boon. He asked that he might always remain with Urvasi, and this was granted, but first they gave him a dish in which was a fire, and with this he was to sacrifice according to the rites. Puru-ravas then departed with his son, and on the way he left the fire in the forest until he could return. When he went back the fire had vanished, and instead there was an Ashwattha tree*, while instead of a dish was a Sami tree. The king appealed to the Gandharvas, and they told him to make a fire by friction between a stick from the upper part of the Ashwattha tree and one from the lower part of the Sami tree. This fire would be like the one they gave him.

He did so, sacrificed, and was made one of the Gandharvas and then dwelt for ever with Urvasi.

Max Müller thought this was a myth showing the love of a mortal and the immortal, of the dawn and twilight. Urvasi symbolises the mist of early morning and Puru-ravas stands for the sun. When the sun is seen the mist vanishes. It is to be noted that the Apsarás are personified vapours which are attracted by the sun and form mists or clouds.

---

* The Ashwattha tree is a sacred tree said to "grow with its roots above and its branches below, the leaves of which are the *Vedas*." It symbolizes among other things the Goddess of Nature, and is similar to the Scandinavian Idrasil, the Egyptian sycamore etc. The Sami tree is also sacred for it is the *acacia suma* used to produce fire by friction. It is the goddess Sami-devi.

# CHAPTER XIV

# DHRUVA, THE POLE STAR

Long, long ago a king Uttānapāda had two wives, Suruchi and Suniti, the former his favourite but a proud and jealous woman, the latter gentle and loving. Both queens had sons, Suniti's son was Dhruva, Suruchi's, Uttama.

Although Suruchi was not the chief queen her son had been promised the throne, and she was so jealous of Dhruva that to save him from possible harm the king and Suniti decided he should be taken from the Court. Mother and son went to live near the edge of a forest. In these peaceful surroundings they were visited by hermits and holy men and in time the queen's wounds were healed. The child grew up to love the blooms that rested on the lotus-ponds and the sounds of the trees in the forest, and often his little mind wondered about them and tried to fathom their secret.

When he was five years old he asked his mother who his father was, and she told him. He asked if he could go and visit him, and as she agreed he set out with a guard for the city. It was a long way to go but in time they reached the palace gates and then Dhruva went on alone. In the great Hall of Audience he saw his father seated on his throne and he rushed into his arms. Uttānapāda was overjoyed to see him and took him on his knee. But, so fleeting is happiness, at that moment Suruchi came in. She angrily reminded the king of his promise to her own son, and she seemed so cruel that the child slipped away, lightly touching his father's feet.

But he was hurt to the core. It was not only the cruel words that hurt him but the fact that his own father had put him down at the words of an angry woman.

Slowly he and the guard returned home to the waiting queen. She looked at the child's face and saw its sadness.

After his meal he told her all that had happened and asked her one question. "Is there anyone stronger than my father?"

"Yes," his mother replied, "there is the Lotus Eyed." He asked where the Lotus-Eyed one lived, and she told him in the very heart of the great forest where the tiger and the bear roamed at will.

In the night the little boy got up. Pausing only to say goodbye to his sleeping mother he went into the forest to find the Lotus-Eyed one. He walked on to the depths of the forest until he reached the centre, and there he waited. A tiger came towards him and he asked if it was the Lotus Eyed? But the tiger was ashamed and turned away. Then a bear came, and went away after it had been asked the same question. And the child waited.

Then the sage Nārada came. He taught the child how to pray to the Lotus-Eyed and how to sit on the ground, unmoved, repeating a verse over and over again. Then he told him the Lotus-Eyed would surely come.

So the child sat, like the midnight sun, unmoving even when the white ants built their great wall round him.

Soon the gods were afraid for owing to the child's persistence and power of concentration the world was in trouble. They went to Vishnu and asked his help. He mounted Garuda and went to the forest. But the child did not see him for he was concentrated on his thought of the Lotus-Eyed, and it was only when Vishnu took away that image from his mind that his eyes saw in front of him the very god himself. His heart was full but he did not know how to praise the god. Vishnu touched his cheek and immediately songs of praise rose up from the child.

Vishnu told him he should go home in order to rule the

kingdom when his father retired and after 60,000 years of rule he would go to heaven.

The child went home, and was greeted warmly even by Suruchi for his fame had gone before him.

When his father retired he took the throne. One day his brother was killed by a Yaksha and to avenge him Dhruva warred against the whole tribe of Yakshas. A dreadful battle ensued and it looked as if Dhruva would destroy the tribe, but Manu, the father of the human race, came to him. He reminded him of the vision of the Lotus-Eyed and pointed out that it was not right to destroy a tribe because one man had erred. Dhruva saw the truth of this and was ashamed that he had forgotten his vision. Thereafter he ruled wisely and well.

After the 60,000 years had gone by a golden car came down from heaven to fetch him, and he ascended to the sky. There he is today as the Pole Star, firm and unchanging, dwelling on the vision of the Lotus-Eyed living in his own heart.

Some say his mother was also transported to a place beyond her son so that he was always at her feet in silent adoration of the Lord of the Universe.

It must be remembered that in the ancient teachings planets and stars and suns were the outer forms of high spiritual intelligences who, through effort and merit had won to those high degrees. Vishnu, the second of the Tri-murti, is said to be in the heart of the planetary sphere which is said to be like a porpoise. In the tail is Dhruva the pole star. As the tail revolves, the sun and other planets turn also. In fact, all the heavenly bodies move round because they are all attached to Dhruva by invisible cords.

# CHAPTER XV

## NACHIKETAS AND YAMA

Once there lived a man, Vāja-sravasa, who kept cows. He wished to sacrifice to the gods in order to reach heaven, but he had little of value to offer for his cows were old and gave little milk and did not seem worthy. But as they were all he had he offered them in sacrifice.

He had a son Nachiketas who saw that his father was distressed at the paucity of his sacrifice, and he reminded him that he had one other possession—his son. Would he not offer him in sacrifice? Then the question arose, to whom should he be offered. Vāja-sravasa said, to Death.

So Nachiketas went to Death. He wondered what it would be like, but he reasoned to himself that others had died before him and others would die after, and therefore what happened to him would be the same. Thus reasoning with himself he arrived at Death's house, but he found that Yama, king of the dead, was away and would not return for three days.

When three days had passed Yama returned, and his servants told him that a Brāhman had been waiting for him, and that it was not good that a Brāhman should be kept waiting without a welcome! They suggested therefore that he should be placated.

Yama therefore went to him and said he would offer him three boons since he had been unwelcomed for three days.

Nachiketas' first boon was that his father should be at peace, and that when they met again his father should recognize him and welcome him back. This was granted.

Nachiketas then asked for the boon of immortality, for he said that in heaven there was no old age or death, and no fear, and he wanted the sacrificial fire which would bring him this knowledge. Yama told him how to make the altar for this fire, and Nachiketas learnt the lesson and thus his second boon was granted.

Then Nachiketas asked what came after death, for some said death was the end and some that life still went on.

This boon Yama was unwilling to grant, for the knowledge was very difficult to attain. He asked the youth to name any other boon save this, for even the gods had difficulty in knowing the answer.

But Nachiketas said there was no other boon equal to this, not even the boons offered by Yama of sons and grandsons, wealth and long life, and the fulfilment of all and every earthly desire. All these were passing things with death at the end. Only the knowledge of death would satisfy him.

Then Yama told him of the causes of death, the knowledge of the "better" and the "pleasanter," of ignorance and knowledge. He told him those who thought the world was real and that there was no other world, came under the control of Death again and again. He taught him by question and answer that the soul is not born nor does it die, but "smaller than the small and greater than the great" it dwells in the heart of every creature. He taught him the body was the chariot of the soul, and to avoid death the soul's chariot needed to be intelligently controlled. He taught him that the mind is higher than the senses, the intellect higher than the mind, higher than the intellect is the Great Self. Higher still is that which is unmanifest. The essential unity of all must be grasped until a man sees the World Soul as his very own.

When Nachiketas had learnt all this he was freed from death.

# CHAPTER XVI

ROHITA

There are many legends about king Haris-chandra and different versions of the same legend. One tells us that the king was childless, and after all else had failed, he worshipped the gods and made a vow that if he ever had a son he would sacrifice him to Varuna, god of the ocean.

In due time a son was born. He was called Rohita, which means red, or a play on the word deer.

All went well, and the kingdom prospered until the boy had grown into a young man and the time had come for the king to sacrifice him to the gods. He, however, delayed so long that famine came and the priests urged him to sacrifice more and more cattle to appease the gods. This he did, but all to no avail, and Rohita was told he must die. Naturally he did not like the idea, and fled to the forest where he remained hidden for six years while famine swept over the country. One day he came upon a hermit and his sons, all of whom were nearly dead of starvation, and he offered to buy one of the sons for one hundred cows if he would take his place as the sacrifice. The second son, Sunah-sephas offered himself for the sake of the family. Varuna was asked if he agreed to the substitution and he assented, so the father was offered another hundred cows if he would take his son to the place of sacrifice and bind him to the altar, and finally, if he would slay him himself he would be given another hundred cows. All this was agreed to.

Now Lakshiì, wife of Vishnu, was on a visit to her sister Varuni, wife of Varuna, and she heard this planning, so she arranged that Viswãmitra should teach the youth two powerful verses which he was to chant as he was lying on the altar. These verses were in honour of Indra and Vishnu, so the gods came to his help.

The sacrifice was arranged near a lake where Lakshmi was going to visit her sister, and the lake was covered with lotus blooms, white and beautiful. Just as the father was striking the fateful blow, the sky seemed to come down and cover the altar with a blue mist, and when it cleared, instead of Sunah-sephas on the altar, there was a deer, bound for the sacrifice. The body of the youth lay on the ground nearby, on a bed of lotuses, a blue lotus growing from his wound. He himself was transported to heaven. Then it was found that the white lotus blooms on the lake had become blue as though they reflected the blue sky.

Some say that Sunah-sephas did not die but entered the family of Viswāmitra.

## INDEX

| | |
|---|---|
| *Ansumat or Ansuman* | Grandson of Sagara. Found the horse of the sacrifice and the sixty thousand slain by Kapila. |
| *Apsaras* | Nymphs in Indra's heaven. |
| *Arjuna* | Son of Pāndu and Prithā. Indra was his divine father. Friend of Krishna. |
| *Asamanjas* | Son of Sagara. |
| *Asura* | Demon. In Vedic times spiritual. |
| *Aswa-medha* | The horse sacrifice. |
| *Aswatthāmān* | Son of Drona. |
| *Aswins* | Sons of the sun; divine physicians. |
| *Babhru-vāhana* | Son of Arjuna and Chitrāngadā |
| *Bāhuka* | Nala's name when a dwarf. |
| *Bala-rāma* | Brother of Krishna. |
| *Bhagavad-Gitā* | Divine Song-discourse between Krishna and Arjuna. |
| *Bhagiratha* | Descendent of Sagara. |
| *Bhāgirathi* | The Ganges. |
| *Bharata* | Son of Dasa-ratha and Kaikeyi. |
| *Bhima* | Son of Pāndu and Prithā—divine father was Vāyu. |
| *Bhishma* | Son of Sāntanu and Gangā. Grandfather of the Pāndus and Kurus. |

| | |
|---|---|
| *Brahmā* | The Creator in the Tri-murti: Brahmā—Vishnu—Siva. |
| *Brihaspati* | Regent of the planet Jupiter. |
| *Buddha* | Gautama, or Siddhartha. |
| *Chhāyā* | Handmaid of Sanjnā. |
| *Chitrāngadā* | Wife of Arjuna, mother of Babhru-vāhana. |
| *Daityas* | Titans, demons, giants. |
| *Daksha* | Son of Brahmā, one of the Prajā-patis. Father-in-law of Siva. Father of Sati. |
| *Damayanti* | Nala's wife. |
| *Dandaka* | Forest in which Rāma and Sitā spent part of their exile. |
| *Dasa-ratha* | Father of Rāma; husband of Kausalya, Kaikeyi and Sumitrā. Also father of Lakshmana and Bharata and Satrughna. |
| *Deva* | A god. |
| *Devaki* | Mother of Krishna, wife of Vasudeva. |
| *Devayāni* | Daughter of Sukra. She fell in love with Kacha. |
| *Devi* | A goddess, wife of Siva, daughter of the Himālaya mountains. |
| *Dharma* | Divine father of Yudhi-shthira. |

| | |
|---|---|
| *Dhrishta-dyumna* | Brother of Draupadi. |
| *Dhrita-rāshtra* | Brother of Pāndu, son of Ambikā, husband of Gāndhāri. |
| *Dhruva* | The pole star. |
| *Dilipa* | Son of Ansumat and father of Bhagiratha. |
| *Diti* | Mother of the Daityas, wife of Kasyapa, daughter of Daksha. |
| *Draupadì* | Daughter of Drupada. Married the five Pāndu brothers. |
| *Drona* | Father of Aswatthāmān, teacher of arms of the princes. |
| *Drupada* | Father of Draupadi and Sikhandin |
| *Duh-sāsana* | One of sons of Dhrita-rāshtra. |
| *Durgā* | A name of Siva's wife. |
| *Dur-vāsas* | A sage. |
| *Dur-yodhana* | Eldest son of Dhrita-rāshtra. |
| *Dushyanta* | Husband of Sakuntalā, father of Bharata. |
| *Dwārakā* | Krishna's city. |
| *Dyaus* | The sky. |
| *Gana-pati* | Name of Ganesa, son of Siva and Pārvati. |

| | |
|---|---|
| *Gāndhāri* | Wife of Dhrita-rāshtra, mother of 100 sons. |
| *Gandharvas* | Singers and Musicians in Indra's Court. |
| *Gāndiva* | Arjuna's bow. |
| *Ganesa* | Son of Siva and Pārvati. |
| *Ganga* | The Ganges or, as a person, daughter of Himavat, sister of Umā, mother of Bhishma. |
| *Garuda* | Vishnu's vehicle. Enemy of serpents. Son of Kasyapa and Vinatā, daughter of Daksha. |
| *Gautama* | Name of Buddha. |
| *Ghatotkacha* | Son of Bhima, killed by Karna. |
| *Gopis* | Cowherds. |
| *Govinda* | Cow-keeper. Name given to Krishna. |
| *Go-vardhana* | Mountain held up by Krishna to shelter the people. |
| *Hanumān* | The monkey chief who helped Rāma. Son of Vāyu. |
| *Haris-chandra* | A king. |
| *Hastinā-pura* | Capital of the Kuru Kingdom. |
| *Indra* | Divine Father of Arjuna. |
| *Indrāni* | Indra's wife. |

| | |
|---|---|
| *Irāvat* | Son of Arjuna and Ulupi. |
| *Janaka* | A king. Father of Sitā. |
| *Jatāyu (or Jatāyus)* | Son of Garuda. The king of the vultures. |
| *Jayad-ratha* | King of Sindhu. |
| *Kacha* | A son of Brihaspati. |
| *Kaikeyi* | Wife of king Dasa-ratha, mother of Bharata. |
| *Kailāsa* | Siva's heaven. |
| *Kāli* | Name of wife of Siva, the goddess Kāli. |
| *Kāli-dāsa* | Great poet, author of Sakuntalā. |
| *Kāliya* | A serpent. |
| *Kalki* | Vishnu's 10th incarnation, yet to come. |
| *Kāma* | Kāma-deva, Eros, or Cupid. God of love, husband of Passion. |
| *Kandu* | Sage. Tempted by Pramlochā, father of Mārishā. |
| *Kansa* | King of Mathurā, cousin of Krishna's mother, persecutor of Krishna. |
| *Kapila* | A sage; destroyed the sons of Sagara. |
| *Karna* | Son of Prithā, father was the sun. Fought with the Kurus and died in the battle. |

| | |
|---|---|
| *Kārttikeya* | Son of Siva; the god of war. |
| *Kasyapa* | Husband of the twelve daughters of Daksha. |
| *Kauravas* | The sons of Dhrita-rāshtra. |
| *Kausalyā* | Wife of Dasa-ratha, mother of Rāma. |
| *Kaustubha* | Jewel which came from the Churning of the Ocean. Worn by Krishna or Vishnu. |
| *Khāndava* | A forest and land given to the Pāndus. |
| *Krauncha* | A pass made in the Himālayas by Parasu-rāma or Kārttikeya. |
| *Kripā* | Wife of Drona and mother of Aswatthāmān. |
| *Krishna* | Son of Dewaki. 8th avatara of Vishnu. |
| *Kumbha-karna* | Brother of Rāvana. |
| *Kunti* | Also called Prithā. Sister of Vasudeva. Mother of the Pāndus and of Karna. |
| *Kuru-kshetra* | Where the great battle took place. Near Delhi. |
| *Kusa* | One of the twins of Rāma and Sitā. |
| *Kuvera* | God of wealth. |
| *Lakshmana* | Son of Dasa-ratha and Su-mitrā. Brother of Rāma. |
| *Lakshmi* | Wife of Vishnu. Goddess of fortune. |

| | |
|---|---|
| *Lankā* | Ceylon and also its capital. |
| *Lava* | One of the twin sons of Rāma and Sitā. |
| *Lingam* | Siva's symbol. |
| *Mādhava* | A name of Krishna. |
| *Mādri* | Second wife of Pāndu. Mother of Nakula and Sahadeva. |
| *Mahā-bhārata* | The great Epic. |
| *Mahā-deva* | Name of Siva. |
| *Mānasa-sarovara* | Lake Mānasa. |
| *Mandara* | Mountain used at the Churning of the Ocean. |
| *Mandodari* | Favourite wife of Rāvana, mother of Indra-jit. |
| *Mantharā* | Deformed slave-nurse of Kaikeyi. |
| *Māricha* | A Rākshasa, minister of Rāvana. |
| *Marichi* | Father of Kasyapa. |
| *Mārishā* | Daughter of Kandu and Pramlachā—mother of Daksha. |
| *Mārttānda* | Sun god. |
| *Maruts* | Storm gods. |
| *Mathurā* | Birthplace of Krishna. |

| | |
|---|---|
| *Matsya* | A fish. The Fish Incarnation of Vishnu. |
| *Māyā* | Illusion. |
| *Menakā* | An Apsarās. Mother of Sakuntalā. |
| *Meru* | A mountain containing the cities of the gods. |
| *Nachiketas* | Sacrificed to Yama. |
| *Nāga* | A snake. |
| *Nakula* | Twin son of Mādri and Pāndu by the gods the Aswins. |
| *Nala* | Husband of Damayanti. |
| *Nanda* | A cowherd, Foster-father of Krishna. |
| *Nandi* | Siva's bull. |
| *Nandini* | Born from Surabhi, the cow of plenty. |
| *Nārada* | A rishi. |
| *Narasinha* | Man-lion incarnation of Vishnu. |
| *Nila* | Blue. |
| *Nila-kantha* | Blue-throated. |
| *Om* | A sacred word. |
| *Panchajana* | A demon. |
| *Pānchajanya* | The conchshell of Krishna. |

| | |
|---|---|
| *Pāndu* | Brother of Dhrita-rāshtra, father of the Pāndus. |
| *Pāndus* | Sons of Pāndu. |
| *Parasu-rāma* | Sixth incarnation of Vishnu. |
| *Pārijāta* | A tree thrown up at the Churning of the Ocean. |
| *Parikshit* | Son of Abhimanyu and Uttarā. |
| *Pārvati* | Wife of Siva. |
| *Paundra* | The conchshell of Bhishma. |
| *Pitris* | Fathers. |
| *Prahlāda* | A Daitya devotee of Vishnu. |
| *Pramlochā* | Nymph who beguiled Kandu and became mother of Mārishā. |
| *Prithā* | A name of Kunti. Mother of the Pāndus. |
| *Purāna* | Ancient Scriptures. |
| *Puru-Ravas* | Married Urvasi. |
| *Pushkara* | A blue lotus. |
| *Pushpaka* | An aerial car. |
| *Putanā* | A demoness. |
| *Rādhā* | Foster-mother of Karna; also devotee of Krishna. |

| | |
|---|---|
| *Rāhu* | Ascending note in astronomy. The cause of eclipses. See Churning of the Ocean. |
| *Rājarshi* | A saint. |
| *Rākshasas* | Evil spirits. |
| *Rāma* | Eldest son of Dasa-ratha. Hero of the Rāmāyana. |
| *Rāmāyana* | The great Epic of Rāma. |
| *Rāvana* | Demon king of Lankā. |
| *Renukā* | Mother of Parasu-rāma. |
| *Ribhus* | Skilful workmen, fashioners of Indra's chariot. |
| *Rishi* | A sage. |
| *Ritu-parna* | A king |
| *Rohini* | A wife of Vasu-deva, mother of Bala-rāma. |
| *Rohita* | *See Legend of the Blue Lotus.* |
| *Rudra* | Terrible. God of storms etc. Sometimes used for Siva. |
| *Rukmini* | Wife of Krishna. |
| *Rumā* | Wife of monkey king Su-griva. |
| *Sagara* | *See descent of Ganges.* |

1. Smiling Bramha
*(Sikar, Rajasthan)*

2. Lord Vishnu
*(Sikar, Rajasthan)*

3. Siva-Parvati marriage performed by Bramha
*(Ajmer, Rajasthan)*

4. Ganesh-Parvati and Kartikay *(Amber, Rajasthan)*

5. Standing Surya *(Amber, Rajasthan)*

6. Seated Lord Vishnu *(Sikar, Rajasthan)*

7. Bearded Lord Bramha *(Ranthambhore, Rajasthan)*

8. Dancing Ganesha and his Consort on the eastern terrace of Harshad Mata-ka-Mandir *(Abaneri, Jaipur)*

9. Chaturambha lings *(Ajmer, Rajasthan)*

10. Standing Vishnu in Harshad Mata-ka-Mandir *(Jaipur, Rajasthan)*

11. Lord Vishnu
*(Jaipur, Rajasthan)*

12. Seated Bramha
*(Sikar, Rajasthan)*

13. Seated Garuna
*(Nahargarh Fort)*

14. Surya in Sun
Temple *(Nahargarh
Fort)*

15. Radha-Krishna
*(Jaipur, Rajasthan)*

16. Standing Lord
Vishnu *(Sikar,
Rajasthan)*

17. Siva-Parvati
*(Jaipur, Rajasthan)*

18. Laxmi Naryan *(Jaipur, Rajasthan)*

19. Standing Lord Vishnu *(Jaipur, Rajasthan)*

20. Bansi Gopal *(Jaipur, Rajasthan)*

21. Sculpture of Siva of Adai-Din-Ka
Jhopra *(Ajmer, Rajasthan)*

22. Lying Lord Vishnu *(Sikar, Rajasthan)*

23. Dancing Siva in Madwa Temple

24. Narasimha — fifth incarnation of Vishnu

25. Parasurama — sixth incarnation of Vishnu

26. Rama — seventh incarnation of Vishnu

27. Krishna — eighth incarnation of Vishnu.

| | |
|---|---|
| *Saha-deva* | Twin son of Pāndu and Mādri, son of the Aswins. |
| *Sakti* | Female energy of the gods. |
| *Sakuni* | Gāndhāri's brother. |
| *Sakuntalā* | Daughter of Viswāmitra and Menakā. |
| *Salya* | Brother of Mādri. |
| *Sāmba* | A son of Krishna. |
| *Sami* | Wood used to obtain fire by friction. |
| *Sampāti* | Brother of Jatāyus, son of Garuda. |
| *Sandhyā* | Twilight. |
| *Sanjaya* | Charioteer of Dhrita-rāshtra. |
| *Sanjnā* | Daughter of Viswa-karma. The sun's wife. Mother of Vaivaswata, Yama and Yami. |
| *Sāntanu* | Father of Bhishma. |
| *Saramā* | Indra's dog, mother of the watchgods of Yama. |
| *Sārameyas* | Children of Saramā. |
| *Saranyu* | Mother of Yama, wife of Vivaswat. |
| *Sāraswati* | River goddess. Wife of Brahmā. |
| *Sati* | Daughter of Daksha, wife of Siva. |
| *Satru-ghna* | Twin brother of Lakshmana. |

| | |
|---|---|
| *Satya-vati* | Mother of Vyāsa by Parāsara. Wife of Sāntanu. |
| *Sāvitri* | Wife of Satyavān. |
| *Sesha* | King of the serpents. |
| *Sikhandin* | See Ambā. Son of Drupada. |
| *Sisu-pāla* | Foe of Krishna. |
| *Sitā* | Wife of Rāma. |
| *Siva* | Destroyer-regenerator. One of the Tri-murti. |
| *Soma* | Sacred drink. |
| *Su-bhadrā* | Wife of Arjuna, sister of Krishna. |
| *Su-griva* | Monkey king. |
| *Sukra* | Venus and its regent. |
| *Su-nandā* | Princess who befriended Damayanti. |
| *Surabhi* | Cow of plenty—from Churning of the Ocean. |
| *Surpa-nakhā* | Sister of Rāvana. |
| *Surya* | The sun god. |
| *Sushena* | Physician of Rāma's army. |
| *Tārā* | Bāli's wife. |
| *Tārā* | Brihaspati's wife. |

| | |
|---|---|
| *Tāraka* | Daitya. Destroyed by Kārttikeya. |
| *Tri-murti* | The Hindu triad. |
| *Twashtri* | Divine carpenter. |
| *Uchchaih-sravas* | Indra's white horse. From the Churning of the Ocean. |
| *Ulupi* | Arjuna's Nāga wife. Mother of Irāvat. |
| *Umā* | Wife of Siva. |
| *Upanishads* | Sacred Scriptures. |
| *Urvasi* | A nymph. |
| *Usanas* | Venus and its regent. |
| *Ushas* | Dawn. |
| *Uttara* | Son of the King of Virāta. |
| *Uttarā* | Daughter of king of Virāta. Wife of Abhimanyu. |
| *Vāhana* | A vehicle. |
| *Vāhuka* | Name of Nala in disguise. |
| *Vaijayanti* | Vishnu's necklace. |
| *Vaivaswata* | Manu |
| *Vajra* | Indra's thunderbolt. |
| *Vajra-nābha* | Discus of Krishna. |
| *Vālmiki* | Author of the Rāmāyana. |

| | |
|---|---|
| *Vāmana* | Vishnu's incarnation as a dwarf. |
| *Varuna* | God of water (formerly king of the universe) |
| *Varuni* | Wife of Varuna. |
| *Vasishtha* | A Sage. |
| *Vasu-deva* | Father of Krishna. |
| *Vāsuki* | King of the serpents. |
| *Vāyu* | The god of wind or air. |
| *Veda* | Divine knowledge. |
| *Vedānta* | A system of philosophy. |
| *Vibhishana* | Brother of Rāvana. |
| *Videha* | North Bihar. |
| *Vidura* | Son of Vyāsa and a slave girl. |
| *Vinatā* | Daughter of Daksha, mother of Garuda. |
| *Vindhya* | Mountain range. |
| *Vira-bhadra* | Son emanated by Siva. |
| *Virāta* | Near modern Jaypur. |
| *Vishnu* | Second of the Tri-murti. |
| *Viswa-karmā* | Divine architect. |
| *Viswāmitra* | A Sage. |

| | |
|---|---|
| *Vivaswat* | The Sun |
| *Vritra* | Drought demon. |
| *Vyāsa* | Author of the *Mahā-bhārata:* son of Satyavati, father of Dhrita-rāshtra and Pāndu. |
| *Yagna* | Sacrifice. |
| *Yakshas* | Supernatural beings. |
| *Yama* | King of the dead. |
| *Yasodā* | Wife of Nanda, foster-mother of Krishna. |
| *Yudhi-shthira* | Eldest of Pāndu princes. |
| *Yuyutsu* | Son of Dhrita-rāshtra by a handmaid. |

2/09/ 267 / 93-99